Essential Linguistics

What You Need to Know to Teach Reading, ESL, Spelling, Phonics, and Grammar

David E. Freeman
Yvonne S. Freeman

HEINEMANN
Portsmouth, NH

Heinemann
A division of Reed Elsevier Inc.
361 Hanover Street
Portsmouth, NH 03801–3912
www.heinemann.com

Offices and agents throughout the world

Library of Congress Cataloging-in-Publication Data
Freeman, David E.
    Essential linguistics : what you need to know to teach reading, ESL,
spelling, phonics, and grammar / David E. Freeman & Yvonne S. Freeman.
        p.   cm.
    Includes bibliographical references and index.
    ISBN 0-325-00274-6 (alk. paper)
    1. Language and languages—Study and teaching.   2. Language acquisition.
3. English language—Grammar.   I. Freeman, Yvonne S.   II. Title.

P51.F694 2004
418'.007—dc22   2003024626

Editor: Lois Bridges
Production: Vicki Kasabian
Cover design: Catherine Hawkes, Cat & Mouse
Typesetter: TechBooks
Manufacturing: Steve Bernier

Printed in the United States of America on acid-free paper

08   07   06   05   04   RRD   2   3   4   5

*We would like to dedicate this book to
Maya Esmeralda, our first grandchild.
She offers living proof that people can acquire more than
one language and become proficient bilinguals.
Not only is Maya acquiring two languages,
she is also acquiring literacy.
We have enjoyed observing her language development.
The process she is going through helps
confirm the theory we present in this book.*

Contents

Acknowledgments

Different groups of people have made this book a reality. The most important contributions came from the many university students who have taken David's linguistics classes over the last sixteen years. Responses, questions, and suggestions from those students led David to develop and teach a linguistics course connecting linguistics to classroom practices. Through student feedback David developed explanations and assignments to help future teachers apply linguistic principles to reading, ESL, spelling, phonics, and grammar. Without the input from students, this book would never have been written.

We also wish to acknowledge the continual support and encouragement of our editor, Lois Bridges. Lois is so responsive to our needs that answers to our queries almost always come in minutes. She is unfailingly enthusiastic, even when we are not sure that what we are writing is worthwhile. In addition, Lois always makes valuable suggestions that shape the final versions of our books. We are privileged to work with such an outstanding and knowledgeable editor.

No book would see the light of day without the efforts of the production team. We were fortunate to work again with Vicki Kasabian and Abby Heim in the Heinemann office in Portsmouth. Not only are Vicki and Abby a pleasure to work with, they always make the perfect choices for the final format of the book. It is through the efforts of these two professionals that our books always receive compliments on their format and general appeal.

Finally, we want to thank our copy editor, Beth Tripp. She did an exceptional job of reading through a dense manuscript and finding many of our errors. In addition, she contributed valuable suggestions that have resulted in a much better book than would otherwise have been produced. It was a pleasure to work with her on this project.

Introduction

Linguistics is a required college course for many students, both undergraduates and graduates. Typically, these students come to the first class session feeling both apprehensive and resentful. They are nervous about having to take the class, and, at the same time, they suspect it will be of no use. No other class, with the possible exception of statistics, triggers these emotions so strongly.

Why do students feel this way? Many students connect linguistics with grammar, which, in turn, triggers thoughts of identifying parts of speech—nouns, verbs, and conjunctions. If these students were not particularly successful at determining whether a word was an adjective or an adverb in the past, they figure that now it will get even harder. They begin the class convinced that they never were very good at grammar and that this class will further expose that weakness.

Other students associate linguistics with activities like diagramming sentences. They are convinced that sentences must be hard to diagram. They aren't sure what a tree diagram is. Or perhaps they have heard from other students that they will need to learn a new writing system called *phonemic transcription*. This system uses unfamiliar symbols to represent sounds. All this can be intimidating. In addition, for students who are studying to be teachers and for those already working in schools, tree diagrams and phonemic transcriptions appear to have little connection to their classrooms. They ask themselves and their instructors questions like "How will this knowledge help me be a better teacher?" and "How will this class give me any practical ideas I can use with my own students?"

We have written this book to help dispel these fears about linguistics. In the chapters that follow, we present the basic concepts of linguistics in everyday language. We focus on aspects of linguistics that have clear classroom connections. We provide examples and suggest activities to help educators apply concepts from linguistics to their own teaching. Our primary goal is to turn key insights from linguistics into what Krashen (1982) calls *comprehensible input*. We hope to provide teachers with the knowledge they need to make informed decisions as they help their students, both native English speakers and students learning English as an additional language, develop literacy.

Why Study Linguistics?

One very good reason for studying linguistics is that language is what makes us distinctly human. Lederer (1991) puts it in the strongest terms: "The birth of language is the dawn of humanity . . . before we had words, we were not human beings" (p. 3). Pinker (1994) writes that humans have a language instinct. Chomsky (1975) argues that language is innate, that it grows in the human mind the same way hair grows on our heads. Other linguists such as Halliday (1975) would debate whether or not language is innate and attribute a greater role to social forces in shaping language. But most linguists agree that language is uniquely human; it is what distinguishes us from other living creatures.

Human communication is qualitatively different from animal communication. A dog might be able to communicate to its owner (or to another dog) that she is hungry, but she can't tell her master what she did yesterday or what she hopes to do tomorrow. However, the claim that only humans have language is debatable. It's a topic students might want to investigate. Do dolphins or apes have language? How is their communication different from communication among humans? Is language what distinguishes humans from other creatures? Linguistics is the scientific study of language, and the study of linguistics gives teachers and students the tools to investigate questions like these.

A second reason for teachers to study linguistics is that the more they know about how language works, the more effectively they can use language to help their students learn. As Halliday (1981) writes, "A child doesn't need to know any linguistics to use language to learn; but a teacher needs to know some linguistics if he wants to understand how the process takes place—or what is going wrong when it doesn't" (p. 9). The greater a teacher's understanding of basic language structures and processes, the easier it is for that teacher to make good decisions on tough topics like phonics, spelling, and grammar. A teacher with an active interest in language will arouse a similar interest in students, who may be surprised to find that *hippopotamus* means "river horse," that the reason commas and periods go inside quotation marks is that typesetters didn't want to lose those little pieces of punctuation as they laid out type for printing, and that the rule about not ending a sentence with a preposition was created in a period of history when teachers decided to try to base English grammar rules on Latin rules. The more teachers understand language, the more effectively they can help their students develop their knowledge of language.

A third reason to study linguistics is that language study is interesting. Students are fascinated to discover that sandwiches got their name from the fourth earl of Sandwich, who spent his days (and nights) playing cards. He also loved to eat meat, but he didn't want to get grease on the cards, so he wrapped the meat in bread, and the sandwich was born! Newspaper columns, radio shows, books, and Internet websites feature information about language. Richard Lederer's books on language are best-sellers. Many of his lines (Why do we park in the driveway and drive on the parkway?) make their rounds on the Internet as friends forward emails with lists of interesting language tidbits. However, even though language is a fascinating topic, the only exposure many students get to language study during their elementary and secondary years is worksheets and exercises that bore them to tears and serve little practical purpose in improving their reading or writing. What students need is a new approach, and teachers who study linguistics can awaken students' interest in language and engage them in linguistic investigations.

A fourth reason for studying linguistics is that a well-educated person should know something about language. Unfortunately, it is usually only when students study foreign languages that they begin to learn how their own language works. Language study should be introduced early in school, and the approach to language study should be scientific. This book is designed to help teachers build the knowledge they need to provide a scientific approach to language study for their students.

A final reason to study linguistics is that "the study of language is ultimately the study of the human mind" (Akmajian, Demers, et al. 1979, p. 5). Although linguists are interested in the structure and function of language, their goal in trying to understand how language works is to gain insights into how the human mind works. Even though scientists cannot examine the workings of the mind directly, they can study language, the unique product of human minds. Language reflects the inner workings of the mind. As Chomsky (1975) puts it, "language is a mirror of mind in a deep and significant sense. It is a product of human intelligence, created anew in each individual by operations that lie far beyond the reach of will or consciousness" (p. 4).

Three Aspects of Language Development

Halliday (1984) argues that we learn language, we learn through language, and we learn about language. Teachers armed with linguistics knowledge can help all their students *learn language*. Whether her students are six years old or twenty-six, whether they speak English as the native language or are learning English as an additional language, a teacher is responsible to help all students develop their language abilities. A first-grade teacher expands his students' language knowledge by representing their experiences in writing during a language experience activity. A middle school language arts teacher helps her students discover the organizational structure of the short stories they read. A high school biology teacher shows her students how to use contextual clues to understand new science vocabulary. Teaching any subject involves teaching the language—the vocabulary and the organizational structures—common to that content area.

The second aspect of language development is *learning through language*. Go into any classroom and what do you hear? The teacher is talking, the students are talking, the room is full of talk. Why is this? It's because one way that humans learn is through oral language. If you look around the classroom, you will also see written language. There are books, lists on the board, student papers on the wall, and words on the computer monitors. Everywhere you look, there is written language. Students constantly learn through language, both oral and written, inside and outside classrooms. And teachers constantly teach their students through language.

Students also *learn about language*. Sometimes they learn that the language they came to school speaking is not valued in the school setting. Sometimes they learn how to make subjects and verbs agree. Or they may learn that when two vowels go walking, the first one does the talking. Every day, students learn about language. In classrooms this language study should be scientific. For example, students might work together to discover why many English words end in a silent *e* and then develop a rule for keeping or dropping the *e* before adding a suffix. This approach to language study is most common in classes where the teacher has studied linguistics. Such a teacher has his students engage in linguistic investigations following the same approach that linguists use. A useful resource for teachers who want to involve their students in language study is Goodman and Helper's book, *Valuing Language Study: Inquiry into Language for Elementary and Middle Schools* (2003).

How Do Linguists Study Language?

We have said that linguistics is the scientific study of language. Linguists study language in the same way that other scientists study their fields. Science always starts with a question. For example, a linguist studying a new language might ask, "What are the meaningful sounds in this language?" or "How do speakers of this language structure sentences?" To investigate a question, a scientist forms a hypothesis and collects data to test the hypothesis. The linguist's goal is to describe the new language.

Akmajian, Demers, and Harnish (1979) explain how a linguist studies language scientifically. Several steps are involved in building a theory to describe a language. When a linguist attempts to describe a new language, the first step is to break the speech stream up into units. It's not hard for people to listen to another person who speaks their language and write down the words that person utters. The language is perceived as being divided into discrete units. But when one tries to determine the units in a language one doesn't speak or understand, the job of picking out meaningful units is a challenge. When we lived in Lithuania, we wanted to learn a few words of the language. However, as we listened to people speak, we had a very hard time deciding where one word ended and the next one began. We invite you to try this yourself with a language you don't speak. See if you can divide the language up into words. It's not easy because the physical speech stream is continuous. Speakers don't pause between words.

Let's imagine that the linguist has collected some data, and when she looks at her field notes, this is what she finds:

Doesyournewhusbandcookwell

First, the linguist must decide how to divide up the stream into discrete units that occur in a sequential order. She might do this by trying to find repeated sequences. After considerable work, the linguist might hypothesize that in this language, the units are these:

Does your new husband cook well

The second task in describing a language is to figure out the differences among the units of speech. They don't all seem to be alike. This leads to forming a hypothesis about categories of words in the language. For example, in English words may be classified as nouns, verbs, conjunctions, and so on. Each of these labels represents a category. Working with this sentence, the linguist might categorize the units this way:

Does   your   new   husband   cook   well

AUX   DET   ADJ   N   V   ADV

She uses AUX for an auxiliary or helping verb and DET for a determiner, such as an article or a possessive pronoun.

The third step in describing a language is to decide how the speech units can be grouped together. For example, in this sentence, *your new husband* might be one group and *does cook well* might be another. The groups of words each play a specific role, so the fourth step would be to determine the function of each group. Here, *your new husband* serves as the subject of the sentence, and "does cook well" is the predicate.

The final step in describing this language would be to find what linguists call *dependencies*. In this sentence, *does* depends on *your new husband*. The subject and verb have to agree in number. If the subject were *your new husbands*, then the auxiliary verb would be *do*, the form used with plural subjects.

Readers shouldn't be worried if they are rusty on their auxiliary verbs, subjects, and predicates. This book doesn't include a test on parts of speech or the parts of a sentence. This example simply illustrates how linguists go about the scientific study of a language. They collect data and form hypotheses about the linguistic units, categories, groupings, functions, and dependencies. They use scientific methods to describe various aspects of a language. Of course, languages are very complex, and no linguist would claim to have described any language completely. Science is always work in progress.

How Do Schools Teach Students About Language?

In most elementary and secondary schools, language study is not approached from a scientific perspective. Linguists work to describe language so that they can study it. However, historically, grammar teachers have prescribed, not described. They have laid down the rules for students to learn and to follow. Teachers have told their classes that subjects and verbs must agree, and they have given students worksheets to practice this skill. Many students have learned that a noun is the name of a person, place, or thing, and they have underlined nouns in a set of sentences. Teachers of grammar, from the earliest days, have been prescriptive, not descriptive.

We want to encourage teachers to take a descriptive approach to language study because prescriptive approaches to natural phenomena like language simply don't work. The laws of physics ensure that if someone drops a pencil, it will fall to the ground, not fly up into the sky. This will occur no matter what rules about gravity great physicists proclaim. In the same way, prescriptive teachers can tell students not to split infinitives, but that won't inhibit a writer who wants "to boldly go" where no person has gone before. In fact, great writers seldom follow the rules in grammar books. In response to a critic who suggested that he rewrite a sentence to avoid ending it with a preposition, Winston Churchill is reputed to have commented, "This is the sort of nonsense up with which I will not put!"

An alternative to the teaching of grammar rules, one a teacher with some linguistic knowledge might choose, would be to involve students in linguistic investigations. For example, students might examine books written by well-known writers to see if they ever end sentences with prepositions. Students could collect examples of such sentences and discuss how each sentence would sound if it were rewritten so that the preposition came earlier. In the course of this investigation, students would need to learn to distinguish between a preposition (He ran *up* a big hill) and a particle (He ran *up* a big bill). They might even discover that what Churchill's critic objected to was a final particle, not a preposition after all.

When teachers understand basic linguistic concepts, they can make informed decisions about how to teach language to their students. Knowledgeable teachers can teach their students about language using a descriptive approach. They also have the knowledge base to determine how to approach topics like phonics, vocabulary, and spelling. We encourage teachers to explore topics in linguistics with their students. We have organized this book to provide the essential linguistics teachers need to boldly go where many teachers have not gone before.

Organization of This Book

One goal for this book is to provide teachers with the linguistics concepts they need to help their students become more proficient in their use of both oral and written language. A second goal is to suggest ways that teachers can help their students to take a scientific approach to learning about language, to conduct linguistic inquiry. The two goals are related. Students who investigate how language works can apply insights from their study to their own reading, writing, and oral language development.

To help teachers apply what they are learning about linguistics to their classroom practice, we begin this book with a chapter on first language acquisition. In Chapter 1 we consider how researchers from different fields of study have approached the topic of language acquisition. Chapter 2 extends the discussion to the acquisition of second and written languages. We argue that people acquire a second language or written language in the same way that they acquire a first language. The following chapters examine different aspects of language.

Chapter 3 looks at the sound system of English. We explain what phonemes are and describe the English phonological system. With the increased emphasis on phonemic awareness and phonics, it is important for teachers to develop a thorough understanding of English phonology in order to make informed decisions about the best way to teach reading. For that reason, in Chapter 4 we consider the implications from phonology for teaching reading and teaching a second language.

Chapter 5 traces the history of writing development and describes the system of English orthography. Teachers with a good knowledge of orthography can better decide how to help their students with spelling. Chapter 6 examines phonics and graphophonics. Phonics rules attempt to state the relationships between phonology and orthography. Graphophonics is the acquired knowledge of these relationships.

Chapter 7 focuses on morphology, the word system of English. We consider how words are structured and how new words are formed. In Chapter 8 we explore the implications from morphology for teaching reading or a second language. In this chapter we discuss vocabulary development and vocabulary teaching. Chapter 9 deals with the structure of sentences. We describe how a linguist develops a theory of syntax. We also consider how syntactic knowledge applies in teaching reading, grammar, or a second language.

Our hope is that readers of this book will keep asking, "How can this knowledge from linguistics inform my teaching?" Teachers are constantly teaching language, teaching through language, and teaching about language. The better they understand English phonology, orthography, morphology, and syntax, the easier they will find it to make good choices about how to structure lessons to enable their students to become proficient language users.

1

First Language Acquisition

- *Is language acquired naturally or is it learned through a conscious process?*
- *How do researchers from different fields study language development?*
- *What do linguists say about first language acquisition?*

At every level, teachers are teaching their students language. A kindergarten teacher might be concerned about whether her children are developing their sounds. A fifth-grade teacher might wonder how to help his students comprehend their science textbooks. An eighth-grade teacher might face the challenge of integrating a student with very limited English and limited formal schooling into his social studies–language arts block. A high school math teacher might question the best way to help her students develop the academic vocabulary needed to do word problems.

Even though the school may not refer to these teachers as language teachers, that is what they are. The task they have in common is helping their students gain the language proficiency they need to succeed in school. Their understanding of how students develop language will guide their curricular decisions. In this chapter, we review the research on language acquisition that comes from different fields of study. We invite readers to reflect on their own beliefs about language development as they study the different perspectives on language presented in this chapter.

First Language Acquisition

When children begin to develop language, they start by babbling. Soon they utter their first word. Not long after that, they begin to produce two-word sentences like "Tommy go" and "Drink milk." And it isn't long before these two-word expressions evolve into full sentences. Parents hang onto every sound infants make. They marvel at how quickly their child learns to understand and speak. But parents aren't really surprised at the development of language in their child because most children accomplish this incredible feat. How do children acquire language? What theory can best account for children's capacity for language development?

Early Views of First Language Acquisition: Behaviorism

During the first half of the twentieth century, the behaviorist view of language development was generally accepted. Behaviorists held that all learning, including language learning, happened as a process of stimulus and response. According to the behaviorists, children's language learning begins when the child produces a sound and a parent or other caregiver reinforces that action positively. For example, if the child, in the babbling stage, utters something like "da da" and the father is nearby, he might pick the child up, smile, and begin talking to the child. This positive reinforcement would lead the child to respond by producing this sound again. This general process of positive reinforcement eventually leads to full adult language proficiency.

This is a simplified account of the behaviorist view. This theory of language development fits popular ideas of learning today. Behaviorists believed that language is learned like anything else. Learning depends on the response of the individual to the environment. Whatever is reinforced is repeated. In this view, children have the potential for language and, given the right circumstances, become proficient language users. The behaviorist view also fits the general idea that language is learned by imitation. Children try to imitate the sounds that adults make. When their attempts are rewarded, they repeat them and eventually learn to make certain sequences of sounds.

In 1959, Chomsky wrote a review of B. F. Skinner's book *Verbal Behavior* (1957). Skinner, the foremost proponent of behaviorism at that time, had written *Verbal Behavior* to account for human language learning. However, Chomsky showed convincingly that language was too complex to be learned through Skinner's behaviorist model. Chomsky's review signaled the end of wide acceptance of behaviorist views of learning. Within a few years, behaviorism was replaced with cognitive views of learning.

The behaviorist view prevailed for a number of years. However, researchers found that behaviorism could not adequately account for learning in general. By the 1970s, behaviorism gave way to cognitive science. Studies indicated that learning is not only the result of the environment acting on the individual. Instead, the new view was that humans are born with innate cognitive abilities, and learning is the result of the child acting on the environment much like a scientist making and testing hypotheses. In addition to this new view of how people learn, careful studies of children acquiring language revealed a number of problems with the behaviorist view.

Lindfors (1987) lists several problems with a behaviorist account of language development. First, if learning is the result of the environment acting on the child, and if learning environments vary, how can one account for the uniformity of the language development sequence in children? Children brought up in very different circumstances all seem to learn to speak at about the same time, and they all go through the same stages. Behaviorist theory would predict different developmental paths for children raised in different circumstances, but this is simply not what happens.

Secondly, if learning is the result of stimulus and response, then why wouldn't other intelligent beings, like apes, also learn to speak? A great deal of study continues to be carried out with apes, dolphins, and other animals, and while some animals seem to be able to develop certain language functions, there is a qualitative difference between human language and the communication systems found among animals. The failure of scientists to teach animals to speak using a behaviorist approach undermines claims for behaviorist learning theory.

A third problem is that close examination of children's language development shows that children don't simply imitate adults. If they did, they would never produce sentences like "I goed home yesterday" because they would never hear sentences like that. At the same time, careful observation reveals that adults seldom correct children's grammar. Instead, they respond to the truth value of what the child says, to the message, not the form of the message. So if a child says something like "I goed home yesterday," a parent might respond, "Yes, and then you watched TV." Transcripts of child-adult interactions show that corrections are not common. And even when parents do correct the form of the child's speech ("You mean you *went* home yesterday") it does little good, as most parents can attest. This is because children are building underlying rules as they figure out how language works. They are not simply repeating what they hear. The child that says "goed" is starting to develop a rule for how English speakers indicate past tense. At an early stage, some children will produce irregular forms like *went*. However, quite soon children overgeneralize the rule for past tense, applying it to verbs that are irregular, and producing forms like *goed*. Later, they realize that some verbs do not follow the pattern, and they begin to use irregular past-tense verbs correctly.

A fourth problem with the behaviorist view is that it can't account for the speed with which almost all children master a complex linguistic system. Children learn language much more quickly than they learn other things. Even though they are not exposed to extensive examples of language, and with only minimal correction, they seem to figure out the system in a very short time. A theory of stimulus and response cannot account for this remarkable accomplishment.

Current Views of First Language Acquisition

The rejection of the behaviorist position on language learning led to renewed interest in child language acquisition. In the last thirty years or so, researchers from fields such as developmental psychology, sociology, anthropology, education, and linguistics have conducted studies to determine how children learn language. Language is complex, and determining just how it is that children develop the capacity to understand and speak the language that surrounds them is no simple task.

Researchers have focused on different aspects of language acquisition. Developmental psychologists have concentrated more on the child and the child's capacity for learning. New studies in brain science have expanded the understanding of how children develop language. Since language is the means by which humans communicate with one another, sociologists and anthropologists have studied the environmental setting to determine how the social context influences language development. Educators have looked at factors that can enhance children's language development and contribute to school success. Linguists have looked closely at just what it is that children acquire. That is, what is the nature of language? Although studies in these areas overlap and provide complementary information, it is helpful to look at them separately. In the following sections, we consider recent research in child language acquisition that has been centered on each of the three areas: the child, the environment, and language.

Insights from Developmental Psychology: Focus on the Child

According to Rice (2002), "any satisfactory model of language development must be compatible with how children learn; their ability to perceive, conceptualize, store, and access information; and their motivations" (p. 21). The question of how language learning is related to developmental psychology, then, might be "Do children learn language in the same way they learn other things, such as how to tie their shoes or how to build with blocks, or do children have a special cognitive capacity for language learning?"

Much of the research in child language acquisition has focused on the early language that children produce. Since researchers can't directly observe what goes on in the brain, and since they can't ask one- or two-year-olds to reflect on how they are learning language, scientists have to rely on children's linguistic output. Researchers who have observed children over time and have transcribed children's speech have identified certain stages in normal language development. This work is very intensive, and the studies are longitudinal.

Brown (1973), for example, studied three children over time. He found that their earliest utterances referred to things of interest to the children (Mommy, ball). He discovered that there were strong parallels between children's language development and the stages of cognitive development identified by Piaget (1955). For example, at an early stage infants focus on objects and actions, and their early speech reflects this in sentences like "mail come" or "see baby."

As researchers continued to collect data, they found that language and cognition seemed to develop separately although the two are related. Rice (2002) comments that there is not a clear temporal order of cognitive insights first, followed by linguistic achievements. Instead, language and related non-linguistic competences appear at the same time. The relationship between language and cognitive development seems strongest at the early stages, but cognitive development and language development, although related, take different courses as children grow. Rice continues, "children at first draw heavily on concepts as a way to master language and later use language to learn new concepts" (p. 22).

Other researchers have continued to conduct detailed studies of early language development. Lindfors (1987), for example, includes a number of examples of transcripts that show how children move from babbling to one-word utterances to two-word sentences and beyond. Although early studies, such as Brown's, were of middle-class white children, subsequent studies have looked at different ethnic and economic groups across a number of languages. The findings have been consistent with the earlier studies, suggesting that children's language development is a universal phenomenon.

Studies of child language development show consistency across children and across languages. During the first year, children develop the physical capacity for speech and begin to babble. Pinker (1994) notes that children's babbling undergoes a change at about seven or eight months. At this age, children begin to produce syllables with a consonant-vowel structure, like "ba" and "dee." At about one year, children start to produce individual words. Researchers have found that nearly all children produce the same types of words. According to Pinker, about half the words are for objects (food, body parts, clothing, vehicles, toys, household items, animals, and people). The words name the people and things that are important to children. Brown's study showed a similar result.

Even though children may produce only one-word utterances at this stage, the single words may represent complex ideas. A word like *bottle* might mean something like "I want my bottle" or "My bottle is empty." On the surface, it appears that language develops from simple forms to more complex forms—from single words to complete sentences. At a deeper level, though, what is happening as children produce longer sentences is that they are discovering how to express complete ideas more fully. At this early stage, the whole idea is represented in a single word. As time goes on, children add more words to express the idea in a form others can understand more easily. Children start with the most important words: nouns to represent objects and verbs to represent actions. Over time they fill in adjectives and adverbs to describe objects and actions (*red* ball, walk *fast*). The last words to come in are the grammatical function words like prepositions, conjunctions, and articles. For this reason, early speech is often referred to as *telegraphic*. Like an adult writing a telegram, a child includes only the key words to express a message.

The next stage of language development comes at around eighteen months. At this age, children start to put together two-word utterances. In English, simple sentences need at least two words (Fish swim), so children at this point are producing sentences and beginning to show an understanding of syntax. That is, they are showing an understanding of how words go together to form sentences. Pinker reports on studies that indicate that children at this stage understand the difference between sentences like "Big Bird is washing Cookie Monster" and "Cookie Monster is washing Big Bird." Infants are seated where they can view two video screens. On one screen Big Bird washes Cookie Monster, and on the other Cookie Monster washes Big Bird. A voice comes over a central speaker saying, "Oh look! Big Bird is washing Cookie Monster. Find Big Bird washing Cookie Monster." The researchers then record where the children look. Even before they can produce two-word utterances, at an age between one year and eighteen months, infants consistently look at the video corresponding to the voice prompt. This shows that very young children are developing syntax. They recognize the difference in meaning between two sentences like "Big Bird is washing Cookie Monster" and "Cookie Monster is washing Big Bird," a difference based on the order of the words.

At about eighteen months, children's vocabulary also begins to grow very rapidly. Pinker (1994) states that at this age, "vocabulary growth jumps to the new-word-every-two-hours minimum rate that the child will maintain through adolescence" (pp. 267–68). Children's ability to learn vocabulary so rapidly along with the ability to recognize and then produce sentences that reflect an understanding of syntax supports the idea that the capacity for language development is either innate or the reflection of a special cognitive processing capacity for language. Children don't learn other things nearly as rapidly as they learn language, and this ability seems to apply to almost all children.

In recent studies, Petitto (2003) discovered that infants exposed to sign language go through the same stages as babies exposed to oral language. Using a sophisticated computerized visual graphic analysis system, Petitto and colleagues are able to record information from babies exposed to sign language and get the same kinds of detailed results that linguists can get by recording oral language on a spectrograph machine. Petitto observes, "In order for signed and spoken languages to be acquired in the same manner, human infants at birth may not be sensitive to sound or speech per se. Instead, infants may be sensitive to what is encoded within this modality" (p. 1). In other words, it is certain characteristics of natural language that humans are able to learn, not just one modality of language. As Petitto states,

> One novel implication here is that language modality, be it spoken or signed, is highly plastic and may be neurologically set after birth. Put another way, babies are born with a propensity to acquire language. Whether the language comes as speech, sign language, or some other way of having language, it does not appear to matter to the brain. (p. 1)

Petitto's research shows that any form of input that has the properties of language can be used to develop a form of language needed for communication.

Studies in child language development have concentrated on the early stages. The problem that researchers face is that beyond the two-word stage, language growth is incredibly rapid and complex. As Pinker writes, "Between the late twos and the mid threes, children's language blooms into fluent grammatical conversation so rapidly that it overwhelms the researchers who study it, and no one has worked out the exact sequence" (1994, p. 269). Children's sentences become longer and more complex as their language approximates adult speech.

Many developmental psychologists view the development of oral or signed language as the result of general cognitive processes. However, language learning differs from other kinds of learning in two ways: most normal children develop language, and they do this very rapidly without instruction. This has led some developmental psychologists to suggest that humans have a special capacity for language. Slobin (1979, in Lindfors 1987), for example, asks, "Does the child have strategies which were specifically evolved for the task of language acquisition, or can one account for this process on the basis of more general human cognitive capacities? . . . I suspect that both general cognitive principles and principles specific to language are at play in the child's construction of his native language" (p. 108). The question of the nature of the child's ability to make meaning continues to be debated among developmental psychologists, but many would agree that children seem to have some sort of special cognitive ability for language learning.

Studies in developmental psychology have contributed a great deal to the understanding of how children acquire language. Early studies attempted to link cognitive stages and stages of linguistic development. However, subsequent studies suggest that cognition and language develop along related but independent paths. Most studies have focused on the early stages of language development. These studies suggest that the stages of early language development are the same for all children, no matter what their ethnicity or economic level. Most studies have been limited to children up until about age two because beyond that point language develops so rapidly that it is almost impossible to document and analyze. Some of the most recent research, using new technology, has revealed that language development may be the same whether the language is oral or gestural. Children learning oral language go through the same stages as children learning sign. The universality and rapidity of language development has led some researchers to suggest that children may have a special cognitive ability in the area of language.

Developmental psychology looks at individual psychological factors involved in language acquisition. However, because we are social beings, humans use language to communicate with others. Studies in sociology and anthropology have focused on the social nature of language development.

Insights from Sociology, Anthropology, and Education: Focus on the Environment

Children develop the ability to understand and produce language because language is essential for social interaction. Hearing children develop the ability to talk, and deaf children develop the ability to sign. The modality is not important. What is important is the capacity for communication. In fact, children don't simply learn the grammar and vocabulary of a language, they learn how to use language appropriately in social settings. They develop what Hymes (1970) termed *communicative competence*, the knowledge of what to say to whom under what circumstances. Language always occurs in a social context, and the meaning of many utterances depends on the context. For example, "Excuse me" could be an apology, but it could also be a means of getting someone's attention.

Many studies of child language development have focused on the interactions between mothers or other caregivers and children. Researchers have analyzed the speech of adults as they interact with children using a kind of language, a register, often referred to as "motherese." Interestingly, adults adjust their language and speak to children in ways that they would never speak to adults. What mother would say to a friend, "Time to go bye-bye"? Children hear this kind of language from their caregivers, and yet, over time, they develop speech that corresponds to adult norms.

Researchers have also looked at how children growing up in different speech communities develop the ability to function in those communities. Communicative competence is the ability to use the language appropriate to a particular social context. Heath (1983), for example, looked at differences in the language development of children in two different communities in the same area of the Carolinas. Roadville is a white working-class community. For four generations, people from Roadville have worked in the textile mills. Residents of Trackton also work in the textile mills. Trackton residents are blacks whose ancestors were farmers. Children from both Roadville and Trackton attend school with mainstream whites and blacks. Heath shows differences between the ways Roadville and Trackton children use language to communicate. For example, Roadville children are taught to always tell the truth. Trackton children are encouraged to be imaginative and entertaining in their speech. Roadville children are to speak only when spoken to. Trackton children learn how to break into a conversation and hold the floor by their creative use of language. Heath points out many differences between these two groups' ways with words and also shows the problems both groups have in interacting appropriately in the school setting, where a different norm for appropriate language use exists.

Wells (1986) followed the native language development of thirty-two children from about fifteen months of age through their elementary years in an attempt to discover what kinds of language support families, communities, and schools provide. Children in the study wore backpacks that contained tape recorders programmed to record at different intervals. Neither the parents nor the children knew when they were being recorded. Wells gathered extensive data from the recordings. He focused his analysis on identifying those factors that facilitated language development.

A key finding of the study was that caregivers who controlled and corrected young children as they were developing English inhibited, rather than aided, language development. Children who were corrected frequently did not use more error-free language. Instead, their language did not develop as well, and they did not succeed to the same degree academically as children whose parents and others focused on understanding and extending the children's meaning.

Wells suggests that the best support adults can give young children is to "encourage them to initiate conversation and make it easy and enjoyable for them to sustain it" (p. 50). Four specific suggestions from Well's work are

- When the child appears to be trying to communicate, assume he or she has something important to say and treat the attempt accordingly.
- Because the child's utterances are often unclear or ambiguous, be sure you have understood the intended meaning before responding.
- When you reply, take the child's meaning as the basis of what you say next, confirming the intention and extending the topic or inviting the child to do so him- or herself.
- Select and phrase your contributions so that they are at or just beyond the child's ability to comprehend. (p. 50)

Wells discusses the implication for teachers. They should encourage children to explore their understandings and use language for making meaning rather than asking students to respond to their specific questions with formulaic answers.

Goodman and Goodman (1990) describe language development as the result of a tension between invention and convention. Children try out different ways of expressing their ideas. They invent words and phrases. As they use language in different contexts, they modify their inventions in light of the responses they receive from the community. Each community has conventional ways to use language. The Trackton and Roadville children developed communicative styles in response to the encouragement of the adults around them. Later, in school, they found those conventions were not the ones teachers expected. To succeed in school, both groups of children had to develop a different language register. The Roadville children needed to learn to use language imaginatively to make up stories that weren't necessarily true. The Trackton children had to restrain their impulse to jump into a class discussion and try to hold the floor. Both groups had to modify their language to fit the new social context of school.

Developmental psychologists, for the most part, have focused their research on the cognitive development of individual children. Sociologists, anthropologists, educators, and sociolinguists, on the other hand, have examined the social nature of language acquisition. Studies from both areas have provided important insights into the nature of first language acquisition.

Insights from Linguistics: Focus on the Language

In their studies of first language acquisition, linguists have focused on the nature of language, on what it is that children acquire. Chomsky, for example, has observed that it is necessary to develop a theory of language before attempting to develop a theory of language acquisition. In other words, linguists are most interested in what it is that children are acquiring when they acquire a language. Researchers in fields such as language teaching and reading have applied the ideas linguists have about language to form theories of language acquisition. Different theories of linguistics have led to different views of language acquisition.

Changes in theories of linguistics have paralleled changes in theories of psychology. For example, during the period that behaviorism was the accepted theory of how humans learn and develop, structural linguistics was the accepted theory in the field of language study. Structural linguists attempted to describe language by looking at sentence patterns, particularly focusing on patterns in oral language. Behaviorism and structural linguistics together formed the basis for beliefs about language development. Children, it was thought, acquired language by learning regularly occurring sentence patterns through a process of stimulus and response.

In the same way that behavioral psychology gave way to cognitive psychology, structural linguistics was superseded by new linguistic theories. The foremost linguist in the United States, Noam Chomsky, developed a theory referred to as *generative grammar*. Chomsky was interested in describing language in terms of a set of rules that could be applied to generate all the sentences of a particular language. Since there is no limit on the number of different sentences that can be expressed in any language, there must be a finite set of rules capable of generating an infinite number of sentences. For this description to reflect psychological reality, the number of rules must be relatively small. Otherwise, humans couldn't acquire them.

By the time they reach school, most children have mastered most of the features of their language and can use it effortlessly to comprehend and produce sentences. As Chomsky comments, "A normal child acquires this knowledge [of language] on relatively slight exposure and without specific training. He can then quite effortlessly make use of an intricate structure of specific rules and guiding principles to convey his thoughts and feelings to others, arousing in them novel ideas and subtle perceptions and judgments" (1975, p. 4). Humans continue to learn vocabulary throughout their life, but the basic structures of phonology and syntax are acquired early.

Generative Grammar

Chomsky's theory is referred to as generative grammar because it is an attempt to develop a small set of rules that could be used to produce, or generate, any sentence of the language. Rather than trying to find a new way to describe the sentence patterns of oral language, Chomsky began to consider a more complex model that contains both a surface structure (what we say or write) and a deep structure (roughly, what we mean, our basic ideas). He argued that there is a limited number of these deep-structure patterns that we acquire. Then we also learn how to move around or transform these basic structures to produce a great number of different surface structures. The task of acquiring a few basic structures and some rules governing how to move the elements of the base structures around to produce different surface structures is much easier than learning all the possible surface structures, and for that reason, Chomsky argued, his model of grammar was psychologically real. In other words, the language system he described, even though it was complex, could be acquired by normal humans in a relatively short time.

Chomsky's idea that language was best described by a model with both a surface level and a deep level came from his observation that many sentences are ambiguous. Some sentences are ambiguous because an individual word has multiple meanings. For example, if someone says, "There's a fork in the road," he might mean that the road divides or that he sees an eating utensil on the road. Other sentences, though, are ambiguous not because of the multiple meanings of individual words, but because the sentence has two possible underlying structures

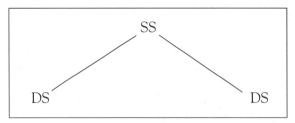

Figure 1–1. Deep and surface structures of ambiguous sentences

corresponding to the two meanings. For example, "Visiting linguists can be boring" is a surface structure that could have come from one of two underlying or deep structures corresponding roughly to these meanings: "Linguists who visit can be boring" and "Visiting a linguist can be boring."

Even though the original sentence is ambiguous, listeners could discern the intended meaning by using context cues. Speakers or writers generally leave out words only when they believe that listeners or readers can infer those words by using other cues that will help them comprehend the intended meaning. Many other ambiguous sentences can be found. When someone says, "The chicken is too hot to eat," a listener has to decide whether the chicken is going to eat once she cools off, or if a person is going to eat the chicken. Chomsky developed his theory of syntax with both a surface and a deep structure based on the presence of structurally ambiguous sentences such as these. Ambiguous sentences can be represented as shown in Figure 1–1.

Not only do some surface-structure sentences relate to (or map onto) two different deep structures; two surface-structure sentences could be derived from one deep structure. For example, someone could say, "My favorite teacher gave me an A," or "I was given an A by my favorite teacher." The meaning (and thus the deep structure) underlying these two sentences is the same. Speakers can choose different surface structures to emphasize different things and for stylistic variation, but the various surface-structure sentences come from the same deep structure.

Linguists have to decide which forms represent the deep structure, or meaning of a sentence, and which forms are derived as the result of moving parts of the sentence around or adding or deleting parts. Generally, linguists assume that active sentences, such as "My favorite teacher gave me an A," are basic, and passive sentences, such as "I was given an A by my favorite teacher," are the result of a transformation of the basic sentence. Active sentences are more common in languages, and passive sentences seem to be a variation. Children acquire active sentences earlier than passives, which are used to create certain effects. For example, by using the passive here, the speaker emphasizes "me" instead of "my favorite teacher."

In cases like this, in which one deep structure can be represented by two or more surface structures, Chomsky's two-level theory seems to work well. Rather than trying to describe all the different possible surface structures for a deep structure, this theory attempts to discover a few basic deep structures and then specify how these can be changed to produce different surface structures.

At first, linguists attempted to write a specific transformational rule for each kind of change. For example, there would be a rule that would govern the way active sentences are transformed into passive sentences. More recently, linguists have focused on the limitations of movements between deep and surface structures. Instead of having to learn a different rule for each kind of change, a speaker simply needs to learn what movements are not possible.

To take one more example, if all sentences at deep-structure level are statements, one change to surface structure would result in a question. There is a consistent relationship between statements such as "Juan can pass the linguistics test" and questions such as "Can Juan pass the linguistics test?" Current approaches would not try to specify the exact changes involved. Rather, linguists would try to specify the changes that are not possible. This approach seems to reflect more accurately what children do when they acquire a language. They develop a set of rules for generating deep structures and a set of rules that limit the possible ways the elements of the deep structure can be moved around to form different surface-structure sentences.

What are the implications of this linguistic theory for child language acquisition? In the first place, it suggests that children don't simply learn language by imitating adult surface-structure utterances and then being rewarded for correct responses. Instead, children must use what they hear to figure out the deep structures of their language and the limits on how those structures can be changed. In this way, they develop a set of rules that allows them to understand and produce a wide variety of sentences including original utterances they have never heard before. How can they do this so quickly with no direct teaching?

Universal Grammar

Chomsky's answer to the question of how children acquire language is that children have an innate capacity for language, what he at first called a *language acquisition device*. This language acquisition device is a specialized area of the brain designed for language. According to Chomsky, humans do not simply have a special cognitive capacity for figuring out language. Rather, humans are born with the basic structures of all human languages already present in the brain. Chomsky calls this innate knowledge of language *Universal Grammar*. Children are not born with knowledge of English or Japanese or any other human language. Instead, they are born with knowledge of those things that are common to all human languages.

As a result, the task facing the child is not to learn how language works, starting from scratch. Instead, since children are born with an implicit knowledge of language in general, they have to figure out how the particular language (or languages) they hear functions. For example, all languages have something like prepositions, words that show relationships among things (The book is *on* the table). In languages like English, these words that show position come in front of the noun, so they are called *pre*positions. In other languages, these words follow the noun, so in those languages, a child would encounter sentences with this pattern: The book is the table *on*. In such languages, these words are called *post*positions because they come after (post), not before (pre).

Children are born with the built-in knowledge that the language they hear will have a word to show position. What children must figure out is whether the position word precedes the noun or follows it. This is a much easier task than starting without any knowledge and having to learn that there are some words that show position and also having to learn where those words go in the sentence. It is much the same as someone who knows how to drive. If that person with this built-in knowledge of driving rents a car, she doesn't have to learn how to drive all over again to operate the new car. Instead, the driver just has to figure out how this particular car works. Is the windshield wiper on the turn signal or on another lever? How does one dim the lights? Which side is the gas tank on? Even though there are a number of things to learn, it is not nearly as difficult a task as learning how to drive in the first place. The knowledge that is already built in makes learning to drive the new car much easier.

If children have a Universal Grammar, this hardwired knowledge, then it is not surprising that most children learn the language that surrounds them. Chomsky has referred to this process of deciding the details of particular languages as *parameter setting*. Learning a language could be thought of as somewhat like setting up a fax machine. The machine already has the ability to receive and send messages, but inside there is a series of switches that can be turned on or off to fit the particular demands of the owner. Learning a language, then, is a process of using the input from the language or languages a child hears to set the switches in a way that allows communication. The process of parameter setting occurs at a subconscious level. The input the child receives from the surrounding language serves to set the switches to correspond to that language.

Not all of language is innate. Certainly, children have to learn individual words. Vocabulary can't be built in because it is not completely systematic and predictable. There is no regular connection between sounds of words and their meanings. Even though there are patterns within vocabulary, as we will discuss in Chapter 7, that enable children (and adults) to develop vocabulary knowledge fairly rapidly, learning vocabulary is different from acquiring the syntax or basic structure of a language. However, Chomsky's claim is that most of language is innate. He and other linguists base this claim on certain facts: (1) most children acquire a first language rapidly and without formal instruction, (2) they do this with only a limited amount of evidence, and (3) they do it with only limited feedback.

How Children Form Linguistic Rules

Children do get evidence of how language works from the models provided by the language of adults and others around them, but linguists who have studied language have consistently noted that there would not be enough evidence in the input for children to formulate the rules of language if the process they were using was the same as the cognitive process for other kinds of learning. For example, if an adult wants to teach a child how to tie his shoes, the adult has to provide very specific demonstrations and give clear instructions. Even when adults do that, children take a long time to learn how to tie their shoes. Adults don't give specific information to children about how language works, but children seem to figure it out quickly.

In addition, if an adult is trying to teach a child how to tie his shoes, the adult will give the child feedback. The adult will correct a child who goes about the process incorrectly and then show how it should be done. None of this happens with language. Adults seldom correct young children. Instead, they respond to what the child is trying to say—to the message, not the form. So if a child said, "I bringed my toy with me," most adults would respond by saying something like, "Oh, I'm glad you brought your toy," not "You mean you *brought* your toy, not you *bringed* your toy." In other words, adults seldom provide explicit feedback showing children which form is wrong and how to correct it. And, as most parents know, even when adults do give this kind of explicit correction, children seem to ignore it. As Wells' (1986) study demonstrated, children develop language much better when adults help them communicate their intended meanings, not when they try to correct what they say.

Studies of child language acquisition show that children develop the rules of language quickly, they acquire the language despite receiving only a limited amount of input, and they do it without much correction. All this suggests that children must have a built-in capacity for language. They seem to learn language in a way that is different from the way they learn other things.

Children's Errors

Perhaps the strongest evidence for Chomsky's claim that language is innate comes from the fact that there are certain kinds of errors that children never make. If learning language were like learning anything else, researchers would expect learners to make many different errors in the process of testing possible hypotheses. A child learning to tie her shoes might twist the strings in a number of different ways. Each attempt could be viewed as a test of the child's hypothesis about the right way to knot the shoe.

Close examination of language learners' errors shows something quite different. When children produce errors, the errors often represent an overgeneralization of a rule. The child who says "bringed" is applying the usual rule for past tense to an irregular verb. Children do make mistakes like this. But there are many other mistakes a child could logically make in testing hypotheses about language. The fact that children never make certain kinds of errors suggests that children are born with some innate knowledge of the rules of language, and their language attempts never violate those basic rules. A child may make mistakes with the parts of language that are unpredictable, like irregular verbs. But children don't make mistakes in some areas where mistakes would be expected.

To take one example, as noted earlier, children learn how to form questions. They might start by just altering the intonation pattern to change "Eat dinner now" to "Eat dinner now?" with their voice rising at the end. Over time, they use the different features of English syntax to produce sentences like "Are we going to eat dinner now?" Children don't immediately form questions that reflect conventional adult usage. Instead, they go through a series of approximations, producing some questions adults would never use. However, during this process there are some linguistic forms for questions that children never produce.

For example, given a statement like "The person who is sitting at the table is a linguist," an older child can form the question "Is the person who is sitting at the table a linguist?" That may not seem like an extraordinary feat, but this transformation from a sentence to a question is complicated. If the rule is something like "Move the helping verb (*is*) in front of the subject," how does the child know which *is* to move? Consider these logical possibilities for this sentence:

The person who *is* sitting at the table *is* a linguist.

Moving the first *is* results in sentence 1:

1. Is the person who __ sitting at the table is a linguist? (the __ indicates where *is* was before it was moved)

To produce the conventional sentence, the child must move the second *is*:

2. Is the person who is sitting at the table __ a linguist?

If children acted like scientists, they would test these two hypotheses to find out which one is right. One might expect, then, to hear children produce two kinds of questions, those like 1 and those like 2. Children could tell which one is conventional by the way people responded. If people seemed puzzled by 1 but

16

answered 2 with no hesitation, then the child would refine the hypothesis and develop an internal rule, something like "Move the helping verb of the main clause in front of the subject to form a question." However, researchers who study children's language never find examples of questions like 1 even though they are a logical possibility. This suggests that children do not develop their understanding of language, their internal grammars, following purely logical cognitive procedures of hypothesis testing the way that scientists do. If they did, children would be expected to produce all sorts of utterances that they never produce.

Pinker (1994) provides additional examples from a number of areas of child language acquisition. For example, children seem to figure out how to divide up speech into words even though there is no physical separation of words in the speech stream. The few errors children make are considered cute because they are so rare. Pinker gives several examples, including one in which a child responds to the adult statement "We are going to Miami" with "I don't want to go to your ami."

Pinker reports on a study by Stromswald, who analyzed sentences containing auxiliaries (words like *do*, *is*, and *will*) from the speech of thirteen preschoolers. The auxiliary system in English is very complex. According to Pinker, "There are about twenty-four billion billion logically possible combinations of auxiliaries (for instance, "He have might eat," "He did be eating") of which only a hundred are grammatical ("He might have eaten," "He has been eating")" (p. 272). Stromswald looked at possible errors children could make that would be logical generalizations based on the English system. Pinker lists examples like the ones shown in Figure 1–2.

Pattern: Adult English	Pattern: Adult English	Similar Pattern	Error That Might Tempt a Child
He seems happy.	Does he seem happy?	He is smiling.	Does he be smiling?
He did eat.	He didn't eat.	He did a few things.	He didn't a few things.
I like going.	He likes going.	I can go.	He cans go.
He is happy.	He is not happy.	He ate something.	He ate not something.
He is happy.	Is he happy?	He ate something.	Ate he something?

Figure 1–2. Children's possible errors

Stromswold analyzed some sixty-six thousand sentences from the preschoolers and found no errors for nearly all the possible patterns that she identified. Research like this strongly supports the claim that children are born with certain built-in linguistic concepts. It would be very difficult to account for the absence of logical errors in any other way.

Language and the Brain

Another way to consider the idea that humans have an innate capacity for language is to say that all human languages are reflections of some properties of the human mind. Linguists study language because it provides a window on the mind. Although scientists cannot see exactly what goes on in the brain, they can study language. What they learn about language gives them insights into the mind. The best evidence that humans are born with an innate knowledge of things like nouns and verbs is that all human languages have something like nouns and verbs. Thus, language must reflect certain properties of the human mind.

Scientific study of the brain has undergone tremendous advances with new technology. As early as 1861, Paul Broca identified an area in the left frontal lobe that was responsible for language. Damage to that area impaired language functioning. This area of the brain came to be known as Broca's area. About ten years later, Carl Wernicke discovered that an area in the posterior of the left hemisphere affected speech comprehension. Subsequent studies have confirmed that most language processing takes place in the left hemisphere. However, the brain is complex. Many of the studies involve patients who have had damage to a portion of the brain. In some cases, other areas of the brain seem to be able to compensate for the damaged area. Thus, although language functions seem to be located in specific areas, the brain is sufficiently interconnected so that other areas can take on certain functions. Despite the advances in brain research, much is still not known. Even though scientists can identify the sections of the brain that process language, that knowledge does not tell them how language is acquired or how it develops.

Studies by linguists complement this brain research. From their study of language, linguists have gained insights into how language is acquired. Chomsky argues that language develops in the mind in the same way that other biological developments occur. From this view, language grows in much the same way that hair does, and particular areas of the brain govern this natural process. This claim continues to be debated, but Chomsky and other linguists hold this position because it is the best way, from their perspective, to account for the fact that nearly all humans develop the ability to use a very complex linguistic system in a short time, and they do this with little evidence of how language works.

Linguists do not claim that children are born with explicit knowledge of language. The knowledge that children have is implicit, not explicit. Children may be born knowing that the language they hear will contain something like nouns and verbs, but they cannot name the parts of speech or underline all the nouns in a sentence. The innate knowledge children have allows them to understand and produce sentences, but it doesn't allow them to explain how they do it. Trying to make this implicit knowledge explicit is the job of linguists. Humans are born with an innate capacity for language, but explaining how language works is a real cognitive challenge. This is why so many students struggle in linguistics courses! Children quickly acquire linguistic knowledge, but they must study to develop metalinguistic knowledge. Metalinguistics is knowledge about language.

Humans know how to do other things that they can't explain. For example, we know how to turn on and off the lights in our house. It's something that was easy for us to learn how to do, and almost anyone living in a house with electricity can turn the lights on and off. But we can't explain to you very well what happens when we turn the switch that results in light or darkness. We can do it, but we can't explain it. Our knowledge of electricity is similar, then, to a child's knowledge of language. The child can use language, but the child can't explain how he does it. In school, children can communicate using nouns and verbs even though they can't underline nouns and verbs on a worksheet.

The implicit nature of linguistic rules is not limited to children. Many adults just know whether or not something sounds right, even though they can't explain how they know. For example, they know that it sounds fine to say, "I wonder when he's at home." But it would seem strange to say, "I wonder where he's at noon." It is perfectly acceptable to use a contraction, *he's*, in the first sentence; however, the second sentence would sound much better without the contraction: "I wonder where he is at noon." Contractions are acceptable in conversational English, but not always. We have a rule in our minds, one we can't explain, that tells us that it is acceptable to use a contraction in the first sentence, but we would never use the contraction in the second sentence. This is what we mean when we say these rules are psychologically real. People can use them even if they can't explain them. The predisposition to learn such rules is best accounted for by saying this capacity is something humans are born with.

This innatist position is supported by the research of Lenneberg, who studied the biological foundations of language development. He noted correlations between stages in language development and stages in physical maturation. As Lindfors (1987) comments, "Lenneberg's work linking language acquisition to biological maturation supported the innatist claim that genetic inheritance for mental abilities was not simply a general ability to learn but, rather, that it included a specific predisposition for language acquisition" (p. 105). Lenneberg recognized that for speech to develop, children had to be surrounded by a speaking community, so language development depends on more than innate factors. Nevertheless, his work strongly supported the innatist position that children are born with a special ability to learn language.

Conclusion

Current studies in the areas of developmental psychology, sociology, anthropology, and education as well as studies in linguistics have contributed to new understandings of the process of first language acquisition. Developmental psychologists have examined the cognitive aspects of linguistic development. Recent studies involving children acquiring sign suggest that the language modality (oral or visual) is not what is important. Instead, humans are able to find patterns in different modes of communication and use this knowledge to understand and produce messages. Children can make meaning through different modalities, and they can adjust their meaning making to different social situations. Studies by sociologists and anthropologists show differences among the ways social and economic groups within a society use language for communication. Children acquire communicative competence, the ability to use language that is appropriate for the group into which they are socialized.

Studies in generative grammar have also contributed to the understanding of first language acquisition. Children are able to internalize a set of rules that lets them understand and produce sentences they have never heard before. This shows that language learning is not simply imitation. The fact that children can develop these rules with minimal input and virtually no correction suggests that humans are born with an innate capacity for acquiring language. Studies have shown that children never make certain kinds of errors that would be logical to make. This evidence further supports the claim that children must have some built-in linguistic knowledge. They are faced with a formidable challenge of figuring out how their language works, but they don't start from scratch. Instead, they seem to already know how languages work in general, and their task is to figure out the workings of the language or languages they hear each day. And children do just this with great success!

Although there is continued debate over just how much of language is built in and how much is learned, most researchers in first language acquisition agree that humans are uniquely adapted for language acquisition. While input from caregivers is essential for the process of language acquisition to take place, no explicit teaching is necessary. Children come to school knowing the language of their community. They still need to develop proficiency in the academic language of school subjects, and they have to learn the conventions of the standard written language, but they can understand and produce language without having to resort to the application of any conscious rules.

Although there is general agreement that spoken (or signed) language is primarily acquired, there is controversy over just how children acquire written language competence. Similarly, there is a debate over whether it is possible to acquire a second language in the same way that a first language is acquired. In the next chapter, we turn to these debates in the areas of written language acquisition and second language acquisition. The ways teachers resolve these controversies have direct implications for how they teach.

Applications

1. Current views of language development are shaped from insights from different fields. Complete a table like the following one to summarize the key points that come from each discipline. Bring this chart to class and create a combined chart for all class members.

Developmental Psychology	Sociology, Anthropology, Education	Linguistics

2. Chomsky's theory of generative grammar is based in part on his observation that many sentences are structurally ambiguous. One surface structure represents two deep-structure meanings. Think of at least three ambiguous sentences, and for each one list the surface structure and the two deep structures as we did in the chapter. For example, you might list

    > The chicken was too hot to eat.
    > a. The chicken was hot, so she didn't eat.
    > b. The chicken meat was hot, so we didn't eat the chicken.

3. Chomsky also noted that two surface structures might have the same deep structure. Think of at least three examples of this phenomenon. Here are three examples:

    > a. The dog chased the cat.
    > b. The cat was chased by the dog.

a. He likes chocolate ice cream best.
b. What he likes best is chocolate ice cream.

a. Thirty children are in his class.
b. There are thirty children in his class.

4. Children's errors reflect at least two things: (1) that they don't always imitate adults, and (2) that they overgeneralize rules. If you can interact with a young child, write down some of the child's errors and then reflect on how these errors contain structures or words the child could never have heard from adults and how the child's speech contains examples of rule overgeneralization.

5. Heath studied the languages of children from different social groups who all went to the same school. If your school has children from different social or linguistic groups, observe their interactions at school. Does their school language reflect the influence of home language practices? If these practices are different from conventional school practices, how do teachers respond to and evaluate the language of those students?

2

Written and Second Language Acquisition

- *Is written language acquired naturally or learned consciously?*
- *Can people acquire a second language?*

Even though researchers debate whether language is innate or whether humans have a special cognitive capacity for language, most researchers agree that children acquire their first language. They do this rapidly and without formal instruction. It appears that children don't have to be taught language the way they are taught to button a shirt. But what about written language? Can children acquire written language in the same way they acquire oral language? There are clear differences between oral language and written language. As Halliday and Hassan (1989) have shown, what appears in a book is not simply oral language written down. Written language contains a different kind of vocabulary and different grammatical structures than oral language.

Questions also arise over whether second languages can be acquired, especially by older students. Once a person has developed one language, can that person develop a second language in the same way as the first? Older second language learners often struggle, especially with pronunciation. Most students who study a second or foreign language in high school or college fail to develop a high degree of proficiency in the language. Is that because of the methods used to teach language, or is it because people acquire a first language and then learn subsequent languages in the same way they learn other subjects in school?

In this chapter we address these questions. Insights from linguistics suggest that both written and second languages can be acquired rather than learned. This has important implications for teaching because the role of the teacher is quite different in an acquisition classroom than in a learning classroom.

Written Language

There is a debate over whether written language is learned or acquired. The question is "Is the ability to develop written language proficiency an innate property of the brain, or do people learn to read in the same way that they learn other things, through a cognitive process that involves hypothesis testing?" As we discussed earlier, most researchers agree that humans have a special capacity for oral language development, and much of the debate is over how much of language is built in and how much is learned. But the proposition that humans may also have an innate ability to acquire written language is more controversial. Some researchers claim that written language is not natural language but a secondary representation of language that the brain is not prepared to acquire. Others hold that written language can be acquired in the same way as oral language or sign language because people have an innate ability for making meaning, and they can do this with different language systems. The question of whether written language is acquired or learned is not merely academic. A teacher's belief about how written language is developed helps determine how he will teach reading and writing.

Two Views of Reading

There is little disagreement that reading success is the key to academic achievement. However, there is a great deal of disagreement about what the reading process consists of and how children should be taught to read. Two current views of reading correspond to the distinction between learning and acquisition. We refer to these two views as a *word recognition view* and a *sociopsycholinguistic view*. The word recognition view is consistent with the belief that written language must be learned. In contrast, the sociopsycholinguistic view is consistent with the claim that the ability to use written language is to some degree innate and can be acquired.

Those who hold a word recognition view believe that the main task during reading is to identify words. Readers learn a set of skills that allows them to make a connection between the black marks on the page and words in their oral vocabulary. Teaching reading involves helping students develop the necessary skills to make this connection. For example, students might learn to sound out letters and then blend the sounds to pronounce and identify words. Once students decode printed words, they recognize them as words in their oral language. Readers combine the meanings of individual words to make sense of what they read.

The sociopsycholinguistic view, on the other hand, emphasizes that reading is a process of constructing meaning. Readers use their background knowledge and cues from three linguistic systems to make sense of texts. This theory holds that readers acquire literacy in the same way they acquire oral language, by focusing on meaning. Krashen (1993, 1999) argues that people acquire the ability to read and write in the same way they acquire a first or second language, by receiving messages they understand. When people read texts that are comprehensible and interesting, they become more proficient readers and writers. Teachers make written language comprehensible when they read to students from big books with illustrations or have students read familiar songs or engaging poetry. As students follow along, they begin to make connections between the oral reading and the print. Eventually, they acquire enough knowledge of written language to read independently. Figure 2–1 contrasts these two views of reading.

Both those who hold a word recognition view and those who hold a sociopsycholinguistic view would probably agree that good readers comprehend texts. The two views might be seen simply as different routes to this common end. However, these different routes translate into very different classroom practices. As Figure 2–1 shows, they involve different goals and different methods of teaching as well as different classroom reading activities. In the next sections we discuss these differences briefly. Then in the chapters that follow, we explain in more detail the linguistic concepts that underlie each aspect of reading. Evidence from linguistics lends strong support to a sociopsycholinguistic model of reading.

Word Recognition View	Sociopsycholinguistic View
Goal: Identify words to get to the meaning of a text	**Goal:** Use background knowledge and cues from three language systems to construct meaning from a text
Method: Use phonics rules to sound out words and learn a set of sight words to identify words that do not follow phonics rules	**Method:** Use graphophonics as just one of three language cueing systems to gain meaning from a text
Learn to break words into parts to identify them	Study word parts only during linguistics investigations
Classroom activity: Learn vocabulary in advance of reading	**Classroom activity:** Read to acquire vocabulary by encountering words in context
Read orally so the teacher can help students learn to identify words and can supply words students don't know	Read silently using the strategies the teacher has helped students internalize to construct meaning from a text

Figure 2–1. Two views of reading

Goal: Word Recognition

The goal for a teacher who takes a word recognition view of reading is to help students learn to identify words. Word identification involves recoding the marks on the paper into words readers already know in their oral vocabulary and then combining the meanings of individual words to get at the meaning of the text. The assumption is that any word a student can pronounce is a word the student can understand. Following Goodman (1996), we refer to this process of identifying words as *recoding* rather than *decoding*. Recoding involves changing from one code to another. In this case, readers change written language into oral language. Decoding, in contrast, involves getting at the meaning. Spies decode secret messages, they don't simply recode them.

There is a possibility with recoding that readers may change written language to oral language without ever getting at the meaning. For example, many students who begin to study linguistics can pronounce the word *morphophonemic*. They can recode this word from written to oral form. However, these students can't decode the word because they don't know what the word means. Even though there is an assumption that word recognition will lead to meaning construction, there is a danger that students will simply learn to say the words without knowing what they mean. This is most likely to occur with English language learners.

Goal: Sociopsycholinguistics

The goal of reading from a sociopsycholinguistic perspective is to construct meaning. Readers are focused on making meaning, not on identifying the individual words. To construct meaning, readers use their background knowledge and cues from three linguistic systems: graphophonics, syntax, and semantics. They go through a process of sampling the text, predicting what will come next, filling in unstated information by inferring, confirming or disconfirming their predictions, and integrating the new information with what they already know. This process occurs rapidly. Readers combine cues from the text with their own knowledge of the world to make sense of what they are reading. Every text has a certain meaning potential, but different readers construct different meanings depending on their background knowledge and their purpose for reading. However, the goal is always to construct meaning.

Method: Word Recognition

If the goal of reading is to recognize written marks through a process of recoding a text, then readers can use several methods to do this. One is learning phonics rules. By applying phonics rules, readers can determine the pronunciation of a string of letters and change the written marks to words in their oral vocabulary. Phonics is the primary tool for word identification. Some common words such as *the* and *of*, however, do not follow regular phonics rules, so readers also need to develop a set of sight words. These are words students recognize automatically. Teachers might use flash cards to help students develop their sight words. The teacher shows a card, and students say the word.

For longer, more complex words, phonics rules do not work well, especially for English. Students can identify longer words by breaking them down into their component parts. For example, they can divide a word into its prefix, root, and suffix. Students can combine the meanings of word parts to determine the meaning of a long word like *transportation* or *reconceptualize*. Teachers sometimes tell students to find the little words inside the big word. This approach to word recognition is called *structural analysis*.

Method: Sociopsycholinguistics

If the goal of reading is to construct meaning, then readers should use all available information, including background knowledge and cues from all three cueing systems. The graphophonic system is just one source of information readers can use. Rather than being the principal means of identifying words, the letters and sounds serve as an important source of information to be combined with information from other sources. Proficient readers learn to sample the visual display and to use visual and sound information as they make and confirm predictions. However, they also use their background knowledge and cues from the syntax and semantics of the written language.

Readers may make use of their knowledge of word parts to construct meaning. However, there are limits on the usefulness of this knowledge. Although studying words is an important part of the language arts curriculum, especially if the word study is undertaken from a linguistic perspective, the ability to break words into component parts and use that information to help construct meaning has only limited value during normal reading. If a student is taking a vocabulary test, knowledge of prefixes and suffixes can help in choosing from a list of possible meanings. However, in the same way that the meaning of a sentence can't easily be determined by combining the meanings of individual words, the meaning of a word can't easily or reliably be determined by combining the meanings of the component parts. For example, it is difficult to decide on the meaning of a word like *transportation* by combining the meanings of its parts: across + carry + state of. Studying word parts can be fascinating, but it may not be too useful for determining the meaning of a word during actual reading.

Classroom Practices: Word Recognition

Beliefs about reading lead naturally to instructional practices. In word recognition classes, teachers often preteach words that they think students may not be able to figure out using phonics, sight word skills, or structural analysis. In some cases, teachers may preteach vocabulary that they think is not part of their students' oral vocabulary. Although it is difficult to decide which words most of the students will not know, teachers who have a word recognition view of reading attempt to help students with words that many of them might not know so that when they encounter those words during reading they will be able to recognize them. Preteaching often consists of defining words for students or giving students a list of words and having them look the words up and write definitions.

Another classroom practice consistent with a word recognition view is to have students read aloud on a regular basis and help students with difficult words. During round-robin reading, teachers or other students usually correct students if they mispronounce a word. They also supply words when the reader does not recognize them. The belief is that giving a student the word helps the student learn that word.

Classroom Practices: Sociopsycholinguistics

The approach to vocabulary from a sociopsycholinguistic view is to have students read extensively so that they can acquire vocabulary as they encounter words in a variety of contexts. When vocabulary is pretaught, students might learn a definition for the word, but knowing a word involves much more than that. By seeing the word several times in slightly different contexts, students can figure out its properties, including what endings it can take (its morphology), what role it plays in the sentence (its syntax), whether it is formal or informal (its pragmatics), along with its meaning (its semantics). Students acquire this information in the process of reading.

In classes in which teachers have a sociopsycholinguistic view of reading, most reading is done silently. Reading aloud is reserved for activities such as readers theatre. For that reason, teachers help students develop strategies to use during silent reading. These strategies are designed to improve comprehension. Teachers often talk with students about different things they can do if they come to a part of a text that they don't understand. Students need a variety of strategies that they can use flexibly to construct meaning. The goal of this instruction is to improve students' abilities to develop higher levels of reading proficiency.

The goals, methods, and classroom practices of teachers with these two views of reading differ. As a result, the way students develop reading proficiency in these two kinds of classes also varies. The two views have very practical consequences. In subsequent chapters, we will look closely at the phonology, orthography, morphology, and syntax of English. As teachers better understand these linguistic systems, they can make more informed decisions about which view of reading to adopt and how to go about helping all their students become proficient readers.

Two Views of Writing

In the same way that there are two views of reading, there are also two views of writing. These two views again correspond to the distinction we have made between learning and acquisition. From a learning point of view, writing, like reading, must be taught directly. From an acquisition perspective, writing, like speaking, is a form of output that reflects the language competence an individual has acquired. Teachers from both points of view include writing in their language arts curriculum, but several aspects of their instruction are different. Figure 2–2 shows these two views of writing.

Learning View: Traditional Writing Classroom	Acquisition View: Process Writing Classroom
Goal: Learn how to produce a good piece of writing	**Goal:** Produce good writing and acquire knowledge of the writing process
Method: Begin with the parts and build up to writing a whole text	**Method:** Begin with a message and develop the skills needed to produce the message
Teacher directly instructs students in how to form letters, then words, then how to combine words into sentences, and then sentences into paragraphs	Teacher creates conditions for authentic written responses and then helps students express themselves in writing
Approach to correctness: Writing product must be conventional from the beginning	**Approach to correctness:** Writing moves naturally from invention to convention
The teacher corrects each piece of writing	Classmates and others, including the teacher, respond to drafts

Figure 2–2. Two approaches to the teaching of writing

Figure 2–2 is adapted from an earlier book, *Teaching Reading and Writing in Spanish in the Bilingual Classroom* (Freeman and Freeman 1996, 1998b), in which we describe in detail how writing develops in both Spanish and English when teachers use a process approach. Here, we briefly describe the major differences between a learning and an acquisition approach to teaching writing.

Goals and Methods: Traditional Classroom

In a traditional class, teachers want students to be able to produce a good story, report, or other piece of writing. To accomplish this goal, teachers break writing down into its component parts and teach each one. For example, teachers of young children show them how to form letters. Students learn to write words, sentences, paragraphs, and then whole stories or reports. In many traditional classes, students learn how to produce a five-paragraph essay that follows a clearly defined structure. Usually, students are given the topics for writing, and they are expected to complete the writing in a fairly short time. This approach can help students perform well on typical tests of writing.

Goals and Methods: Process Classroom

One goal in a process writing class is the production of good pieces of writing. However, teachers also want students to internalize the process involved. This includes choosing a topic, writing drafts, conferencing to get feedback on the writing, doing final editing, and sharing the finished piece with others. Teachers provide many opportunities for students to produce different kinds of writing—a story, a letter to a friend, a list of books they have read. Rather than giving students topics, teachers help students understand that there are many situations in which they can express their ideas most effectively by using written language. For example, students who investigate a topic during a theme study might accompany their oral report with a written handout for classmates.

Teachers set aside time on a regular basis for writing. During writers workshop they teach minilessons to help students express their ideas more effectively. Teachers who take an acquisition view realize that students must read frequently. The reading provides the input needed for written output. As they read, students come to understand the different organizational structures writers use to communicate ideas.

Approach to Correctness: Traditional Classroom

Teachers in traditional classrooms emphasize the importance of producing writing that follows conventions in handwriting, spelling, punctuation, and organization. Often, handwriting and spelling are major components of the writing program. Students memorize lists of words and are tested each week on their spelling words.

To help students learn to produce correct writing, teachers correct each piece a student writes. In many traditional classes, the form of the writing becomes much more important than the content. Students who focus on form may not even try to use new words for fear of misspelling them.

Approach to Correctness: Process Classroom

Process writing teachers believe that writing will move from individual invention to conventional forms. For example, students may begin by spelling most words the way they sound. Over time, they begin to produce more conventional spellings. Teachers help students keep the focus on the content of what they are writing, not just the form. At the same time, as writers share their writing with classmates and the teacher, they realize that some ways of spelling words or punctuating sentences confuse their audience, so they start to use more conventional forms to communicate more effectively. When students have written something they want others to read, they are motivated to put their writing in a form that follows social conventions. Teachers give minilessons on all areas of writing, including spelling and punctuation. Rather than giving students lists of words to memorize, they help them discover the patterns in the spellings of English words. Conventional writing is a goal of a process classroom, but teachers emphasize that the content of the message is more important than the form.

The Reading and Writing Connection from an Acquisition View

A teacher's view of whether written language is learned or acquired determines, to a great extent, the classroom practices the teacher follows. If teachers believe that reading and writing are learned, they divide the skills into their component parts and teach each of the parts directly and systematically. Reading is accomplished by recognizing words, so teachers teach phonics rules, sight words, and structural analysis. Writing consists of producing words, so teachers focus on handwriting, spelling, punctuation, grammar, and conventional organizational forms, such as the five-paragraph essay.

When teachers view reading and writing from an acquisition standpoint, they do a number of things to make written language comprehensible. They read to and with students and teach students strategies they can use to comprehend texts. They believe that written language, like oral language, develops best when students focus on the message, not the form. They recognize that reading provides the input needed for writing output. They provide many opportunities for students to produce and share their writing. They help students understand all the steps involved in the writing process.

From an acquisition standpoint, reading and writing are closely related. Students acquire much of their ability to write by reading. However, writing and talking about what they have written play an important role in students' writing development. Brown and Cambourne (1987) describe a method teachers can use to help students become more proficient in reading and writing. This method is called *read and retell*. Students read a number of articles or stories from a single genre. For example, they might read several different fairy tales over time. After reading a short fairy tale, they would turn the paper over and do a written retelling. Then, working in pairs or small groups, they would share and compare their retellings.

Brown and Cambourne found that many of the features from the readings showed up in the children's writing. Not only did children use some of the same phrasing and vocabulary, but they also used punctuation and spellings they had never used before. Brown and Cambourne refer to this effect as *direct spillover*. When they interviewed the children, they discovered that this inclusion of text features was not conscious. Children were focused on representing the meaning of the story, and in the process they used several of the text features. In fact, these features also showed up in other writing much later, a phenomenon the authors call *delayed spillover*.

Brown and Cambourne conclude that spillover is the result of the retelling process. They write, "The retelling procedure, as we define it, coerces learners to bring to their conscious awareness many features of text structure on which they would not typically focus, or upon which they would not typically reflect" (p. 27). Doing a written retelling and discussing how one retelling is similar to or different from another helped these students internalize features of written text that they later used. This suggests that while input from reading is necessary for students to acquire written language, output in the form of writing and talking brings some aspects of written language to the conscious level and enables students to use these features later. Teachers in an acquisition class may not directly teach spelling and vocabulary, but they plan activities such as read and retell that require students to focus on language forms as part of a meaningful language activity.

Teachers who take an acquisition view of reading and writing have different goals, use different methods, and respond to errors differently from teachers who take a learning view. In the same way, teachers who adopt an acquisition view of second or foreign language teaching approach their task differently from teachers who believe that a second or foreign language must be learned.

Two Views of Second or Foreign Language Development

In the same way that there are two views of how people develop literacy, there are also two views of how people develop a second or foreign language. One view is that

Traditional Learning View	Current Acquisition View
Goal: Teach language directly so students can produce correct language forms	**Goal:** Make language comprehensible so students can use language for different purposes
Method: Break language into component parts and teach each part	**Method:** Use various techniques to make the linguistic input understandable
Classroom activities: Students do drills and exercises to practice language	**Classroom activities:** Students use language in communicative situations
Attitude toward errors: Teachers correct errors to help students develop good language habits	**Attitude toward errors:** Errors are natural, so teachers keep the focus on meaning and help students understand and express ideas

Figure 2–3. Two views of language teaching

a second language is learned. Traditional methods of second and foreign language teaching follow the learning model. The second view is that second languages are acquired. Current methods incorporate more activities designed to foster acquisition. Even though traditional practices prevail in many classrooms, current theory supports methods based on an acquisition view. Figure 2–3 lists some of the differences between learning and acquisition views of second language teaching.

Goals and Methods: Learning View

The goal of instruction is to produce students who speak and understand the language. This is best accomplished by teaching each part of the language—the pronunciation, grammar, and vocabulary—directly and systematically. Teachers break each language area into parts to make learning easier. For example, early lessons might all be in present tense to teach that part of language. Later lessons might introduce past or future tense.

Goals and Methods: Acquisition View

The goal of instruction is to enable students to use language for a variety of purposes. Students should be able to understand, speak, read, and write the language in different settings. For example, they should be able to read a menu and order food in a restaurant. To accomplish this goal, teachers provide students with a great deal of language input and use various techniques to make the new language comprehensible. These techniques might include using gestures, pictures, and real things or reading a book with a predictable pattern and clear pictures of key words.

Classroom Activities: Learning View

Students practice language by engaging in oral drills and written exercises. They might also learn dialogues and practice them in pairs or small groups. Each drill, exercise, or dialogue would reinforce the grammar and vocabulary the students are learning.

Classroom Activities: Acquisition View

At first, students listen and read to build up a store of language. They focus on making sense out of the new language. Later, they use the language to accomplish different things. For example, they might introduce a new student to the class or retell a story the teacher has read to them.

Attitude Toward Errors: Learning View

Since the emphasis is on developing correct language forms, teachers correct errors immediately. They often do this directly. This helps students avoid developing bad habits of grammar or pronunciation. Much of the class focus is on producing correct language forms.

Attitude Toward Errors: Acquisition View

All students make errors. However, if their intent is to express their ideas, they will modify their language to make it more understandable to their listeners or readers. Teachers help students say what students want to say and also give them strategies so they can continue to communicate when they don't have the linguistic resources yet. For example, teachers might show students how they can use circumlocution to talk around a word they have not yet acquired using words they do know and still get their idea across.

These two views of second language teaching are much like the two views of written language development. In each case, the traditional view is based on a model of learning that comes from behavioral psychology, and the current view is based on a model of acquisition that is consistent with cognitive psychology and also assumes that at least some parts of language may be innate. There is still debate over how much of language is acquired and what has to be learned, but current methods are based on the belief that, to a great degree, a second language can be acquired in the same way that a first language is acquired. In the sections that follow, we explain the most widely known theory of second language acquisition and also examine the role that the social context plays in the language acquisition process.

Krashen's Theory of Second Language Acquisition

Krashen (2003) has developed a theory of second language acquisition that forms the basis for much of the teaching methodology in ESL, EFL, and bilingual classes as well as mainstream classes with second language students. Krashen has written and spoken extensively to show how his ideas about language acquisition translate into classroom practice. Across the country, teachers have attended workshops and staff development sessions in which Krashen's ideas were presented. Coursework for preservice teachers in states with high numbers of English learners usually includes Krashen's theory. Many teachers have adopted methods consistent with Krashen's theory because it makes sense to them and works with their students. Krashen's theory of second language acquisition consists of five interrelated hypotheses. In the sections that follow we explain each of these hypotheses briefly. For a more extensive discussion of Krashen and other second language theorists, see *Between Worlds: Access to Second Language Acquisition* (Freeman and Freeman 2001).

The Learning/Acquisition Hypothesis

Krashen makes a distinction between two ways of developing a second language. The first, which he calls learning, is what many students experienced in high school or college foreign language classes. Learning is a conscious process that involves studying rules and vocabulary. Students who attempt to learn a language approach language study in the same way they might approach the study of any other school subject. They break the subject down into manageable chunks and try to memorize and practice the different parts of the language with the goal of being able to use the language to communicate. A student might study vocabulary lists or verb conjugations. Students would practice using this knowledge by doing different exercises and drills. Learned knowledge can be tested. Unfortunately, many students who are able to pass quizzes in French or Spanish are not able to use the new language to communicate with native speakers or to understand TV shows or movies in the language. In addition, this learned knowledge is quickly forgotten if it is not used.

The second way of developing language is what Krashen calls acquisition. In contrast to learning, acquisition is subconscious. Students acquiring a language may not even be aware that they are picking up vocabulary or sentence structures. Acquisition occurs as students use language for a variety of purposes. For

Learning	Acquisition
Conscious: We are aware we are learning	Subconscious: We are not aware we are acquiring
It's what happens in school when we study rules and grammar	It's what happens in and out of school when we receive messages we understand

Figure 2–4. Learning and acquisition

example, students can acquire a language at the same time that they are learning some academic subject area content if the teacher uses techniques to help make the instruction understandable. While learning is usually restricted to the school context, acquisition can take place in or out of school. Acquisition is what happens when someone goes to another country and picks up the language in the process of day-to-day living and interacting with native speakers of the language. Figure 2–4 summarizes the key differences between acquisition and learning.

The Natural Order Hypothesis

Krashen reviews research that shows that language, both first language and second language, is acquired in a natural order. Simply put, some aspects of language appear in the speech of language learners before other features. For example, babies acquiring English first produce sounds with vowels (usually the low, back "ah" sound) and later add consonants beginning with consonants formed with the lips, like *p* and *m*. This helps explain why the first word of many infants is something like *mama*, much to the delight of a parent. Sounds like "r" come later. That's why young children might say, like Elmer Fudd, "wabbit" instead of "rabbit." Other parts of language also appear in a natural order. Statements come before questions. Positive statements come before negatives, and so on.

Researchers in second language found the same phenomenon. The natural order of second language acquisition differs slightly from that of first language, but there is a definite order. Dulay and Burt (1974) studied Spanish and Chinese speakers acquiring English. They looked at the order in which certain morphemes appeared. They noted that the plural *s* in a word like *toys* showed up in children's speech earlier than the third-person *s* of present-tense verbs in sentences like "He plays." Whether researchers look at the acquisition of sounds, word parts, or sentence patterns, they find an order of acquisition that is the same even for children whose first languages are different. The order seems to be determined by the language being acquired, not by a transfer of features from the first language.

When languages are taught and students attempt to learn language, the sequence seldom matches the natural order of acquisition. This helps explain why students can produce correct sentences in class or do well on a written test but have trouble using the same forms correctly a short time later. Students may have learned the form, but they have not acquired it, so it is not a part of their long-term ability to use the language.

In addition, since language is so complex, linguists have not been able to describe the order of acquisition of the different parts of language in sufficient detail so that teachers could use the order to create a sequence of lessons that follows the natural sequence of acquisition. Even if linguists were able to specify the natural order, trying to teach it would probably fail because different students in any class are at different levels of acquisition. Besides, any attempt to sequence and teach parts of language is consistent with a model of language learning, not with language acquisition. It is helpful for teachers to be aware of normal developmental patterns of acquisition so they can support students, but teachers can't change the sequence through direct teaching.

The Monitor Hypothesis

This hypothesis helps explain the role of learning in the process of language acquisition. Acquired language forms the basis for the ability to understand and produce language. The phonology, morphology, and syntax are acquired. Acquisition is what enables native English speakers to tell what sounds right in the language. They may not be able to explain why "He is married to her" sounds better than "He is married with her," but because native speakers have acquired the language, they can make these kinds of judgments.

Learned knowledge also plays a role in language competence. The rules that people learn can be used to monitor spoken or written output. In other words, people can use these rules to check what they say or write. In order for monitor use to be effective, language users must have time, they must focus on language form, and they must know the rules. Even in the first language, most people monitor their speech in formal situations such as giving a speech to a large group of people. However, there are effective and ineffective ways to use the monitor.

In the flow of rapid conversation, speakers generally don't have time to check what they are saying and correct themselves. In addition, monitoring involves focusing on how something is being said rather than on what is being said. Unfortunately, it is almost impossible to concentrate on both the ideas and the correct pronunciation or grammar at the same time. The more a speaker thinks about the message, the less the speaker can concentrate on the language. Further, to use the monitor effectively, one must know the rules. Is it "different from" or "different than"? Unless the speaker knows the right answer, he can't monitor the output very well.

Effective monitor users steer a middle course. Overusers try to correct everything, and the result is halting speech or even a hesitation to enter a conversation. Underusers charge ahead, but at times their errors make their discourse incomprehensible. Optimum use of the monitor involves checking to avoid major errors, all the while keeping the focus on the message.

Spoken language is more difficult to monitor than written language. Editing during the writing process represents an ideal situation to apply the monitor because there is time and one can focus specifically on the correctness of the language to be sure that sentences are complete and words are spelled right. However, if writers monitor while they are drafting, the focus on form may interrupt the flow of their ideas.

The Input Hypothesis

How does acquisition take place? According to Krashen, the key is comprehensible input—messages, either oral or written, that students understand. A teacher's job is to find ways to make the input comprehensible. Not all input leads to acquisition. Krashen says that students acquire language when they receive input that is slightly beyond their current level. He refers to this as i+1 (input plus one). If students receive input that is below or at their current level (i+0), there is nothing new to acquire. However, if the input is too much beyond their current level (i+10, for example), it no longer is comprehensible.

Providing comprehensible input is not an exact science. Teachers can't possibly ensure that everything they say or write will be exactly at the i+1 level for every student. The students in a class are all at different levels of proficiency. Nevertheless, as long as students understand most of what they hear or read in a new language, they will acquire the language. Different students will acquire different parts of the language depending on their current level. To ensure that the input is comprehensible, teachers can use pictures, gestures, tone of voice, and hands-on activities. Teachers can also avoid using idioms, they can pause often to slow down the rate of speech, and they can recycle vocabulary by planning curriculum around themes so that certain words are repeated naturally in the process of studying the theme through different academic content areas. These techniques give students comprehensible input at the i+1 level (Freeman and Freeman 1998a). Krashen is an especially strong advocate of reading for language acquisition. He cites research showing that reading provides excellent comprehensible input and is the source of one's knowledge of vocabulary, grammar, and spelling (Krashen 1993).

Output It should be noted that while Krashen argues that acquisition is the result of receiving comprehensible input, other researchers have claimed that students also need opportunities to produce "comprehensible output" (Swain 1985). Van Lier's (1988) model of second language acquisition includes meaningful language use. It may be that speaking and writing a second language help bring aspects of the language to a conscious level, and, as a result, students can use those language forms in the future. This would parallel what Brown and Cambourne (1987) found with first language writing.

One of the benefits of output is that it produces more input. In fact, good acquirers learn how to manage conversations so that they get comprehensible input from others. These acquirers have developed what is called *strategic language competence*. They use different strategies both to understand a second language and also to make themselves understood. For example, a person trying to communicate in another language might learn or use phrases such as "Could you repeat, please?" and "I don't understand exactly" and "Could you show me?" These kinds of strategies encourage the native speakers to respond with language that the acquirer can better understand. In other words, the language becomes comprehensible input.

The Affective Filter Hypothesis

How do affective factors such as nervousness, boredom, and anxiety influence language acquisition? If language is acquired when a person receives comprehensible input, that input has to reach the part of the brain that processes language. That part of the brain is what Chomsky calls the language acquisition device. Boredom and anxiety are affective factors that can serve as a kind of filter to block out incoming messages and prevent them from reaching the language acquisition device. As a result, even though a teacher may present a very comprehensible lesson, some students may not acquire the language of the presentation because their affective filter operates to block the input. Students cannot acquire language that never reaches the language acquisition device. On the other hand, when the filter is open, when students are relaxed and engaged in a lesson, even messages that are not easy to comprehend will trigger the acquisition process. This is why, for example, students often acquire language when singing or when involved in an interesting hands-on activity such as cooking or an interesting science experiment.

Krashen's hypotheses help explain why many people who had trouble learning language in school were able to acquire a language living abroad. They acquired the language in a natural setting in which they received lots of meaningful and relevant comprehensible input. Nevertheless, schools can be good places for acquisition if teachers recognize that there is a natural order and thus support students at different levels; if they encourage students to use their learned rules appropriately, especially when they edit their writing; when they use various techniques to make sure each lesson contains comprehensible input; and when they create classroom conditions that lower students' affective filters. When teachers do these things, students acquire a second language in much the same way they acquired their first language.

Schumann's Theory of Second Language Acquisition

Krashen's theory of second language acquisition accounts for the psychological process of language development. Other researchers have considered the broader social context. Schumann (1978), for example, studied one adult immigrant whose English acquisition was very limited. Schumann found that a number of social factors helped explain the low rate of acquisition. These factors created a considerable social distance between the student and members of the mainstream society.

Schumann has identified several factors that contribute to social distance. For example, distance is greater when there is only limited integration of the two cultural groups, when the minority group itself is large enough to be self-sufficient, when the group is very tight-knit, when the group has characteristics very different from those of the mainstream culture, when the majority group has a negative attitude toward the minority group, and when the learner intends to stay only a short time in the country. One example might help illustrate social distance. The Hmong, a nomadic people from Laos, came to the United States after the war in Vietnam to escape persecution for helping the United States. The first generation settled mainly in Minnesota and central California. Their numbers there were so large that they were able to support one another, buy at stores that catered to them, and live with minimal contact with the mainstream. All these factors contribute to social distance, and the greater the social distance between the minority group and the mainstream, the less likely that minority group members will acquire the language of the mainstream culture. At first, then, many adult Hmong people did not acquire English quickly. As the next generations have attened U.S. schools and come into closer contact with the U.S. culture, this social distance has descreased and not only have they learned English, but many are losing their ability to speak Hmong fluently.

Schumann also considered psychological factors, such as motivation, attitude, and culture shock. Students with low motivation and a negative attitude toward members of the mainstream culture are less apt to acquire the language of the mainstream, especially when students are going through culture shock as they adjust to living in a new country. Many Hmong teens arriving after the war were adjusting to the huge change in lifestyle from an agrarian society to the modern life of cities in the U.S. They felt resentment because of the persecution of their people and the lack of understanding they perceived from both teachers and other students. Many dropped out of school, joined gangs, or did both. Psychological factors can create psychological distance, which, combined with social distance, helps explain a slow rate of acquisition. Social and psychological distance helped explain why the student Schumann studied developed very limited English despite being an intelligent and capable person.

Schumann's concepts of social and psychological distance complement Krashen's theory. Social distance limits opportunities for students to receive the comprehensible input needed for acquisition. Psychological distance serves to raise the affective filter and prevent input from reaching the language acquisition device. Immigrants who have limited contact with native English speakers are not likely to develop high levels of English proficiency. Valdés (2001) has shown that many middle school and high school students are segregated from native English speakers much of the day and, as a result, they fail to develop the academic English required for school success. If these students also have limited contact with native speakers outside school, then they will not develop the language of everyday communication either.

The Critical Period Hypothesis

Krashen has developed a theory of second language acquisition. But is there a time limit on acquisition? Researchers from a number of fields have debated this issue for both first language and second language acquisition. In the case of first languages, there have been cases of children who have been brought up under very unusual circumstances that included isolation from other humans. Such children have often exhibited considerable difficulty in developing language later in life. However, in almost every case, the children have experienced physical and psychological trauma that may account for their later language learning difficulties.

Although cases of someone failing to develop a first language are rare, there is a general belief that children are better language learners than adults. Children are able to speak a second language with little or no foreign accent, but adults usually retain an accent. This has led researchers to investigate the possibility that there is a critical period during which language can be acquired. Once past that period, people are not able to acquire a second language.

Before examining the idea of a critical period more closely, it is important to point out that the discussion is generally limited to accent or pronunciation. There are two reasons that children appear to be better language learners than adults. In the first place, adults have more to learn. If an adult went to a new country and learned to speak the language like a competent six-year-old, most people would rate the adult as deficient in the language. Adults are expected to have a much more developed vocabulary, and adults frequently use complex syntax. Nobody expects this of a six-year-old.

Not only do adults have more to learn, but they usually have less time to learn it. Most adults who go to live in a foreign country go there to work. Usually, at work the adult speaks his or her native language. Outside work, the adult may socialize with others who speak the native language as well. For many adults living in a foreign country, opportunities to use the foreign language are limited. An English speaker will spend much of the day in contexts where English is the medium of communication. Children acquiring a second language, though, have fewer responsibilities and many more chances to interact with speakers of the foreign language. As a result, children receive more comprehensible input in the foreign language than adults do.

Even though adults are good language learners, they usually retain an accent. Does this mean there is a critical period for the acquisition of phonology? Researchers from different disciplines have investigated this question, and although no definitive answers have emerged, there are several possible explanations. The three most common explanations as to why most, although not all, adults speak a second language with a foreign accent are based on neurological factors, cognitive factors, and affective factors.

Neurological Factors

Studies of the brain have shown that different areas of the brain are associated with different functions. Brown (1994) notes that "there is evidence in neurological research that as the human brain matures certain functions are assigned—or 'lateralized'—to the left hemisphere of the brain and other functions to the right hemisphere. Intellectual, logical, and analytic functions appear to be largely located in the left hemisphere while the right hemisphere controls functions related to emotional and social needs" (p. 53). Language is one of the functions located in the left hemisphere.

Lateralization of the brain begins at about age two. Not all researchers agree about when lateralization is complete. However, many researchers have concluded that by puberty, the different functions of the brain have been lateralized to the two hemispheres. Children who acquire a second language before puberty usually speak the new language without an accent. Older learners, however, generally speak the second language with an accent. Since people who learn a second language after puberty generally retain an accent, researchers have hypothesized that people are no longer able to acquire some aspects of language, such as the phonology, once the brain is lateralized and language is located in the left hemisphere. They hypothesize that the critical period for the acquisition of phonology is the period prior to changes in the brain associated with lateralization.

Cognitive Factors

Young children who develop a second language with nativelike pronunciation have not yet reached what Piaget identified as the *formal operational stage*. This stage begins for most children at around age eleven, and it is the point at which more abstract thought is possible. Perhaps the ability for more abstract thought changes the way people go about the task of learning a second language. Children in the *concrete operational stage* may be able to acquire the language without needing to analyze the structure of the language. Older learners may not be able to suppress formal thought processes. To use Krashen's terms, younger children have not reached a point where learning is possible (learning involves knowing and applying abstract rules about language), so they develop a second language through a process of acquisition. Older learners have difficulty turning learning off. They use cognitive processes to analyze language, and, as a result, they have more difficulty acquiring a language, particularly nuances of pronunciation.

Affective Factors

The fact that most adults retain an accent may be due more to affective factors than to neurological or cognitive factors. For one thing, adolescents or adults learning a second language may be more self-conscious than children. Older learners may be hesitant to try out a new language for fear of appearing incompetent. Krashen hypothesizes that affective factors may filter out input and prevent it from reaching the language acquisition device. There may also be a kind of output filter. Nervousness, for example, could inhibit an older learner from producing the new language.

Guiora, a psychologist, has suggested that each person has a language ego. A person's language forms an important part of that person's identity. The way someone talks helps define who she is. Learning a new language, at a subconscious level, may threaten the language ego. By retaining an accent, a person keeps part of her identify. A British English speaker, for example, who speaks Spanish with a British accent sends the message that she is still a person from England.

The idea of a language ego is related to general attitudinal factors. Older learners who acquire a second language and speak with little or no foreign accent are often people who admire and identify with people who live in a country where the language is spoken. On the other hand, if a person has a somewhat negative attitude toward people who speak a certain language, that attitude might serve to block the acquisition of a nativelike accent in the language. The learner might not want to be identified as a native of a country where the language is spoken.

A great deal has been written about a critical period. For an excellent review, see Brown (1994). However, it is important to recognize that the critical period applies primarily to pronunciation. Adults can acquire a second language, and some adults also develop a nativelike accent. In some cases, though, adult learners also make persistent errors in vocabulary and syntax when they speak in the second language.

Fossilization

The presence of certain kinds of errors that persist in the speech of adult second language learners is referred to as *fossilization*. For these learners, some errors seem to have become a permanent part of their new language. In many cases, these older learners are highly educated, and they may have spent years in the country in which the language is spoken. Instruction doesn't seem to solve the problem.

A good example of fossilization comes from an older Japanese student. This student studied and taught English in Japan. He came to the United States and completed an M.A. degree in English teaching. He has lived in the United States for several years. Yet, consider this excerpt from an email he sent: "I miss a cozy, sunny weather in Fresno. I have to put on a heavy down jacket, a glove, and a cap. The strong, chilly wind attacks me. I am in the process to get used to a mean weather."

Even though this student has advanced vocabulary and syntax, his writing has a number of errors. He could probably explain the rule for each error, but when he uses English, errors like this keep coming up. Fossilization is characteristic of the language of many adults who have acquired a second language. Perhaps the best explanation for this phenomenon is that people like this student have acquired enough of the language to communicate any idea. The language serves their needs very well. Although they may say that they want to speak English perfectly, at a subconscious level, at least, they may feel that their English is good enough.

A Note on Bilingual Programs

If students acquire English primarily by receiving comprehensible input in English when their affective filter is low, one might conclude that structured English immersion programs such as the ones that Ron Unz and other antibilingual education campaigners advocate would be the solution to the poor academic performance of many English language learners. In these programs English learners are given all their instruction in English. Krashen (1996) and many others have pointed out the problems with structured English immersion and the benefits of bilingual education.

The debate over bilingual programs tends to be more emotional than pedagogical. Often, parents of English language learners want their children in all-English classes because they recognize the importance of learning English. However, students who continue to receive instruction in and develop their first language while they are learning English do much better in school than those who are placed in structured English immersion programs. English immersion is not supported by theories of second language acquisition, and such programs ultimately disadvantage English language learners. Some students do make short-term gains in English, but their test scores and academic performance fall rapidly as they move up through the grades (Thomas and Collier 2001). English language learners need to develop both their first language and English. Unfortunately, children in structured English immersion seldom develop either their first language or English to the levels needed for academic success.

Bilingual programs promote English acquisition in several ways. First, native language instruction, when used appropriately, enhances English instruction by making the English more comprehensible. When teachers preview a lesson in the student's native language and then review it using the first language again, students are more apt to understand the English instruction that makes up the major part of the lesson. Preview, view, review is a technique that many bilingual teachers use (Freeman and Freeman 1998a).

Secondly, students in bilingual programs receive some content area instruction in their first language. This instruction builds the necessary background for understanding lessons in the content areas given in English. For example, a student who has learned about the water cycle during native language instruction can better understand a lesson in English that builds on the concept that water passes through different states as it is heated and cooled. For students without that background, the English instruction might be incomprehensible. Teachers have often noted how quickly some recent immigrants acquire English. In many cases, these students have already built strong academic content knowledge in their first language, and this knowledge makes the English instruction more comprehensible.

A third way in which bilingual programs contribute to English language acquisition is that students in these programs more fully develop their first language. Studies have shown that when students have full native language proficiency, including the ability to do academic reading and writing, they can transfer this knowledge from their first language to the second (Cummins 2000). This helps explain why older students with adequate schooling in their native countries do quite well in school while students who do not develop their first language tend to struggle (Freeman and Freeman 2002).

Bilingual programs have other advantages, but they directly support English language acquisition by making the input more comprehensible. Students in well-designed and well-implemented bilingual programs succeed in school at higher rates than students in structured English immersion programs (Collier 1995). Effective bilingual programs provide the comprehensible input students need for second language acquisition.

Conclusion

We began this chapter by posing two questions:

1. Is written language acquired naturally or learned consciously?
2. Can people acquire a second language?

In our discussion of each question, we pointed out that there is a debate over two views of language development. One view is that language is learned. Teachers who hold a learning view break language into its component parts and teach them directly. They correct errors to help students develop good language habits. They keep the focus on correct language form and pay less attention to the content. How students say or write things is more important than what they say or write. This approach applies to both written and second or foreign language teaching.

The second view is that language is acquired. Teachers who hold an acquisition view attempt to make written or oral language comprehensible. They use different techniques to help students understand what they read or hear. The focus always stays on making meaning. Students develop conventional language forms once they have messages they wish to communicate.

Current research supports an acquisition view, although there is still debate over how much of language can be acquired and what can be learned. In the following chapters we present relevant aspects of phonology, orthography, morphology, and syntax. Concepts from these areas of linguistics can help inform readers as they decide what their view of language development is and how they can organize instruction to help all their students become proficient users of oral and written languages.

Applications

1. In this chapter, we distinguish between learning a language and acquiring a language. If you have studied a second language, evaluate your experience.

Was the teaching method used consistent with a learning view or an acquisition view? Write down some reasons for your answer and prepare to discuss these with classmates.

2. Reflect on the writing instruction you have received. Different teachers may have used different approaches. Which view of writing described in this chapter corresponds most closely to each of your experiences? Make some notes on your experiences and bring them to class for discussion.

3. Brown and Cambourne have written a book that is an excellent resource for teachers at any grade level who wish to use the read and retell strategy. In their book they describe spillover as a phenomenon in which students' writing reflects aspects of texts they have read, responded to in a written retelling, and discussed. Do you see evidence of spillover in your students' work? Try out this strategy over a couple weeks. Reflect on the experience.

4. We discussed in some detail the two views of reading that correspond to acquisition and learning views of language development. Following is a list of a classroom activities. Mark each one as typical of what goes on in a word recognition class or a class with a sociopsycholinguistic perspective. Bring your marked form to class to discuss with classmates. Some items could fit either view depending on how a teacher carries out the activity. Be prepared to defend your marking decisions.

Directions:
Label each activity (L) for learning/word recognition or (A) for acquisiton/
sociopsycholinguistic view.
Some activities can have both labels.
Be prepared to explain your choices.

The students:

_____ look up words in the dictionary to write definitions
         make a Venn diagram to compare two stories
_____ practice sounding out words
_____ read in round-robin fashion
_____ correct peers when they make a mistake during reading
_____ identify words on a big book page that start with the same sound
_____ group cards with classmates' names by a criterion on such as first or last letter
_____ write rhyming poetry and then discuss different spellings for the same sound
_____ ask the teacher how to spell any word they don't know
_____ read a language experience story they have created with the teacher
_____ work in pairs to arrange words from a familiar chant into sentences
_____ divide words into syllables
_____ on a worksheet, draw a line from each word to the picture that starts with the same sound
_____ make alphabet books on different topics

The teacher:

_____ preteaches vocabulary
_____ does a shared reading with a big book
_____ makes sure that students read only books that fit their level
_____ has students segment words into phonemes
_____ writes words the students dictate for a story and has students help with the spelling of difficult words
_____ asks students to look around the room and find words starting with a certain letter
_____ uses decodable texts
_____ sets aside time for SSR (sustained silent reading) each day
_____ teaches Latin and Greek roots
_____ has students meet in literature circles
_____ conducts phonics drills
_____ chooses predictable texts
_____ teaches students different comprehension strategies
_____ does a picture walk of a new book
_____ uses a variety of worksheets to teach different skills

3

English Phonology

- *How do people understand and produce language?*
- *What is phonology and what are the phonemes of English?*

Human Communication

Humans love to talk. Whether it is face-to-face or on the phone, people constantly communicate with one another. In fact, with the increasing use of cellular phones, it seems like some people never stop talking!

Oral communication is something most people take for granted. Few people ever stop to think about how they are able to produce and understand language. A commonsense view is that a speaker starts with an idea and encodes it into language. Since the channel of communication for most people is oral language, producing language involves pushing air from the lungs up into the mouth and using the lips and tongue to produce different sounds. Understanding a message requires the listener to decode the acoustic signal into language to understand the original idea. All this seems to happen effortlessly. Speakers and listeners concentrate on what they are saying, not on how they are accomplishing the task. Communication with oral language seems so easy that, for most people, it is almost like breathing. Figure 3–1 represents this commonsense view of how communication takes place.

Human communication is considerably more complex than the commonsense view would suggest. Sending and receiving messages involves much more than encoding and decoding. For example, listeners predict what they will hear and then sample the acoustic signal to confirm their predictions. Listening is not a precise process. Otherwise, people would always hear exactly what others say. Communicating depends on listeners being able to make inferences to fill in information not included in the message. The social context also helps determine the meaning. Listeners' predictions are often based more on the setting than the acoustic signal. For example, at a store a customer might predict that the clerk

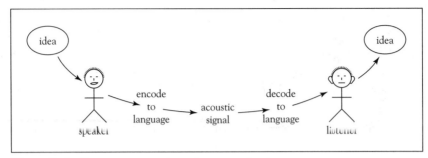

Figure 3–1. Commonsense view of communication

will say, "Have a nice day," at the end of the transaction and not listen carefully to the words the clerk utters.

In addition to the context, listeners get other clues that help them understand messages. Speakers often use gestures to clarify their ideas. They point to things or people. Further, natural language includes a great deal of redundancy. Listeners get more than one clue when, for example, a speaker declares, "No! I won't." The two negatives here don't signal a positive message. Instead, the speaker is giving two strong clues that he will not do something. The redundant nature of language allows people to communicate even when they miss some of the available clues.

Human communication is complex indeed. Even the same words, uttered with a different tone of voice, can signal different meanings. The boyfriend who doesn't notice the difference between "Marry my daughter, will you" spoken in a threatening tone and the same phrase delivered in a pleading tone is in for a great deal of trouble. The situation and the roles and status of the speaker and listener all affect the meanings of messages.

Linguists have developed complex models to describe human communication (Bach and Harnish 1979). Speech acts theory attempts to account for the different factors involved in communication. For example, successful communication depends on speakers and listeners sharing knowledge of references. If a speaker refers to the Pentagon, he will assume that the listener knows that the reference is to the building that houses the central offices of the military of the United States. The speaker and listener may also share common feelings about people or places that are mentioned.

In addition, listeners have to decide if an utterance is literal or nonliteral, direct or indirect. "I have a frog in my throat" would normally be interpreted nonliterally, for example. And a question like "Is there any salt on the table?" is not simply a question, it is also an indirect request to pass the salt. If a listener treats this utterance as a question and answers, "Yes, the salt is right in front of me," communication will break down. Many utterances have both direct and indirect meanings. "The garbage is full" and "The potatoes are boiling over" are more than simple reports, they are indirect requests for the listener to do something.

Peggy Parish (1976) has written an amusing series of books whose main character, Amelia Bedelia, is a nonnative speaker of English. Amelia takes everything literally. She works as a maid for a family. When the husband tells her to "go fly a kite," she does just that. When she reads a recipe that says the bread will rise, she watches the pan carefully to see if it will lift off the counter. Fortunately, Amelia always redeems herself with her wonderful cooking. What makes this series of books so amusing is that these kinds of communication breakdowns are quite rare. Most listeners know whether to interpret a message literally or nonliterally. However, English language learners like Amelia sometimes do not realize that certain expressions carry nonliteral meanings.

Even though the process is complex, most humans use language to communicate effectively each day. In this chapter we look at the physical process of producing meaningful sounds, but first we might ask why sound developed as the principal means of communication for most people.

Why Use Sound to Communicate?

Humans are social beings who seem driven to communicate. Deaf people develop the ability to communicate with gestures. Hearing people use sounds. Why did sounds, rather than visual signals, develop as the means of communication for hearing individuals? There are several practical reasons: In the first place, if people use sounds to express and receive ideas, their hands are free for other tasks. Thus, they can talk (not just whistle) while they work. In addition, sound travels around corners, so a wife in one room can tell her husband in another room that he should take out the garbage. Sound also works much better than gestures in the dark. For humans, then, communication using sounds has many practical advantages over other means of exchanging messages.

Humans use sounds to communicate even though using sound means changing the way people breathe and eat. Akmajian and colleagues (Akmajian, Demers, et al. 1979) point out that "the rhythm of respiration during speech is radically different from the rhythm of respiration during normal breathing" (p. 72). To speak, a person must control the outflow of air. For that reason, during speech rather than breathing in and out in a normal pattern, a person extends the period of exhalation. "One of the greatest distortions of the breathing rate occurs during speech: breath is drawn in rapidly and let out over a much longer period than during normal breathing" (p. 72). People do this without any conscious awareness. Humans seem to naturally adjust their breathing to accommodate speech.

Young babies can nurse and breathe at the same time. If adults try to drink and breathe simultaneously, though, they begin to choke. That is because at birth, the larynx is higher so that the passage for food and the passage for air are clearly separated. A baby can breathe through the nose while taking in milk through the mouth. Once the larynx drops down, there is the possibility of food or drink going into the lungs rather than the stomach. Why would humans develop in a way that makes choking possible? The reason seems to be that once the larynx drops down, there is more room in the oral cavity for humans to produce sounds. In other words, the development of a greater capacity for speech outweighs the dangers of food or drink going into the lungs.

The Complexity of Sound Production

Speech production is sufficiently complex that most researchers agree that it is an acquired capacity. During normal communication, humans produce an average of eight phonemes (distinctive, meaningful sounds) per second (Akmajian, Demers, et al. 1979). Speakers are able to maintain this rate of production over a long period of time without fatigue. During phoneme production the brain sends signals to the lungs, vocal cords, tongue, and lips to contract or relax the muscles. Even the production of a single phoneme can be complex. For example, in producing a word like *construe*, a speaker starts to round the lips to make the sound represented by *ue* even before starting the *str* sequence. Some messages from the brain have to travel farther than others to the muscles that control speech. At the same time, some nerve bundles transmit messages more rapidly than others because they are thicker. For that reason, the command to round the lips is sent out earlier than the command to start the *str* sequence so that when it is time to produce the *ue* sound, the lips will be ready. In other words, "the lip rounding in the last vowel in 'construe' arrives three phonemes early" (Akmajian, Demers, et al. 1979, p. 74). The details of this complex operation are not important here. What is important is that the messages the brain sends out to tighten and relax the muscles that control speech are so complicated that they must be acquired. Akmajian et al. sum up this point: "These features of speech are complex and automatic physical gestures which cannot be learned, but are among the biologically innate features that facilitate the acquisition of speech by the human species" (p. 74).

Even though hearing individuals use sounds to communicate, the biologically innate features that facilitate communication among humans may not be tied to sounds. What humans seem to have is the ability to use language to comprehend and produce meanings. Petitto (2003), from her study of children learning sign, suggests that this capacity is not specifically an ability to deal with sound: "I propose that humans are born with a sensitivity to particular distributional, rhythmical, and temporal patterns unique to aspects of natural language structure" (p. 1). Humans are equipped to understand and produce messages. This capacity develops in the process of natural communication.

Using Linguistic Concepts to Evaluate Methods of Teaching People to Communicate

Linguistics is the scientific study of language, and linguists study different aspects of language. For example, historical linguists study how language has changed over time. Sociolinguists study how people use language to communicate in social settings. Neurolinguists study language and the brain. Some linguists focus on specific aspects of language and specialize in studies of phonology, morphology, or syntax. Each area of study contributes important information.

In this book, we are especially interested in examining those aspects of linguistics that provide insights into how people learn to read and write and how people learn a second language. In the area of reading there has been a division between methods based on the idea that reading should be directly taught and learned and methods based on the view that reading is acquired. A current approach to teaching reading that has been supported by the U.S. Department of Education relies heavily on directly teaching the small parts of language—the phonemes and morphemes. Nevertheless, many teachers read to and with children in the belief that children can acquire literacy without direct instruction in parts of the language. Early approaches to second language teaching were based on the idea that second languages are learned. Instruction focused on the parts of the language, the grammar and vocabulary. Current methods are based on an acquisition model of second language development. Instruction focuses on providing comprehensible messages.

We believe that information from areas of linguistics such as phonology, morphology, and syntax can inform educators as they evaluate methods of teaching reading and methods of teaching second languages. We begin by discussing English phonology in this chapter. We then use linguistic concepts from phonology to evaluate methods of teaching reading and methods of teaching a second language.

English Phonology

Phonetics is the study of sounds across languages. Many linguists use the International Phonetic Alphabet to describe sound systems. This alphabet has symbols to represent all the sounds that have been found in human languages. *Phonology* is the study of the sounds used by speakers of a particular language. A *phoneme* is a sound that makes a difference in meaning in a language. Different languages use different sets of phonemes to communicate ideas. English has about forty phonemes while Spanish has about twenty-two.

To determine whether a sound functions as a phoneme in a language, a linguist tries to find two words that differ by just one sound. For example, in English, *pet* and *bet* are words that signify different meanings, and the only difference in sound is the difference between the "p" sound in *pet* and the "b" sound in *bet*, so a linguist might hypothesize that "p" and "b" are two phonemes in English. The linguist would then look for other pairs of words like *pan* and *ban* to confirm the hypothesis that "p" and "b" are phonemes of English. These words are referred to as *minimal pairs* because they differ by just one phoneme. The presence of a minimal pair is evidence that a sound functions as a phoneme in a language.

No language has a writing system that uniquely represents each sound in the language. That is, no alphabet has a one-to-one correspondence between sounds and letters. Instead, one letter may represent different sounds, and one sound may be represented by different letters or letter sequences. In English, for example, the same sound is represented by the *c* in *cat* and the *k* in *kite*. At the same time, the letters *ea* have different sounds in *tea*, *bread*, *steak*, and *idea*. Linguists wishing to study the sound system of a language need a more consistent method to analyze the sounds than an alphabet provides. For that reason, they use phonemic transcription.

In phonemic transcription, each sound is represented by one and only one written mark. Phonemic transcription makes use of many of the letters of the alphabet but uses them in a consistent way. For instance, the first sound of *cat* and *kite* is always written with a /k/. Phonemes are indicated by putting them between slash marks. To show the first phoneme in *pet*, a linguist would write /p/. A linguist could also show more details in the pronunciation of a sound by using phonetic transcription. The first sound in *pet* could be written as [pʰ]. Phonetic transcription is written within square brackets. The small raised *h* represents a puff of air that speakers produce as they make the /p/ sound at the beginning of a word. This feature, aspiration, is phonetic, not phonemic, because in English, aspiration is never used to signal a change in meaning.

Linguists describe phonemes by telling where and how they are produced. Each phoneme has unique articulatory properties. For example, /p/ is produced by stopping the air with the lips. The place of articulation is referred to as bilabial (the two lips), and the manner of articulation is called a stop, since the air is completely stopped for a moment and then released to make the sound. During the production of this sound, the vocal cords do not vibrate, so this type of sound is called voiceless or unvoiced. Each phoneme can be described by its place and manner of articulation and whether or not it is voiced.

Even though phonemes have physical properties that can be studied, a phoneme is a perceptual unit, not a physical entity. Phonemes actually differ in their physical production depending on the other sounds around them. For example, although the /p/ in *pet* is aspirated, the /p/ in *sip* is not. Listeners ignore this physical difference and perceive both sounds as the phoneme /p/. The phonemes of a language don't sound the same each time they are produced, but all the variations are perceived as instances of the same sound by speakers of a language. That is why linguists claim that phonemes are perceptual, not physical units. In the next section, we explain how the phonemes of English are produced.

The Physiology of Speech

The speech sounds of English and other languages are formed by changes in the vocal tract, the area between the vocal cords and the lips. Figure 3–2 shows the key physical features involved in speech production. As air comes up from the lungs, it passes through a narrow area, the glottal region, which contains the vocal cords. These are elastic bands of tissue located in the larynx. They can be brought close together so that the air passing through causes them to vibrate. This causes what is referred to as *voicing*. Or they can be held apart so no voicing occurs.

The air continues up through the pharynx into the oral cavity. If the flow of air is not constricted, a vowel sound is produced. Different vowel sounds result from movements of the tongue and lips. These change the shape of the oral cavity so that different sounds are produced. For all vowels, the air flows freely. Consonant sounds are formed when the air is constricted as it moves toward the lips. This constriction can involve simply slowing the air down or stopping it completely. The different consonant sounds depend on how and where the air is slowed or stopped. For English consonant sounds, the air may be constricted at the lips, the teeth, the alveolar ridge (the hard ridge behind the upper front teeth), the hard palate, and the soft palate, or velum. Air can also pass though the nasal cavity if the velum is lowered.

Linguists may refer to vowel sounds as *syllabics*, because each syllable contains a vowel, and consonant sounds as *nonsyllabics*, because consonants by themselves do not constitute a syllable. Syllables consist of a series of alternating vowel and consonant sounds. There is a limit on the number of consonant sounds that can be produced in sequence because consonants involve blocking the air in different ways. In English, syllables can begin with up to three consonant sounds. In *stream*, for example, the three consonant phonemes are /str/. Linguists use the terms *vowel* and *consonant* to refer to sounds rather than letters of the alphabet. However, since the vowel sounds of English are usually represented by a small set of letters,

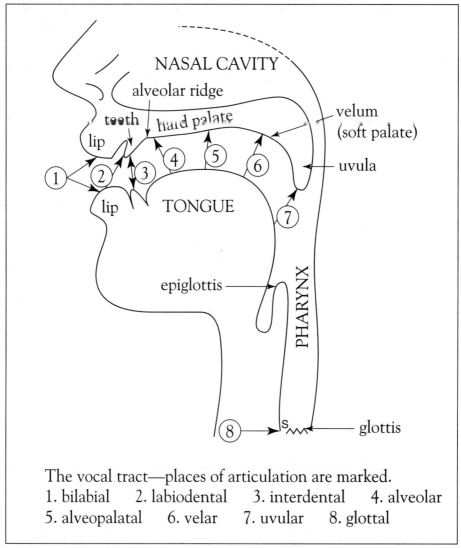

The vocal tract—places of articulation are marked.
1. bilabial   2. labiodental   3. interdental   4. alveolar
5. alveopalatal   6. velar   7. uvular   8. glottal

Figure 3–2. Physiology of speech production

those letters are often referred to as vowels, and the other letters are called consonants. In the sections that follow, it is important to keep in mind that we are referring to the sounds, not the letters.

In the following sections, we describe the physical aspects of producing the vowel and consonant phonemes of English. Knowing where sounds are produced can be helpful in understanding students' spelling. For example, if a student spells *ten* as *den*, it is useful to know that /t/ and /d/ are produced in the same place in the mouth. Educators who know something of the physiology of speech production can better understand invented spellings that emergent writers produce.

English Vowels

English has a complex system of vowels consisting of short, long, and reduced vowels. The short vowels are also called *lax* vowels, and the long vowels are called *tense*. These terms reflect the relative tension of the muscles as the sounds are produced. Reduced vowels occur in unstressed syllables. All vowels in English are voiced. The vibration from the vocal cords provides the energy needed for a vowel sound. Different vowels are formed by changing the shape of the vocal tract as the vibrating air molecules pass from the vocal cords toward the lips.

Vowels vary considerably across dialects, and the number of vowel phonemes varies as well. For example, some people pronounce *cot* and *caught* with two different vowel sounds. For others, these words are pronounced the same. Speakers who distinguish *cot* and *caught* by their pronunciation have two different phonemes, while other people have only one. In our description of vowel sounds, we have chosen to present the phonemes common to most dialects of American English.

Short vowels   There are six short vowel sounds. English spelling usually represents each of these short sounds with just one letter. Figure 3–3 shows where the short vowels are produced. The table represents the areas of the mouth when looking from the left side as in Figure 3–2. For example, /ɪ/ is made in the front of the mouth, high up. What does that mean, though? Although there is considerable variation among speakers, and although the placement of a vowel depends on the other sounds in the word, in general this vowel is produced by moving the tongue toward the front of the mouth and raising the tip of the tongue up toward the roof of the mouth. In a word like *sit*, this is the movement of the tongue for the vowel. For each vowel phoneme, we include a word in parentheses that contains that vowel sound.

A good way to feel the differences among these vowels is to say the words on the chart in sequence from high front to low back: *pit, pet, pat, putt, put, pot*. In

	Front	Central	Back
High	ɪ (pit)		u (put)
Mid	ɛ (pet)	ʌ (putt)	
Low	æ (pat)		a (pot)

Figure 3–3. Short vowels of English

the first three words the tongue moves toward the front of the mouth, and the vowel sound is made by moving the tongue slightly lower for each phoneme. For *pat*, most speakers open their jaw slightly to make this lower vowel sound. The word *putt* is produced with the tongue in the middle of the mouth. For *put*, the tongue moves slightly up and back and the lips are rounded, which has the effect of lengthening the vocal tract. The last word, *pot*, is produced with the tongue low and back.

Many native speakers of English have difficulty in feeling these variations in tongue position. Native speakers of English produce these sounds effortlessly without conscious awareness of the tongue movements. It may help to make these sounds in front of a mirror to try to observe where the tongue is for each sound. English language learners often have difficulty distinguishing between words that differ by just one of these vowel sounds. However, during normal conversation, they can use other cues to determine the meaning. Trying to distinguish minimal pairs by saying two sets of words (*sit* and *set*, *sit* and *sit*) and determining if the two words in the sets are the same or different in exercises does not seem to help improve listening comprehension because this exercise removes normal context clues.

Long vowels   The seven long vowels of English are all made by starting with a vowel and adding a glide. As the vowel is produced, the tongue moves from one part of the mouth to another. These vowels are also called *diphthongs*, from Greek roots meaning "two sounds," because the sound quality changes as each long vowel is produced. The long vowels are indicated with two letters in the transcription system being used here. The first letter indicates the tongue position at the beginning of the sound, and the second letter shows the direction of the glide. The tongue glides up and toward the palate for vowels represented with a /y/ and up and toward the velum for those with a /w/ (see Figure 3–2 for these parts of the mouth). Figure 3–4 lists the long vowels of English.

The long vowel phonemes are present in the words *beet*, *bait*, *boot*, *boat*, *boy*, *bite*, and *bout*. English spelling, in most cases, reflects the length of these vowels, representing them with two letters. The tongue starts toward the front

	Front	Central	Back
High	iy (beet)		uw (boot)
Mid	ey (bait)		ow, oy (boat, boy)
Low			ay, aw (bite, bout)

Figure 3–4. Long vowels of English

and moves slightly up for *beet* and *bait*. To produce *boot*, a speaker moves the tongue from the high back position slightly higher and farther back, and, at the same time, enhances the effect by rounding the lips to lengthen the vocal tract. The tongue starts in the middle back area and moves up and toward the front for *boy*. To produce the vowel in *boat*, the tongue starts in the middle back area and moves up toward the roof of the mouth in the back. It starts down low in the back for *bite* and then glides up toward the roof of the mouth as the vowel is produced. For *bout* it also starts low in the back, but then it glides up to the back.

Reduced vowels English has two other vowels, which are called *reduced vowels*. These vowels are produced with a weaker airflow, so the syllables in which they appear do not receive stress. Reduced syllables occur in words with two or more syllables. For example, in the first syllable of *about*, the vowel sound is a kind of "uh" that is unstressed. This is the same sound that occurs in a one-syllable word like *putt*, where it gets some stress. This mid, central unstressed or reduced vowel is called a *schwa*. It is a very common sound in English. It is the sound many English speakers make when they are trying to think of something to say. The mouth is relaxed, and the tongue is in a neutral position. The symbol for the schwa is an inverted *e* and is written as /ə/.

The other reduced vowel in English is produced with the tongue slightly higher up in the mouth. It is a high, central vowel. This sound occurs in unaccented or unstressed syllables of words with two or more syllables. For example, it is the vowel sound in the second syllable of *medicine* and the last syllable in *jumping*. This sound is like the /ɪ/ sound in *sit* except that it is produced with less force of air. This vowel is often called a *barred i* and is written as /ɨ/. One of the difficulties of English spelling is that many different vowel sounds are reduced to schwa or barred *i*, and these sounds can be spelled with almost any vowel letter. Figure 3–5 summarizes the

	Front	**Central**	**Back**
High	iy (beet) ɪ (pit)	(ɨ) (jump**i**ng)	uw (boot) u (put)
Mid	ey (bait) ɛ (pet)	(ə) **a**bout ʌ (putt)	ow (boat) oy (boy)
Low	æ (pat)		a (pot) ay (bite) aw (bout)

Figure 3–5. Vowel phonemes of English

information about vowels. The chart represents a speaker's mouth from a side view, with the speaker facing left. The two reduced vowels are placed in parentheses. A key word for each vowel sound is written to the right of the phoneme. Educators may wish to learn to use this system to transcribe English vowels. Phonemic transcription is a useful first step in analyzing sound-to-spelling correspondences.

In total, there are fifteen vowel phonemes, six short vowels, seven long vowels, and two reduced vowels. This system is further complicated by the effect of an /r/ phoneme following a vowel. Vowel sounds are made by slight adjustments of the tongue up or down and front or back. The /r/ phoneme is made by raising the tip of the tongue and curling it back somewhat. This action has an effect on the preceding vowel, giving it a quality it does not usually have. Which vowel phoneme best represents the sounds in *dear*, *four*, and *tour?* We won't attempt to make the fine distinctions needed to represent these vowel sounds here, but it is not surprising that children have trouble learning to spell English words with these so-called *r*-controlled vowels. Other factors can influence vowels as well. For example, when a vowel is followed by a nasal sound, the vowel picks up some of the nasal quality. The vowel sound in *wet* is different from the same phoneme in *went*. Children learning to spell English often leave out the *n* in *went* because they perceive the nasal sound as part of the vowel, not as a separate phoneme.

Educators who understand the complexity of the English vowel system can better appreciate the difficulty children have as they attempt to represent these sounds as they write. Since there are about fifteen sounds, American English spelling uses various combinations of the available letters to represent them. In addition, English learners often have difficulty learning the vowel sounds of English. Spanish and Japanese, for example, have only five vowel phonemes, and none of them corresponds exactly to any English vowel. An understanding of the vowel phonemes of English can be helpful for any educator working with English learners or students learning to spell English words. This knowledge is also useful for educators trying to decide on the best way to teach students to read. We should add here that the best way to help students become more proficient spellers is to involve them in problem-solving activities so they can make sense out of the English spelling system. We return to this topic in Chapter 5. In addition, students who read extensively are much better spellers than those whose reading is limited.

English Consonant Phonemes

Consonant phonemes are produced by restricting or stopping the flow of air as it passes through the vocal tract. Consonants can best be described by telling where and how the air is constricted and by noting whether the sound is voiced

		Bilabial	Labio-dental	Inter-dental	Alveolar	Alveo-palatal	Velar	Glottal
Stops	voiceless	p			t		k	
	voiced	b			d		g	
Fricatives	voiceless		f	θ	s	š		h
	voiced		v	ð	z	ž		
Affricates	voiceless					č		
	voiced					ǰ		
Nasals	voiced	m			n		ŋ	
Liquids	voiced				r, l			
Glides	voiced					y	w	

Figure 3–6. English consonants

or voiceless. Consonants generally appear in matched pairs, one voiced and the other voiceless. Figure 3–6 shows the consonant phonemes of English. The place of articulation is indicated along the top of the chart, and the manner of articulation is shown on the side. In the sections that follow, we describe each type of phoneme.

Stops

There are three pairs of stops. Stop phonemes are formed by completely blocking the air for an instant and then releasing it. The first two stops, /p/ and /b/, are formed by stopping the air by closing the lips. Thus, they are called bilabials (two lips). These are the sounds at the beginning and end of *pop* and *bib*. Bilabials are some of the first sounds babies produce, so that is why parents and grandparents, in many languages, are called by words starting with /p/, /b/, or /m/, as in *papa*, *bapa*, and *mama*. Note that all these names also contain the low, back vowel /a/, which is one of the first vowels children produce. The only difference between /p/ and /b/ is in voicing. English uses voicing to distinguish these sounds, and English speakers attend to this meaningful clue. In other languages, such as some dialects

		Bilabial	Labio-dental	Inter-dental	Alveolar	Alveo-palatal	Velar	Glottal
Stops	voiceless	p			t		k	
	voiced	b			d		g	

Figure 3–7. Stops

of Arabic, the two bilabial stops are simply two ways of producing one phoneme, so speakers of those languages do not pay attention to the voicing difference since it doesn't signal a change in meaning. Arabic speakers learning English, then, might have trouble hearing the difference between words like *pig* and *big* if they are presented the words in isolation. Of course, context clues would prevent them from getting these two words confused during normal communication.

The next two stops are /t/ and /d/. These phonemes are present at the beginning and end of words like *tot* and *dad*. The sounds are made by placing the tip of the tongue behind the front teeth along the alveolar ridge to block the air for a moment. Many of the consonants of English are produced in the alveolar region. In other languages, like Spanish and Japanese, these sounds are produced by placing the tongue against the back of the front teeth to form a dental stop. For that reason, the /t/ and /d/ phonemes sound slightly different in Spanish and Japanese than they do in English.

The last stops, /k/ and /g/, are formed by raising the blade of the tongue up against the velar region in the back of the mouth to temporarily block the air. These phonemes occur at the beginning and end of words like *kick* and *gig*. The three pairs of stops are set apart in the vocal tract. One is made with the lips at the front of the mouth, one in the middle, and the other at the very back. This separation helps listeners distinguish the stops from one another.

Fricatives

Fricatives are produced by constricting the airflow through the vocal tract. The resulting friction sets the air molecules in motion as they pass through the narrow opening. This action produces a sound. The fricatives also come in pairs, except for /h/. There are nine fricatives in English.

The labiodental pair, /f/ and /v/, are made by biting down on the lower lip. This slows the air and produces the sounds heard at the beginning and end of *fluff* and *verve*. The interdental fricatives, /θ/ and /ð/, are made by putting the tongue between the teeth and forcing air through the opening. Even though people have different spaces between their teeth, the tongue can be used to produce a similar sound for people with quite different tooth gaps. The names for these two

		Bilabial	Labio-dental	Inter-dental	Alveolar	Alveo-palatal	Velar	Glottal
Fricatives	voiceless		f	θ	s	š		h
	voiced		v	ð	z	ž		

Figure 3–8. Fricatives

phonemes come from the Greek words *theta* and *eth*. The difference in sound between these two phonemes is more difficult to hear than some of the others, but it is evident in pairs like *thigh* (the /θ/) and *thy* (the /ð/). Words like *with* can be pronounced using either sound depending on the speaker's dialect and on the sound that follows. These phonemes can also occur at either the beginning of words or the end, as shown in *thin* and *bath* for /θ/ and *then* and *bathe* for /ð/.

The phonemes /s/ and /z/ are made by putting the tip of the tongue against the alveolar ridge, as in producing /t/ or /d/, but unlike the stops, the tip of the tongue is lowered enough to let some air go through. These phonemes occur at the beginning of words like *sip* and *zip* and the end of words like *kiss* and *fuzz*. It is easy to hear the difference in voicing in this pair. The vocal cords vibrate during /z/ but not in making an /s/. One way to detect voicing in more difficult cases is to block the ears while making the sound. That makes the vibration of the vocal cords easier to perceive.

The next two sounds, /š/ and /ž/, have a small mark above them called a haček. This diacritic mark distinguishes these sounds from /s/ and /z/. They are produced by flattening the tongue along the roof of the mouth, the alveopalatal area. The /š/ phoneme occurs at the beginning or end of many words, such as *ship* and *dish*, but the /ž/ is less common. It never starts a word, except for a borrowed word or a name, like *Zsa Zsa*. Speakers of some dialects pronounce this sound at the end of words borrowed from French, like *garage* and *rouge*. Most commonly, this /ž/ occurs in the middle of a word, like *confusion*. It is often represented by *si* in spelling.

The /h/ phoneme is a special case. It can be produced in different ways, but it is often made by slowing the air as it passes through the glottal area. In a word like *hop*, the /h/ can be felt in the throat, causing some vibration before the onset of the vowel sound. This sound is voiceless.

Affricates

Affricates are formed by briefly stopping the air and then releasing it with some friction. Thus, affricates are a combination of a stop and a fricative. English has two affricates, /č/ and /ǰ/. The /č/ is a combination of /t/ and /š/, while the /ǰ/

		Bilabial	Labio-dental	Inter-dental	Alveolar	Alveo-palatal	Velar	Glottal
Affricates	voiceless					č		
	voiced					ǰ		

Figure 3–9. Affricates

combines /d/ with /ž/. The /č/ can be heard at the beginning and end of *church* and the /ǰ/ occurs twice in *judge*. English spelling reflects the combined sounds in affricates by spelling some words that end in /č/ with *-tch* as in *watch* and /ǰ/ with *-dge* as in *badge*. However, English words do not begin with *tch* or *dg*, and this is something that children learning to spell need to figure out.

Stops, fricatives, and affricates generally come in voiceless and voiced pairs. The last three types of consonant phonemes, nasals, liquids, and glides, have more the quality of vowels because the air is not stopped or constricted as much, and all three of these kinds of phonemes are voiced.

Nasals

English has three nasal consonants. These are /m/, /n/, and /ŋ/. The first two have the sounds of the letters *m* and *n* in words like *Mom* and *Nan*. The last one has the sound of *ng* in *ring*. In fact, the symbol looks like an *n* with the tail of a *g*. This sound occurs only at the end of a syllable in English, never at the beginning.

English nasals are voiced. They are produced by stopping the air in the oral cavity and lowering the velum so that the airflow can pass through the nasal cavity. The phoneme /m/ is produced by blocking the air with the lips, the /n/ by stopping the air at the alveolar ridge, and the /ŋ/ by blocking off the velar area. Thus, these three nasals are produced in much the same way as the stops /b/, /d/, and /g/. This can be shown by making a sound like /m/, stopping the air from going out of the nose, and then opening the mouth. The result should sound like a /b/. The relationship between stops and nasals is also noticeable when a person has a cold. Then an /n/ comes out sounding like a /d/ because air can't flow smoothly through the nasal cavity.

		Bilabial	Labio-dental	Inter-dental	Alveolar	Alveo-palatal	Velar	Glottal
Nasals	voiced	m			n		ŋ	

Figure 3–10. Nasals

Liquids

There are two phonemes called *liquids*, a descriptive term to denote the smooth sounds associated with /l/ and /r/. The sounds of these phonemes are those that occur at the beginning and end of *lull* and *roar*. To form the /l/, a speaker places the tip of the tongue against the alveolar ridge and lowers one side of the tongue

		Bilabial	Labio-dental	Inter-dental	Alveolar	Alveo-palatal	Velar	Glottal
Liquids	voiced				r, l			

Figure 3–11. Liquids

to let the air pass through on that side. Since the air passes on one side, the /l/ is referred to as a lateral. It is possible to tell which side of the tongue a person lowers by making the kind of clicking sound used to signal a horse. Most speakers can make that click best on one side, and that is the side the speaker also lowers to produce an /l/.

We mentioned earlier that /r/ affects following vowels. The American English /r/ is produced by curling the tongue tip back slightly. The tongue does not touch another part of the mouth, but raising and curling the tongue changes the shape of the oral cavity. As the tongue uncurls, a vowel sound is produced, but the action of the tongue colors that vowel. Many other languages make the *r* sound by flapping the tongue against the back of the front teeth. Spanish also has a trilled or rolled *r*, but neither of the Spanish *r* sounds is the same as the English /r/.

Glides

The final two consonant phonemes, the glides, are sometimes called *semivowels* because they are produced with very little constriction of the air passage, more like a vowel. These two phonemes are the /y/ sound at the beginning of *yes* and the /w/ that occurs at the start of *wet*. The sounds of words like *day* and *saw* have glides that are part of vowel diphthongs, but these are considered vowels, not consonant phonemes. The glides that are consonants occur only at the beginning of a syllable in English or as part of a blend, like the *sw* in *swing*. They are produced by moving the tongue up toward the alveopalatal or velar region. In the case of /w/, the lips are also rounded.

In all, American English has twenty-four consonant phonemes: six stops, nine fricatives, two affricates, three nasals, two liquids, and two glides. The consonant phonemes are relatively easy to learn to transcribe. Only seven

		Bilabial	Labio-dental	Inter-dental	Alveolar	Alveo-palatal	Velar	Glottal
Glides	voiced					y	w	

Figure 3–12. Glides

consonant sounds are represented by special marks. The rest use letters from the alphabet. For example, the /p/ phoneme represents most words that begin with *p* in written English (except for words like *ptarmigan* in which the *p* is silent). The seven special marks are represented in spelling by digraphs. Digraphs are two letters used to indicate one sound. Since there is only one sound in each case, linguists represent the sound with a single character. The phonemes that correspond most often to two-letter spellings (digraphs) are /θ/ and /ð/, which represent the voiceless and voiced "th" sound; /š/ and /ž/, which represent the "sh" and "zh" sounds; /č/ and /ǰ/, which represent "ch" and "dg," and /ŋ/ for the sound of "ng" in *ring*. The /ǰ/ is also spelled with a single *j* at the beginning of a word.

Digraphs are two-letter spellings for one phoneme. They differ from blends, such as *bl* and *st*. In blends, two letters are used to represent two different phonemes. When pronounced, each of these phonemes maintains its sound. For example, a word like *blend* is transcribed as /blɛnd/. The two consonant phonemes at the beginning and at the end are both pronounced. In contrast, a word like *thing* contains digraphs, not blends. It is transcribed as /θɪŋ/ because the *th* represents the first phoneme, and the *ng* is the last phoneme. Digraphs are also used to spell long vowel sounds (diphthongs). For example, the phoneme /iy/ is represented by the digraph *ee* in *see*. The term *diphthong* refers to a sound, and *digraph* refers to a spelling.

The twenty-four consonant phonemes, together with the fifteen vowels, make thirty-nine phonemes in the system we are describing. Speakers of English acquire the ability to produce and understand these sounds early in life. Some of the phonemes, the bilabials and the low, back vowel, are acquired early, and others, such as the /r/, come later. However, by the time they reach school, most children have good control over the complex phonological system of English. Teachers of young children sometimes worry that their students don't yet "have their sounds," but this concern usually reflects an inability of students to identify or produce certain sounds as part of a classroom exercise. Often, young children simply don't understand what they are being asked to do. On the other hand, observation of children in natural communicative situations generally reveals that they do "have their sounds."

Phonotactics

People who acquire English not only acquire the ability to comprehend and produce English phonemes but also acquire knowledge of the distribution of the sounds. The linguistic term for possible phoneme combinations is *phonotactics*. For example, in English, /ŋ/ appears only at the end of a syllable, never at the beginning. English speakers know that English words don't start with /ŋ/. An English speaker who tries to pronounce the common Vietnamese name *Nguyen* typically experiences difficulty. Even though English speakers have no trouble pronouncing words that end in /ŋ/, they find it difficult to pronounce words starting with /ŋ/. This helps confirm that phonemes are perceptual, not physical units, since English speakers have no trouble with the physical production of the sound /ŋ/ unless it begins a word.

This knowledge of sound distribution, or phonotactics, allows an English speaker to decide that /glark/ is a possible English word, but /tlark/ or /dlark/ is not. Every language puts constraints on how the phonemes can be combined. In English a number of different consonant blends are possible at the beginnings of words, but some combinations never occur. For example, if the first consonant phoneme in an English word is a stop, the second can be a liquid. This is true for all the possible combinations except /tl/ and /dl/. Figure 3–13 shows how this pattern works.

English allows up to three consonant phonemes at the beginning of syllables. However, there are constraints on the kinds of phonemes that can be combined. Figure 3–14 lists the possibilities. What is interesting, from a linguistic perspective,

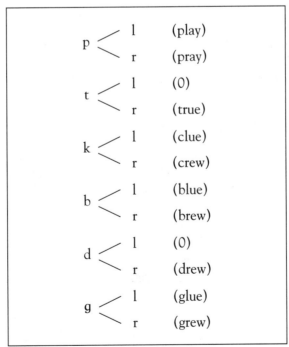

Figure 3–13. Initial blends combining stops and liquids

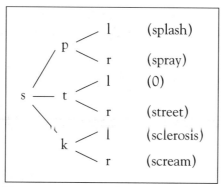

Figure 3–14. Initial combinations of three-consonant phonemes

is that the kinds of phonemes that can be combined fall into certain classes. The first phoneme must be /s/. The second phoneme must be a voiceless stop, and the third phoneme must be a liquid or a glide, the two kinds of consonants that are most like vowels.

English spelling doesn't reflect these consonant combinations, but each of the example words would be transcribed using the phonemes that are listed. Not all the possible combinations occur, but the only words in English that start with three consonant phonemes start with one of the combinations listed in Figure 3–14.

There are also constraints on vowels. For example, while any kind of vowel can go at the beginning or middle of a syllable, only long vowels and reduced vowels can end a syllable. Many words, such as *free* and *stay*, end with a long vowel sound. English words like *idea* end with the schwa sound. Long and reduced vowels are sometimes referred to as *free vowels* because they occur freely in any position in English words. Short vowels, also known as *checked vowels*, cannot end a word. No word or syllable in English ends in /a/, for example. These constraints on vowels constitute part of a speaker's knowledge of English phonotactics.

Young children who grow up in an English-speaking environment acquire knowledge of English phonotactics. This is subconscious knowledge. They use this information as they speak, but they can't explain how they know that certain combinations are possible and others are not. Part of acquiring a language is acquiring the phonemes, but people also acquire the knowledge of how to combine the phonemes into words.

Tongue Twisters

People have fun trying to pronounce tongue twisters. In his book *A Twister of Twists, a Tangler of Tongues*, Alvin Schwartz (1972) has collected tongue twisters from many different regions of the United States as well as from different languages. He begins the book by presenting a very difficult example: "One of the hardest tongue twisters in the English language is 'Peggy Babcock.' Try to say it five times as fast as you can. If you are like most people I know, your tongue won't cooperate" (p. 9).

Most people can't even say this name twice in a row. Just what makes tongue twisters like this one so difficult? Part of the difficulty comes from the physical movement of the tongue, but part also comes from the mixed patterns the brain has to deal with. A phonological analysis of *Peggy Babcock* reveals both difficulties.

The name would be transcribed as /pɛgiy babkak/. To produce these sounds, the tongue must move rapidly from front to back. Both /p/ and /b/ are bilabials, produced as far forward in the mouth as possible. The other two consonant phonemes, /g/ and /k/, are produced at the back of the mouth. The sequence of consonant phonemes is /p/, /g/, /b/, /b/, /k/, and /k/. In other words, the tongue goes front, back, front, front, back, back. The brain is sending messages to the tongue, lips, and other parts of the mouth to control these movements.

At the same time, the brain is sending messages to the vocal cords. They vibrate to produce the voiced consonants, /b/ and /g/, and they are held apart to make the voiceless phonemes, /p/ and /k/. Here is the pattern of voicing: voiceless, voiced, voiced, voiced, voiceless, voiceless. Now consider where most people run into trouble. For many speakers it is the second time through, when the first name comes out as "Pebby" instead of "Peggy." Why might this occur?

Two different patterns (at least) are at work here, the front-back movement of the tongue and the on-off pattern of the voicing. Figure 3–15 shows the relationship between these two patterns.

Phoneme	p	g	b	b	k	k
Position	front	back	front	front	back	back
Voicing	voiceless	voiced	voiced	voiced	voiceless	voiceless
Front = − Back = +	−	+	−	−	+	+
Voiceless = − Voiced = +	−	+	+	+	−	−

Figure 3–15. Peggy Babcock

As shown by the last two rows, in which front or back and voiceless or voiced are represented by a plus or a minus, the two patterns start out the same, but then change with the first /b/. The brain is very good at picking up patterns. People can repeat rhymes rapidly. But here the two patterns seem to conflict and speech is short-circuited. Speakers who say "Pebby" the second time through produce the right voicing but in the wrong position. Other tongue twisters, like "Rubber baby buggy bumpers," also play on these same alterations between front and back, voiceless and voiced.

Some tongue twisters, such as "She says she shall sew a sheet," require rapid movement between two points in the mouth that are close together, /s/ and /š/. Several tongue twisters use this contrast. Again, this alteration seems to cause problems primarily because the pattern is complex. Speakers do not have trouble shifting between /s/ and /š/ as long as the two sounds alternate following a regular pattern. However, here the pattern is irregular. In addition, *says* contains a voiced phoneme, /z/, that is produced at the same place as /s/. The result, for most people, is a twist of the tongue.

Several Internet websites that deal with linguistics feature tongue twisters. One site that is a good resource for a discussion of tongue twisters from different languages is www.geocities.com/Athens/8136/tonguetwisters.html.

Native speakers of a language can produce phonemes at rapid rates. The brain sends a series of messages to the muscles that control speech, and the desired sounds are produced almost effortlessly. Tongue twisters suggest the upper limits on human capacity, but they are interesting primarily because they occur so seldom in natural communicative situations.

Conclusion

Despite the complexity of phonology, speakers of a language can produce sounds that convey meanings to listeners, and listeners can interpret these sounds. They do this while focusing their attention on what they are saying, not on how they are saying it. Linguists argue that speech production and comprehension are so complex that they must be acquired, not learned. Most young children have mastered the phonology of one or more languages by the time they enter school, and they have done this without receiving any instruction.

Humans are born with a drive to communicate. They acquire the ability to comprehend and produce language to receive and express ideas. Hearing individuals rely on sound to communicate because communicating with sounds offers practical advantages. However, deaf people communicate with signs. The modality is not important. What is important is the capacity to make and share meanings. Oral language and sign language are simply two systems humans can use to comprehend and express meanings.

Linguists study different aspects of language. Phonology is the study of speech sounds. Linguists have examined both the acoustic and articulatory aspects of speech. The meaningful sounds of a language are called *phonemes*. One way to test for phonemes is to find minimal pairs, two words that differ by just one sound. English has about thirty-nine phonemes.

Phonemes can be described by their place and manner of articulation. Vowel phonemes are made by moving the tongue and lips into different positions as the air passes through the vocal tract. Consonant phonemes are made by constricting the air in different ways as it passes from the lungs and out past the lips. Words in any language consist of combinations of vowel and consonant phonemes. As people acquire the phonology of a language, they also acquire knowledge of phonotactics, the possible combinations of phonemes in that language.

Language production is a complex process, but most speakers are not aware of the complicated series of messages the brain sends to the various muscles that control speech. The process seems to occur automatically as people produce and comprehend ideas. Tongue twisters help show the upper limits on this capacity to produce language so easily. Most tongue twisters require the brain to send out different patterns to the muscles at the same time, and this may overload the capacity to produce meaningful language.

Insights from linguistics in the area of phonology can be helpful for educators evaluating methods of teaching reading or methods of teaching a second language. In the following chapter, we apply the concepts presented here to written and second language development.

Applications

1. Look back at Figure 3–1, the simple model of communication. Make a list of different facts about communication that this model fails to capture. Sketch out a model that would include some of these missing features.
2. Try saying "It's Friday" in different ways using different intonation and emphasis to convey different meanings. How many different meanings can you convey?
3. Read one or more of Parish's Amelia Bedelia books and list the expressions she fails to understand. Make a table like the following one that lists the expression, Amelia's interpretation, and the conventional interpretation.

Expression	Literal Meaning	Nonliteral Meaning
dust the furniture	put dust on the furniture	remove dust from the furniture

4. Describe in detail how the following phonemes are produced: /d/, /m/, /l/, /w/, /ey/, and /u/.

5. Find a minimal pair of words for each phoneme. The consonant phonemes are listed on p. 61 and the vowel phonemes on p. 59. Minimal pairs differ by just one phoneme. Transcribe your answers. Add boxes to complete the chart here.

/p/	pat	kat	/iy/	biyt	bayt
/b/	tuwb	tuwn	/u/	put	pat

6. Try analyzing your favorite tongue twisters to see why they are difficult to say. Use the procedure explained in this chapter for your analysis.

7. Transcribe the following words:

play	chance	dread
crazy	shout	bath
just	yes	ring
bridge	five	toy
mast	then	taste

8. What are the possible combinations of consonant phonemes that can begin English words? This is one feature of English phonotactics. Complete the following chart by putting an X in each cell that represents a possible English word. Write a word for each X. Then try to make some generalizations about classes of words (voiceless stops, nasals, etc.) that can be combined. The first row is done. Possible words are *play*, *pray*, and *pew* (/pyew/). It would be possible to mark /pw/ if you include borrowed words like *pueblo*. However, it would be best to mark combinations that exist only in words that are not borrowed. Even though some words are spelled with *ps-*, no words begin with the sounds /ps/. Remember to mark possible sound combinations, not possible spellings. Only mark boxes for initial consonant combinations.

	p	t	k	b	d	g	m	n	ŋ	f	v	θ	ð	s	z	š	ž	h	č	ǰ	l	r	y	w
p																					X	X	X	
t																								
k																								
b																								
d																								
g																								
m																								
n																								
ŋ																								
f																								
v																								
θ																								
ð																								
s																								
z																								
š																								
ž																								
h																								
č																								
ǰ																								
l																								
r																								
y																								
w																								

4

Implications from Phonology for Teaching Reading and Teaching a Second Language

- *What is the role of phonological and phonemic knowledge in learning to read or in learning a second language?*
- *What insights from phonology can help in evaluating a method of teaching reading or a method of teaching a second language?*

As babies acquire their first language, they acquire the phonology of that language, as long as they have normal hearing. Phonology also plays a role in both written language and second language development. There may be some debate over whether oral language is innate or whether humans have a special cognitive capacity for language, but humans acquire their first language without instruction. When it comes to learning to read or learning a second language, though, there is less agreement. As we discussed earlier, some researchers argue that written language or a second language can be acquired in the same way that a first language is acquired. Others claim that written language or a second language must be learned.

In this chapter, we consider how insights from the linguistic area of phonology can help inform these debates. We examine the role of phonology in the methods of teaching reading and in the methods of teaching a second language. Evidence from linguistics can help educators evaluate different methods and the theories underlying those methods.

Reading and Phonology

The two models of reading we have described each place a different value on the role of sounds. Sounds play a central role in the word recognition view because identifying words involves recoding written marks into the sounds of oral language. To convert written marks into sounds, readers need to understand that words in oral language are made up of individual sounds. This knowledge is referred to as *phonemic awareness*. In addition, readers need to learn how sounds correspond to the marks used in writing. Phonics rules attempt to capture these correspondences.

Sounds play a lesser role in a sociopsycholinguistic model of reading. Readers use *graphophonic cues*, a combination of visual and sound information, as they sample texts and make and confirm predictions. Graphophonics is just one of three language cueing systems readers use to make meaning from written texts. Graphophonic knowledge develops as children, who already can distinguish among sounds to make sense of oral language, combine their knowledge of sounds with their emerging understanding of written language to construct meaning from written texts.

In this chapter we consider two views of phonemic awareness, one consistent with a word recognition view of reading and the other aligned with a sociopsycholinguistic view. We then discuss linguistic factors from phonology that can help educators evaluate these views of phonemic awareness and of reading. In Chapter 6, we turn from phonemic awareness to phonics and consider insights from phonology that can inform educators as they make decisions about how to teach phonics.

Phonemic Awareness: A Key to Word Recognition

The word recognition view of reading is a model based on the idea that identifying words involves recoding written language to oral language. This process requires that readers first develop phonemic awareness. *Phonemic awareness* is defined within this paradigm as the ability to perceive and manipulate the sounds (phonemes) that make up words in oral language. Readers use phonemic awareness, along with knowledge of letter sounds and names, to learn phonics rules and apply those rules to identify words.

Researchers have tried to break reading down into its component parts and to determine factors that can help predict reading success or failure in young children. A very important early paper by Stanovich (1986), titled "Matthew Effects in Reading," reviewed a number of research studies. Stanovich used the biblical concept found in the book of Matthew that the rich get richer and the little the poor have will be taken away from them for his title. Stanovich noted that good readers read more, and the benefits of reading, such as increased vocabulary, make these good readers better. On the other hand, poor readers read less over time, and because they read less, they fall farther behind their classmates.

In his review of the research, Stanovich identified phonemic awareness as the key factor that differentiated good from poor readers. Children with phonemic awareness became good readers, and those who lacked phonemic awareness struggled with reading. The studies did not clearly show whether phonemic awareness was needed in order for someone to learn to read or whether it was developed as a result of reading. Good readers have phonemic awareness, but this correlation does not show clearly which factor is the cause and which is the effect. Stanovich used the term *reciprocal causation* to account for a bidirectional relationship. According to Stanovich, phonemic awareness appears to help children learn to read, and reading helps build phonemic awareness.

When phonemic awareness is defined as the ability to perceive and manipulate the phonemes that make up words, the concept of phonemic awareness fits neatly into the word recognition model of reading. In the next section, we discuss in more detail how this concept has been elaborated.

Phonological Awareness and Phonemic Awareness

Researchers often distinguish between phonological awareness and phonemic awareness. *Phonological awareness* is the ability to distinguish larger units of speech, such as words and syllables. *Phonemic awareness* is a type of phonological awareness. It is the ability to identify the phonemes in a word and manipulate them in various ways, such as adding a phoneme, deleting a phoneme, or substituting one phoneme for another. Thus, a child with phonemic awareness could change /æt/ to /sæt/ by adding an /s/, or change /sæt/ to /ræt/ by substituting /r/ for /s/ during an oral language exercise.

Adams (1990) identified five levels of phonemic awareness. These included the ability to

1. hear rhymes and alliteration in nursery rhymes
2. do oddity tasks (picking out a word that starts with a different phoneme from others in a series, for example)
3. blend or split syllables
4. perform phonemic segmentation (count the number of phonemes in a word like *cat*)
5. perform phoneme manipulation tasks (adding, deleting, substituting a phoneme)

Items 1 and 3 above appear to be phonological, rather than phonemic, awareness tasks because they involve working with units bigger than phonemes. However, all these tasks involve students in manipulating parts of language. Some of the tasks can be described in simple terms that most young children would understand, such as telling which words sound the same, or rhyme. However, other tasks, such as adding or deleting a phoneme, involve more abstract thinking.

As a result of research summaries by Stanovich, Adams, and others, which showed that children with greater phonemic awareness at a younger age were better readers by third or fourth grade, some reading researchers operating from a word recognition orientation called for direct instruction to improve children's phonemic awareness. This movement was buttressed by a report of a national reading panel. The panel's report supported the claims for the importance of phonemic awareness and phonics. This report has been severely critiqued (see Garan [2002] for a good summary), but, at the same time, the results have been widely disseminated and have helped shape educational policy at national, state, and local levels.

What were originally research tasks, such as deleting a phoneme, became suggested instructional practices. For example, a summary document, *Put Reading First* (Armbruster and Osborn 2001), claims that phonemic awareness can be taught and learned. The specific activities for teachers and students include

1. phoneme isolation (What is the first sound in *van?*)
2. phoneme identity (What sound is the same in *fix, fall,* and *fun?*)
3. phoneme categorization (Which word doesn't belong— *bus, burn,* or *rug?*)
4. phoneme blending (Combine individual phonemes to form a word.)
5. phoneme segmentation (Divide a word into its phonemes and say each one.)

These are all phonemic awareness tasks because they require students to deal with phonemes. Even though phonemic awareness is an aural ability, the writers of *Put Reading First* claim that "phonemic awareness instruction is most effective when children are taught to manipulate phonemes by using the letters of the alphabet" (p. 7). Once letters are introduced, the instruction involves phonics, not purely phonemic awareness.

This tendency to combine phonemic awareness and phonics is common. Perhaps this is because for literate adults who conduct research studies, it is difficult to conceptualize sounds apart from the letters that constitute them. Krashen (personal communication), for example, has informally tested groups of teachers on the common task of phoneme deletion. He asks them what word results if they delete the first sound in a word like *trip*. Then he asks them how they carried out the task. Most teachers report that they pictured the spelling of the complete word and then the spelling of the word without the *t*. In other words, the teachers used their knowledge of letters to talk about sounds. This was not a test of phonemic awareness for them.

It is apparent that phonemic awareness, as it has been defined and operationalized, fits very well into a word recognition model of reading. Proponents of this model claim that reading is primarily a process of identifying words and that this ability can be taught and learned. Learning is best accomplished by breaking a task down into its component parts and teaching each part systematically. A logical teaching sequence, from this perspective, would include teaching

1. phonemic awareness skills
2. names and sounds of letters
3. phonics rules
4. sight words
5. structural analysis skills

All of these abilities help students identify marks on paper as words they know in their oral vocabulary. These subskills can also be further broken down and taught individually. Phonemic awareness, as shown earlier, can be divided into different levels, and each level can be taught and learned. One of the most commonly used tests of phonemic awareness, the Yopp-Singer test (Yopp 1992), asks students to segment words into phonemes. Since segmentation is considered the most difficult skill in the phonemic awareness hierarchy, students who can score well on this test are assumed to have developed the other, less difficult phonemic awareness skills.

Phonemic awareness is a key to word recognition. It is the first skill in a hierarchy that students must learn to identify words. Phonemic awareness may develop in some children as the result of early literacy experiences. However, other children come to school without phonemic awareness, so the best solution is to teach phonemic awareness directly and systematically. This is the perspective of those who take a word recognition view of reading. However, phonemic awareness is defined differently and is thought to play a different role in the sociopsycholinguistic model of reading.

Two Views of Phonemic Awareness

Researchers who take a word recognition view of reading have defined phonemic awareness as the ability to perceive and manipulate the sounds (the phonemes) that make up words in oral language. This definition fits into a word recognition view of reading because phonemic awareness, by this definition, is a metalinguistic ability. *Metalinguistics* refers to knowledge about language. This is conscious knowledge, something that can be taught and learned. It can also be tested in isolation from meaningful language use. For example, children can be tested on their ability to segment nonsense words into their phonemes.

Researchers who take a sociopsycholinguistic view of reading, guided by insights from linguistics, would define phonemic awareness differently. They would say that this awareness is subconscious. It is a natural part of oral language development.

The speech stream is not physically segmented. Instead, it is a continuous flow of sound, as a speech spectrograph, a machine that visually represents speech, can show. To understand a language, a person must acquire the ability to perceive this continuous stream of sound as being made up of component parts.

Native speakers must be able to divide up speech into words or parts of words in order to understand what is being said. That is, they must develop phonological awareness. They do this effortlessly. The raw data from the speech stream is perceived as being composed of clearly differentiated units. To appreciate the difficulty of this task, one needs only to listen to an unfamiliar language. When most English speakers listen to Chinese or Arabic, for example, they have great difficulty in dividing the speech up into individual words. An important part of acquiring a language is developing this ability to differentiate the speech stream into its component parts.

The process of separating out the parts of speech goes from a perception of whole phrases, to the perception of words, and then to parts of words. To understand messages, people must be able to perceive differences among phonemes. That is, they must develop phonemic awareness. Otherwise, they couldn't distinguish between "I saw a *house*" and "I saw a *mouse*." Even though context clues can help listeners construct meaning, listeners must also be able to distinguish among individual phonemes. In this respect, anyone who can understand a language has phonemic awareness.

Children acquiring their first language and people acquiring a second language develop the ability to perceive differences in meaning that are signaled by variations in phonemes. They do this by attending to the meaning, not to the sounds themselves. Their knowledge of the differences among sounds is subconscious. They can use this knowledge to construct meaning, but they can't explain how they do it. A five-year-old understands the difference between "Eat your peas" and "Eat your bees" even though he wouldn't be able to explain that the difference in meaning is signaled by a change in the voicing of the initial consonant phoneme in the words *peas* and *bees*. A five-year-old would attend to the difference in meaning, not the difference between /p/ and /b/.

Linguists and researchers who work from a sociopsycholinguistic view of reading conceptualize phonemic awareness and its role in reading quite differently from those who take a word recognition view.

If reading is seen as a process of recognizing words, then phonemic awareness is regarded as a subskill readers must develop in order to make sense of phonics rules and apply those rules to recode texts. Phonemic awareness is conscious knowledge that can be taught and tested outside the context of meaningful reading. On the other hand, if reading is viewed as a process of constructing meaning, phonemic awareness is considered a component of one of the three linguistic cueing systems:

the graphophonic system. Readers use both visual and sound knowledge as well as the knowledge of correspondences between letters and sounds as they sample texts and make and confirm predictions to construct meaning from texts. However, they also use cues from syntax and semantics as they read.

We should note here that although graphophonics combines aural and visual information, readers can acquire reading proficiency with just one of these modalities. After all, deaf children learn to read without being able to hear words, and blind children learn to read without seeing words. Humans have an innate capacity to make meaning of oral or written language, and they manage to do this even under circumstances in which the input is limited.

Developing Conscious Awareness of Phonemes

For the purposes of reading, children don't need to be consciously aware of phonemes. However, to produce writing, children need to be aware of sounds and of how sounds connect to letters. Studies of children's spelling development (Wilde 1992; Freeman and Freeman 1996) show that young writers of English begin by representing words with single letters. Later, they use one letter for each syllable. Eventually, writers begin to represent each sound with a letter: they discover the alphabetic principle. As they attempt to communicate using written language, children become conscious of how sounds relate to spellings.

An early study by Read (1971) provides dramatic evidence from children's spelling of their knowledge of phonology. Their acquired knowledge is revealed in different ways in their spelling. For example, they use letter names to spell long vowels. The sound of /iy/ is spelled with the letter e in words like egle and fel, and the sound of /ay/ is spelled with the letter i in lik and mi.

Children's spellings reflect phonetic details in the language. For example, children often omit nasals that precede consonants and write a word like and as ad, leaving out the n. As we discuss in Chapter 6, in English when a nasal precedes a stop consonant, the two sounds are produced in the same place in the mouth. Children feel where the sound is being produced and use just one letter to represent the two sounds that are produced in one place. Similarly, they use the letter d to represent the sound of /t/ in a word like letter. This spelling (leder) more closely corresponds to the way speakers pronounce /t/ in this position.

Read's study showed that children's spellings reflect their knowledge of many details of English phonology and phonetics. Children acquire phonology in the process of comprehending oral language. They can use this acquired knowledge to learn to read. Then, when they begin to write, their spelling reflects this knowledge.

Their awareness of how sounds relate to spellings, which developed as they were read to and with, is brought to a conscious level as they attempt to represent their own ideas using invented spelling.

From a sociopsycholinguistic perspective, then, awareness of phonemes develops as children acquire oral language. When they are read to, children connect this knowledge of sounds to letters. However, their focus is on making sense of text, and they are not consciously aware of how sounds connect to spellings. Then, as children begin to write, their spellings reflect their acquired knowledge of the relationship between sounds and spellings. It is not until children attempt to produce conventional spellings that they become consciously aware of the relationships between sounds and spellings. At this point, teaching about spelling can be effective. In Chapter 5 we discuss in more detail the English writing system, and we suggest ways teachers can help students improve their spelling by investigating patterns in the ways words are spelled.

Research Support for the Two Views of Phonemic Awareness

If phonemic awareness develops as a result of being read to and of reading, as proponents of a sociopsycholinguistic view claim, then research should examine the effects of reading on phonemic awareness rather than the effects of phonemic awareness training on reading. That is, instead of giving groups of students practice in various phonemic awareness skills and then testing the children on some aspect of their reading ability, researchers would expose some children to more reading than others and then measure differences in the phonemic awareness of the two groups.

Neumann (1999) reports on one such study, a read-aloud project she conducted. Teachers were provided with high-quality children's books and inserviced on methods of reading these books aloud effectively to young children (Trelease 2001). Krashen (in press) summarizes the results of these read-alouds:

> Tests of phonemic awareness were given six months after the project ended. In the rhyme test, children were asked to indicate which word of three did not rhyme with the others. In the alliteration task, children were asked to indicate which word of three did not begin with the same sound. Children in the Books Aloud group were better than controls on both: I calculated effect sizes of .57 for rhyme and .54 for alliteration, which are quite substantial, and especially impressive considering that the tests were given long after the treatment ended. Citing Ehri, Neumann notes that this result suggests that "these skills may indeed be a by-product of exposure to books and learning." (p. 305)

More studies such as Neumann's would be helpful in determining whether classroom time spent on phonemic awareness training could effectively be replaced with read-aloud activities. As Krashen points out, reading aloud to children is pleasurable and has many benefits in addition to helping them gain phonemic awareness.

The idea that phonemic awareness develops as the result of being read to is consistent with the concept of graphophonics. Children can develop graphophonic knowledge only by hearing books read to them while looking at the print. This allows them to make connections between oral and written language. This approach is supported by the advice from *Put Reading First* that "Phonemic awareness instruction is most effective when children are taught to manipulate phonemes by using the letters of the alphabet" (Armbruster and Osborn 2001, p. 7).

As noted earlier, most studies in the area of phonemic awareness has been conducted by researchers with a word recognition orientation. Krashen (2001) carried out an extensive review of this research. He limited this review in two ways. First, he considered only studies that involved phonemic awareness and did not also include phonics instruction. Second, he looked only at studies that reported differences in reading comprehension. Many studies of phonemic awareness test children on their ability to carry out phonemic awareness tasks or to pronounce words, but if reading involves constructing meaning, then the best evidence for the benefits of phonemic awareness would come from gains in reading comprehension.

Krashen found just six studies that met his criteria. Of these, three dealt with English-speaking children, and just one was conducted in the United States. Most of the studies involved small groups of children. For example, a study by Bradley and Bryant (1983), which has been widely quoted, had only thirteen children in the experimental group. The results of these six studies were mixed. Only one showed clear gains in comprehension from phonemic awareness training. This was a study carried out with fifteen Hebrew-speaking children in Israel. Krashen concluded that he found no studies using English that were clearly and strongly supportive of training in phonemic awareness. Krashen's review reveals that the research base that supports phonemic awareness training is limited.

Phonology plays a role in reading. Those who hold a word recognition view of reading claim that phonology plays a very important role. Phonemic awareness is the key to word recognition. Those who hold a sociopsycholinguistic view of reading claim that phonology plays a more limited role. They argue that hearing children acquire phonemic awareness naturally as part of their oral language development, and then children can use this subconscious knowledge as part of one cueing system to help them construct meaning as they read. Before evaluating these two views of the role of phonology in reading, we turn to the role of phonology in second language teaching and learning. Then we consider certain linguistic factors that can help teachers determine the best approach to teaching reading or teaching a second language.

Second Language Teaching and Phonology

Students learning English as a second language must develop the ability to comprehend and produce the sounds of English. That is, they must develop control over English phonology. Different methods of second language teaching have approached phonology in different ways. In this section, we discuss how three widely used methods of second or foreign language teaching have presented English sounds.

In Chapter 2, we discussed two views of second language development: a learning view and an acquisition view (see Freeman and Freeman 1998a for an extended discussion of second language teaching methods). Early methods of second language teaching, such as the grammar translation method, were based on a theory that language must be learned. Therefore, students studied parts of the language, the grammar and the vocabulary, and used that knowledge to translate texts from the foreign language into the native language or from the native language into the foreign language. The goal of instruction was to enable students to read and write the language. Little attention was paid to speaking and listening, so phonology, the study of speech sounds, did not play a role in instruction.

Later, other methods were created to help students develop oral proficiency in a second language. These were also based on a learning model. The most widely used method, the audiolingual method (ALM), involved students in learning dialogues and practicing language with exercises and drills. The dialogues, exercises, and drills were all based on linguistic analyses contrasting the native language and the second language. Classroom activities presented parts of the language—sounds, vocabulary, and grammar—in context so that students could develop proficiency in using the language. Students memorized and recited dialogues and different drills to practice language structures. Emphasis was placed on correct production of language forms. Meaning was a secondary focus. Students learned to pronounce phrases and sentences correctly in the new language, and little attention was given to meaningful communication.

The linguistic base for ALM was contrastive analysis. Linguists contrasted the native language with the second language. Their analyses were very thorough. For example, to contrast the phonological systems of two languages, a linguist would first describe each language. Then she would contrast the two systems. For phonology, this would include a phoneme-by-phoneme comparison. For each phoneme, the linguist would ask

Does the native language have a phonetically similar phoneme?
Are the variants of the phonemes similar in both languages?
Are the phonemes and their variants similarly distributed?

As these questions show, the comparison was very detailed.

Results of contrastive analyses were used to develop teaching materials. For example, to develop materials to teach Spanish to English speakers, linguists would compare English and Spanish phonology, morphology, syntax, and so on. Lado (1957) even contrasted the two cultures. The assumption was that if a certain sound or vocabulary item was the same in the two languages, that part of the language would be easy to learn. On the other hand, in areas where the two languages differed, learning would be more difficult. Over time, linguists developed a hierarchy of difficulty. The most difficult case was a situation in which one item in the native language was represented by two or more items in the second language. For example, English has one /r/ phoneme and Spanish has two different /r/s.

Linguists identified these problem areas and then developed exercises to give students practice with the difficult forms. However, many of the predictions based on the linguistic contrasts between languages were not borne out as students attempted to learn the language. Students had trouble learning some items that were predicted to be easy, and they easily learned some items that were predicted to be difficult. Even though linguists had performed careful analyses of the two languages, the results were not helpful in planning instruction. The attempt to analyze language, divide it into parts, and present the parts in the context of exercises and drills simply did not work very well. Students had a hard time learning language when instructors used methods like ALM (Brown 1994).

These earlier methods of language teaching, based on a learning model, have been replaced by current methods that are based on an acquisition model. The Natural Approach, for example, is consistent with Krashen's theory of second language acquisition outlined in Chapter 2. The teacher uses a variety of techniques to make the language input comprehensible. Students focus on constructing meaning as they use the language. There is no grammatical sequence built into the curriculum or materials. According to the natural order hypothesis, any student learning English, for example, will develop parts of the language (the phonology, morphology, and syntax) in a natural order as long as he receives messages he understands. In the case of phonology, the hypothesis is that second language learners, like babies acquiring their first language, will pick up correct pronunciations of the sounds of the language as they hear and use the language in natural communication. A premise of The Natural Approach is that English phonology is simply too complex to be learned through either direct, explicit teaching or implicit teaching in the context of carefully sequenced drills. Instead, students acquire phonology in the process of developing the ability to communicate in a new language.

There is no attempt to identify parts of the language and present them in sequence for two reasons. First, linguists have not identified the components of any part of the language in enough detail to suggest a sequence of teaching. Even though linguists can list the phonemes of a language, many of the details of how speakers vary these phonemes along with how they use stress and intonation are not fully known. Second, even if the components were known, it would not be useful to sequence the parts because they are too complex to be learned as the result of direct teaching. Instead, they are acquired. What is important is to involve students with meaningful language, not to present the parts of the language either directly or in context to be learned.

Early versions of The Natural Approach delayed reading and writing until students had developed oral language proficiency. Now, teachers introduce reading from the beginning. In many classes, teachers teach language through academic content and organize curriculum around themes. This is referred to as *sustained content language teaching* because students are involved in extended themes in which the different subject areas are integrated (Pally 2000). Students learn language as they read, write, and talk about content and become involved in investigations and studies of interest to them.

Figure 4–1 summarizes the relationships between these methods of teaching a second language and phonology.

Linguistic Considerations for Developing Proficiency in a Written or Second Language

We have described the system of English phonemes and have considered how different views of reading and of second language teaching take phonology into account. There is a division between those who believe second and written languages are learned and those who believe they are acquired. Methods based on a learning perspective attempt to break language into its component parts and teach these parts either in context or directly. The belief is that students can develop language skills through various kinds of exercises and then use this knowledge to comprehend written language or a second language.

Methods based on an acquisition perspective keep the focus on meaning construction. Students develop control over parts of the language, such as the phonology, in the process of attempting to communicate. Knowledge of phonology is subconscious, but students can use it to comprehend language. Later, as students use writing to communicate, they become consciously aware of sounds and how they are represented by spellings. Those who take the acquisition view believe that areas of linguistics such as phonology are too complex to be divided into skills to be taught and learned.

Insights from linguistics can help inform educators as they evaluate these two views of language development. In the following sections, we discuss three linguistic factors that should be taken into account. The first is that English phonemes occur in variant forms called allophones. Second, speakers from different dialect

Method of Second Language Teaching	View of Language Development	Role of Phonology	How Phonology Is Developed
grammar translation	learning	almost no role; emphasis on written language	not included; other parts of language are learned as the result of direct teaching
audiolingual method	learning	major role; sounds are presented in sequence based on contrastive analysis	learned by practicing pronunciation of words in the context of drills and exercises
Natural Approach	acquisition	minor role; focus is on understanding messages	acquired by using language to communicate
sustained content language teaching	acquisition	minor role; focus is on learning interesting content	acquired by using language to learn content

Figure 4–1. Second language teaching and phonology

regions use different phonemes. Third, phonemes vary across languages. This last point is especially important to consider when trying to test English language learners for phonemic awareness.

Allophones: Phonetic Variations

As we discussed earlier, English has about thirty-nine phonemes. These phonemes are perceptual units. They are sounds that make a difference in meaning in English. Linguists test for phonemes by finding minimal pairs, words that differ by only one sound. Since words like /sæt/ and /mæt/ differ by only their initial sounds, those sounds must be phonemes in English. They signal a difference in meaning. Phonemes, however, are not always pronounced in the same way. They undergo changes in pronunciation depending on their position in words and the other sounds around them.

Allophones of /k/, a case of assimilation   Each phoneme in English or any other language is actually a group of sounds, called *phones*. The phones that make up one phoneme are called its *allophones* ("all the phones"). The particular allophone that a speaker produces depends on the preceding or following sound. For example, when English speakers say, "Keep cool," they produce two /k/ phonemes, one at the beginning of each word. The /k/ phoneme, as we explained earlier, is produced by bunching the back of the tongue up to block the air at the velum.

We invite readers to say "Keep cool" and to notice exactly where the tongue hits the velum in each word. Most speakers will feel that the point of contact is farther forward for *keep* than for *cool*. Thus, the /k/ phoneme is produced at a slightly different place in the mouth for each instance of this phoneme. Adults are good at ignoring this physical difference because what matters is that this is an instance of /k/. The word is *keep*, not *beep* or *seep*.

The allophones of /k/ are the result of a general process in language called *assimilation*. Phonemes assimilate to neighboring sounds. Just as immigrants may change some habits to become more like the people in their new country, phonemes become similar to the phonemes next to them. In this case, the /k/ in *keep* is produced farther forward in the mouth because the following vowel sound, /iy/, is a high, front vowel. The brain sends a message to block the air at the velum to form /k/, but even as the tongue is moving to that position, it is preparing for the next sound in the sequence. The tongue doesn't go all the way back along the velum because it is getting ready to move to the front.

In producing *cool*, the tongue blocks the air to form /k/ at a point farther back in the mouth because the following vowel, /uw/, is a high, back sound. By stopping the air farther back along the velum, the tongue is moving closer to the position to make the /uw/ sound. Thus, the /k/ is assimilating to the /uw/. Assimilation is a common process in all languages. It is a kind of physical shortcut between two tongue positions, a more efficient way of producing phonemes. Since speakers generate some eight phonemes per second, this kind of economy is necessary and natural. The production of /k/ is conditioned by the anticipation of the following sound, in much the same way that a person might eat a light meal if a heavy meal is to follow later in the day.

All phonemes have allophonic variations. Phonemic awareness, from a learning perspective, involves the ability to perceive and manipulate phonemes. This would be easier if phonemes were constant physical realities. Educators can reasonably expect their students to learn to perceive and manipulate classroom objects. For example, a kindergarten teacher who wishes to teach colors and shapes can give students colored blocks and ask his students to arrange them in different ways. Students could arrange the blocks in different orders by color or shape.

They could also learn to delete one block from a sequence or replace a red square block with a blue triangle. This sort of thing would be relatively easy to teach and learn because a blue triangular block maintains its properties whether it is at the beginning of a sequence or at the end. It is still a blue triangle.

Phonemes are not constant physical realities like colored blocks. They are perceptual units that differ from one another by the fact that they signal differences in meaning. The allophones of a phoneme are all perceived as the same sound despite the physical differences in their production. As a result, it is a more difficult task to teach children to perceive and manipulate phonemes than to rearrange blocks. During phonemic awareness exercises and tests, children are asked to focus on the physical aspects of phonemes, not on the meanings of the words they constitute. During phonemic awareness exercises, variations between allophones may cause confusion. Since phonemes, by definition, are sounds that make a meaning difference, it is difficult to perceive phonemes in situations in which meaning is not the concern, and that is precisely what children are being asked to do on tests of phonemic awareness.

From an acquisition perspective, allophones do not pose a problem because in classes in which teachers organize instruction to help students acquire a written or second language, teachers keep the focus on making sense. They try to make the new language comprehensible. Students acquire phonemes and their allophones as they attempt to make meaning. Their knowledge of phonology and graphophonics is subconscious. Students in acquisition classes develop linguistic knowledge, although they may not develop the metalinguistic knowledge needed to talk about phonemes that occur in tests of phonemic awareness.

Allophones of /t/, a complex case   The phoneme /k/ has two allophones. Some phonemes are much more complex. In English, /t/ has six variations, depending on its position in a word and the other phonemes around it. The following words each contain a different /t/ allophone: *top*, *pot*, *kitten*, *letter*, *train*, and *stop*. Using phonetic transcription, linguists represent these allophones and describe the conditioning environment (the neighboring sounds that influence the pronunciation) of each as shown in Figure 4–2 (Farmer and Demers 1996, p. 75).

All six allophones of /t/ involve physical differences. We described /t/ as a voiceless, alveolar stop that is made by blocking the air with the tip of the tongue at the alveolar ridge. The first allophone, [tʰ], is produced when /t/ starts a syllable. As the sound is released, an extra puff of air is produced. This is called *aspiration* and is represented by a small raised *h*. At the end of a word, though, the /t/ is not released. In addition, the air is partially blocked in the glottal region before being stopped in the mouth. This process of blocking the air in the throat is called

Articulatory Description	Phonetic Symbol	Conditioning Environment	Example
released, aspirated	[tʰ]	syllable initial	top
unreleased, preglottalized	[ʔt]	word final after a vowel	pot
glottal stop	[ʔ]	before a syllabic /n/	kitten
flap	[D]	between vowels when the first vowel is stressed	letter
alveopalatal stop	[ť]	syllable initial before /r/	train
released, unaspirated	[t]	when the above conditions are not met	stop

Figure 4–2. Allophones of /t/

preglottalization. This allophone is represented by [ʔt]. The ʔ is the symbol for a glottal stop. The third allophone [ʔ] is not simply preglottalized, it is a glottal stop produced by stopping the air in the glottal region, not in the mouth. One can produce a word like *kitten* without pressing the tongue against the alveolar ridge for the /t/, but the tongue does move there for the /n/ that follows. The next allophone, [D], is called a *flap* because the tongue taps or flaps against the back of the front teeth. The symbol is a capital D, and the sound is much the same as /d/. Words like *metal* and *medal*, the first with a flapped [D] and the second with a /d/, sound identical to most native English speakers. As we mentioned previously, children learning to spell often represent this allophone of /t/ with a *d* in their writing.

The next phoneme, [ť], is similar to an affricate. The air is stopped with the tongue pressing against the alveolar ridge and then released into an /r/ sound. What happens is that the tongue flattens along the top of the mouth to block the air. Physically this tongue movement is very similar to the motions used to produce the voiceless alveopalatal affricate, /č/. Young children can feel that these two phonemes are produced in a similar manner, and they sometimes spell a word like *train* with a *ch* instead of a *t*. The final allophone, [t], occurs whenever none of the conditions for producing the first five variations is present. For example, in *stop*, there is no aspiration because air is already being released as /s/ is produced, there is no constriction of air in the glottal region, and the tongue doesn't flap against the front teeth.

The allophones of a phoneme are in complementary distribution. This means that each instance of /t/ falls into one and only one of the six categories. Together, these categories make up all the possible allophones of /t/. No allophone can fit into two different categories. For example, if the /t/ is followed by /r/, it is affricated and written as [ť]. This is the only category for /t/ followed by /r/. The alternative to complementary distribution is overlapping distribution. If categories overlap, an allophone could be in either of two categories. Although allophones of phonemes are in complementary distribution, as we will explain in Chapter 5, spellings of some phonemes are in overlapping distribution. There is more than one possible spelling for the same sound even in the same conditioning environment.

We have described all these allophones of /t/ in some detail to show how complex phonemes can be. Depending on the other sounds around them, phonemes are produced in different ways. During normal communication, speakers of English ignore all these allophonic variations and focus on the meaning differences that phonemes signal. As young children learn to read, they begin to connect sounds with letters. They ignore the physical variations among allophones of a phoneme as long as their focus is on making sense of written language. However, allophonic variations may pose difficulties when children are asked to perceive and manipulate phonemes during exercises and tests of phonemic awareness because then the focus is on the phonemes themselves, not on the meaning differences they signal.

Although adults are good at ignoring allophonic variations as they listen to a language they speak well, they may experience difficulties in perceiving the phonemes in a language they are trying to learn. Language learners often complain that speakers of the new language talk very fast. Actually, even though there are individual differences in rate of speech, speakers of one language don't talk faster than those of another language, because speech rate is constrained by human physiology. The reason that language learners think that speakers of the new language talk fast is because language learners are not so good at ignoring variations in phonemes. Like children taking a phonemic awareness test, adults learning a new language may try to pay attention to all the physical differences among the sounds they hear, and, as a result, they become overloaded with information. The effect of attending to all these details is similar to trying to understand someone speaking very rapidly.

Dialect Differences

All speakers of a language speak some dialect of that language. Dialects can be regional or social or both. People in different parts of the country speak differently, but even within one area, people of different social classes may speak with different dialects. Dialect study is fascinating, and several excellent books have been written on the topic (Wolfram and Christian 1989; Wolfram 1991; McWhorter 2000). In general, dialects are variations in language marked by certain ways of pronouncing words, particular choices of vocabulary, and even variations in syntax. For example, people from Texas might pronounce "you all" as "y'all," midwesterners drink "pop," not "soda," and some Minnesotans will ask, "Are you going with?" An Internet website that provides information about dialects is http://polyglot.lss.wisc.edu/dare/dare.html.

Although dialect study is an important area of linguistics, we wish to examine ways in which variations in dialect could influence people learning to read or learning a second language. Dialect is not an issue in learning to read if instruction is based on an acquisition view. Studies have shown that when proficient readers read aloud, they often translate the written text into their own dialect (Goodman 1984, 1993). On the other hand, even readers who speak a particular dialect may stumble through texts in which the writer has attempted to represent that dialect through unconventional spellings. From a sociopsycholinguistic view, readers use graphophonic cues not to recode words to sounds, but to construct meaning. Trying to rewrite a text so that it represents a reader's pronunciation of words may simply confuse the reader.

In the case of second language teaching, students will generally acquire the dialect of their instructors. This is most notable in settings in which people choose between British and American schools in which to study English. Students coming out of a British school sound quite different from those coming from an American school. If schools are teaching language through content with the belief that students will acquire language, then dialect difference is not an issue. Students will simply acquire the dialect they hear.

Although dialects are not a problem from a sociopsycholinguistic view, they are potentially a problem from a word recognition view. The difficulties surface in exercises or tests of phonemic awareness. For example, many native English speakers from the south do not differentiate between the vowel phonemes in /pɪn/ and /pɛn/. For speakers of this dialect, these two words are homonyms. They rely on the context, not the sounds, to distinguish between them. However, if a child from the south is asked to identify the middle phoneme in one of these words, the answer the child gives may be considered wrong. Similarly, if the child is asked to substitute /ɪ/ for /ɛ/ in these words during a phonemic awareness exercise, the child may be confused.

For many speakers of English, the vowels in *caught* and *cot* are the same. However, speakers of some dialects distinguish between these sounds, and linguists represent the two vowel phonemes as /ɔ/ and /a/. Again, if children speak a dialect that doesn't include both phonemes, they may have trouble with exercises or tests that involve these sounds.

One of the well-known features of the dialect of speakers from Maine and some other parts of New England is the deletion of /r/. These speakers may declare, /ay pakt may ca ın havad yad/, in the process leaving their /r/s parked at home. This feature gets a bit more complex. Mainers do pronounce /r/ in many contexts. They have no trouble with the /r/ in *red* or *Fred*, and they may even add an /r/ at the end of a word like *idea* or *tuna*. The /r/ is regularly deleted when it follows a vowel, as it does in *park*, *car*, *Harvard*, and *yard*. For speakers of this dialect, exercises in identifying phonemes could be difficult. For example, if children who speak this dialect are asked how many phonemes there are in *car*, they might answer, "Two." These children might be confused if asked to delete an /r/ from a word like *park* because they don't perceive that phoneme in the word. In short, children who speak different dialects of English may have difficulty with exercises or tests that involve phonemes that do not occur in their dialect.

English language learners also face problems when trying to do exercises or take tests of phonemic awareness. The difference between the variety of English they speak and Standard English is often greater than the difference between the dialect spoken by someone from the South or someone from Maine and Standard English. In addition, English language learners have already developed the phonology of one language, and that knowledge may influence their perception of English sounds.

Language Differences

A third linguistic factor to consider when evaluating approaches to teaching reading or a second language is the phonological differences among languages. Phonemes, as we have explained, are the sounds used in a particular language to signal differences in meaning. Each language uses a different inventory of sounds. As a result, some phonemes from one language may be identical to those in another language, and some may be different. At the same time, sounds that are phonemes in one language may be allophones of a phoneme in another language.

The potential problems caused by differences between languages are minimized when the focus of instruction is on meaning construction. When an English learner is trying to use English to understand some academic content area, that student can use background knowledge and cues from syntax and semantics to supplement phonological cues in making meaning. Students can acquire both oral and written English in classes in which language is learned through content area study.

However, language differences are a potential source of difficulty in classes in which instruction focuses on aspects of language itself. Some methods of second language teaching and testing ask students to determine whether two sounds are alike or different. Often, tests of English require students to distinguish between minimal pairs. Since phonemes are perceptual units, speakers of some languages may regard two sounds as the same if they are allophones of one phoneme in their language, even though they are separate phonemes in English. For example, in English /d/ and /ð/ are two phonemes. English has minimal pairs such as *den* and *then* and *breed* and *breathe*. Spanish has these same two sounds, but they are allophones of one phoneme. There are no minimal pairs of words in Spanish that differ by these two sounds. In other words, the sounds do not signal a difference in meaning in Spanish.

In words such as *dedo* and *dado*, the first sound is more like the English /d/ and the second sound is like the English /ð/. In Spanish, the voiced interdental fricative [ð] is an allophone of /d/. These two sounds occur in different environments. The stop occurs at the beginning of a syllable or following a consonant phoneme, and the fricative follows a vowel. This is one instance of a general rule in Spanish that voiced stops (/b/, /d/, /g/) become voiced fricatives in these environments. The two types of sounds are allophones.

A Spanish speaker learning English has acquired the subconscious knowledge that the difference between the sounds [d] and [ð] never makes a meaning difference, so the physical differences between the sounds can be ignored. However, in English, the difference can't be ignored because /d/ and /ð/ are separate phonemes. Spanish speakers acquiring English will come to understand this difference between the two languages, again at a subconscious level, in the process of trying to make sense of the new language. This is not a problem as long as the focus is on making meaning. Spanish speakers may still spell some English words, like *that*, with a *d* instead of a *th* while they are acquiring English spelling conventions. The Spanish spelling reflects the fact that in Spanish, both sounds are spelled with a *d*.

However, exercises or tests that focus on the sounds themselves may cause problems for Spanish speakers being tested in English. These students may already have developed phonemic awareness in Spanish, but they may not have developed phonemic awareness in English yet. Exercises involving /d/ and /ð/ could be confusing. Spanish speakers may still perceive these two sounds as variations on one phoneme. If asked to substitute /ð/ for /d/, the Spanish speaker might not perceive these as different sounds. In addition, because Spanish doesn't contain words that start with /ð/, students might pronounce a word like *then* the same as *den*.

To take one other example, English has the two phonemes /č/ and /š/, and Spanish has only one of these phonemes, /č/ (although some dialects of Spanish may also include [š]). Linguists using contrastive analysis might predict that Spanish speakers learning English would have difficulty producing /š/ because

Spanish lacks that phoneme. However, Spanish speakers learning English often pronounce words like *chair* as "share." Perhaps, once they realize that English has the /š/ sound, they decide that this sound replaces the /č/ sound and overgeneralize its use.

Jane Medina (1999) has written a poignant poem, "T-Shirt," that plays on these two sounds. Jorge calls his instructor "Teacher," but she interprets his pronunciation as "T-shirt" and says, "Besides, when you say it, it sounds like 't-shirt,' I don't want to turn into a t-shirt" (p. 25). Jorge uses the /š/ sound where a native English speaker would use /č/. Jorge would probably have trouble with exercises and tests of phonemic awareness involving these two phonemes. English spelling is not too helpful, either, since some English words, those borrowed from French, like *machine* and *Chevrolet*, retain the *ch* spelling to represent the /š/ sound.

Additional Concerns About Phonemic Awareness

Proponents of a word recognition view encourage teachers to contextualize phonemic awareness exercises. They suggest the use of songs, rhymes, poems, and language games. However, teachers sometimes involve students in decontextualized exercises simply because they don't have the time to develop the creative activities needed to contextualize phonemic awareness exercises. As a result, with the focus on the phonemes, the exercises become quite abstract, especially for younger children and English language learners.

Another problem is that phonemic awareness exercises and tests often include nonsense words. The use of nonsense words ensures that students focus on the sounds, not the meaning. However, children and English language learners may not realize that these are nonsense words. The exercises may confuse them if they are attempting to make sense out of nonsense.

Perhaps the greatest problem with exercises and tests of phonemic awareness is that in some schools a great deal of time is devoted to these activities. Time spent on phonemic awareness is generally time taken away from authentic reading experiences. From a sociopsycholinguistic perspective, it is these reading experiences that promote acquisition. Teachers who conduct phonemic awareness activities for part of their language arts time have less time to read to and with children, and children have less time for independent reading. As a result, children have fewer opportunities for written and second language acquisition.

Conclusion

Phonology plays different roles in the two models of reading we have described. Phonology plays a major role in a word recognition view. Students are expected to develop phonemic awareness, the ability to perceive and manipulate phonemes, and then use this knowledge as a base for learning phonics rules. Application of phonics rules helps readers recode written language to oral language.

Phonology also plays a role in a sociopsycholinguistic view of reading. However, phonemic awareness is defined differently in this model. Phonemic awareness is an acquired ability that allows people to distinguish between words. Children come to school with this ability. Then, when teachers and others read to and with them, they develop graphophonic knowledge. Graphophonics combines their subconscious knowledge of sounds with knowledge of letters and knowledge of the correspondences between sounds and letters. During reading instruction, the focus stays on making meaning, not on the specific properties of phonemes. Later, as children learn to spell words, they become conscious of the connections between sounds and letters.

Phonology also plays a different role in various methods of teaching a foreign or second language. In the grammar translation method, for example, phonology plays a minimal role because the focus is on translating the written language. On the other hand, in the audiolingual method, phonology plays a major role because the goal is to enable students to understand and speak the language. ALM is based on a learning model. Linguists helped develop materials for ALM by contrasting the native language with the second language and then developing drills to practice areas predicted to be difficult. By engaging in drills and exercises and practicing memorized dialogues, students are expected to learn the skills needed to master the second language.

Phonology plays a less important role in approaches to teaching a second language that are based on an acquisition model. In The Natural Approach and sustained content language teaching, the emphasis is on making the instruction meaningful. The phonology of the second language, like that of the first, is acquired in the process of using the language for meaningful communication and content learning. No attempt is made to present the phonemes of the second language in a particular sequence. Instead, the emphasis is on using the language to communicate.

Insights from linguistics can help educators evaluate the claims of those who take different views of reading or teaching a second language. Three linguistic factors to consider are allophones, dialect differences, and language differences. Studies in linguistics have shown that phonology is complex. Phonemes are not stable, physical realities. Instead, they are perceptual units. Phonemes differ in their physical properties depending on the sounds around them. Phonemes often assimilate to preceding or following sounds. These variations are called *allophones*. The fact that phonemes are perceptual units that vary in their physical production has implications for methods of teaching reading or a second language. In addition, differences among dialects and differences between languages also influence learners as they cope with written language or a second language. Generally speaking, these differences do not pose problems if students are focused on making meaning, but they do constitute potential roadblocks when instruction focuses on language itself.

Applications

1. Much has been written about the value of phonemic awareness. Find a current research article on phonemic awareness from a journal such as *Reading Research Quarterly*. Evaluate the study that is reported. Does the study link phonemic awareness with comprehension or only with ability to do phonemic awareness tasks?

2. Michael Opitz' book *Rhymes and Reasons: Literature and Language Play for Phonological Awareness* (2000) contains a good explanation of the difference between phonological and phonemic awareness. The book also lists a number of books that can be used to help students develop phonological and phonemic awareness. Try out some of his suggested activities and report on the effects of helping students acquire phonological awareness through exposure to literature.

3. Charles Read's early studies of spelling development show how children's knowledge of phonological awareness is revealed in their writing. Read his 1971 article "Pre-school Children's Knowledge of English Phonology" or another article or book (Freeman and Freeman 1996, Wilde 1992) on children's spelling development, then collect some writing samples of emergent writers and analyze how their spelling reveals their growing awareness of how letters represent sounds.

4. Linguists have carried out extensive studies comparing languages. Observe English language learners you work with. Is there some feature of their speech that seems to reflect their first language? For example, Spanish speakers might pronounce words like *Spanish* with an /ɛ/ sound at the beginning, before the /s/. Some Asian students may simplify final consonant clusters and pronounce words like *walked* without the sound of the ed. Identify one or two features, and then find some information about the students' first language. Is there something in the first language that helps account for the way the students pronounce English? In evaluating these students, how does the school treat these features of the English learners' speech?

5. This chapter explains that allophones are variations on a phoneme. Take another phoneme of English, such as /p/, and try to find the allophones of the phoneme. For English language learners, if they have this phoneme in their first language, do they also produce the same allophones?

6. Dialect study is fascinating. Study the speech of someone who speaks a dialect different from yours. List the differences in pronunciation, vocabulary, and syntax that you find. Discuss with classmates how they regard people who speak different dialects. Do they associate certain dialects with greater intelligence or prestige than others? Some agencies offer classes in dialect reduction so that people who speak a regional dialect can develop standard speech. Discuss how you feel about the concept of dialect reduction. Should people try to speak with some sort of standard dialect?

5

English Orthography

- *How did the English writing system develop?*
- *Should the spelling system be reformed?*
- *How can teachers help students take a scientific approach to spelling?*

One thing that most people agree on is that English spelling is not very logical. Why does English have silent letters? Why does English allow words like *great* and *grate*, in which one sound, /ey/, is spelled in different ways? Why does English have words like *through* and *though*, in which one set of letters, *ough*, represents different sounds?

Many writers have called for spelling reform. Mark Twain, for example, wrote a clever essay proposing a number of changes to make American English spelling more regular. Plans for changes in the way words are spelled are often circulated on the Internet. These proposals point out the inconsistencies in the system. Most of the suggestions are more humorous than serious. Nevertheless, there is a widespread belief that English spelling is haphazard at best.

Although the writing system is often referred to as the spelling system, *orthography* is a more general term used to refer to all aspects of writing, including the spelling, the punctuation, the spacing, and special features, such as boldface and italics. With the widespread use of computers, writers have many choices of fonts and special effects. Punctuation and special marks attempt to capture the intonation features of oral language. In this chapter, our focus is on the way letters are used to spell words and not on the other aspects of English orthography.

We begin this chapter by tracing the history of writing from early systems to alphabetic writing. We describe the development of American English spelling and explain the logic behind the current system. Both native English speakers and English language learners need to cope with English spelling as they read and write. When teachers understand how the writing system works, they can better assist all students as they attempt to use written language. We describe several ways that teachers can involve students in investigating the spelling system.

The Development of Writing Systems

Many of the world's writing systems, including English, are alphabetic. In these systems, one letter represents each sound. Even though no language uses a writing system that has a complete one-to-one correspondence between letters and sounds, all alphabetic systems follow the general principle that each letter in a word represents one of its sounds. Alphabetic writing evolved gradually.

Sumerian Cuneiform

Humans have used written marks for communication for centuries. According to Samoyault (1998), "Though people all over the world have been writing for more than 5,000 years, the first true alphabets weren't developed until the period between 1700 and 1500 B.C. in areas bordering the eastern shores of the Mediterranean" (p. 1). Before that, writing consisted of pictures or symbols that represented ideas. These writing systems are referred to as *pictographic* or *ideographic*. Early writing was usually connected to religion or magic. Generally, only priests or their scribes could write or interpret the written marks. In fact, the word for early Egyptian writing, *hieroglyphics*, means "priest writing."

In addition, merchants used writing to record business transactions. The earliest known writing system is *cuneiform*, invented by the Sumerians living in Mesopotamia around 3300 B.C. This system used marks to record the number of different kinds of items that the Sumerians traded. The word *cuneiform* means "wedge-shaped." Sumerian writers used sticks or reeds to make marks on clay. When they pressed a stick into the clay, the resulting mark was a triangular wedge shape.

The Sumerian cuneiform writing system could be read by people who spoke different languages because the pictures and more abstract symbols represented numbers and items that were traded. Speakers of different languages interpreted the marks in their own language. This was a useful system for trade across different language groups. Pictographic or ideographic writing has the advantage of communicating ideas directly to people who speak different languages or different dialects of a language. Since there is no correspondence between the written marks and sounds, speakers of different languages can all interpret the message. Samoyault (1998) tells us, "From the Sumerians, cuneiform writing spread to Akkadians, Babylonians, and Assyrians, and eventually became the writing system of the entire Middle East" (p. 5). Chinese writing is a modern-day example of a largely ideographic writing system, and it can be read by both Mandarin and

Cantonese speakers. The disadvantage of pictographic writing is that a writer has to learn a great number of different symbols, one for each idea.

Egyptian Hieroglyphics

The writing system that developed in Egypt around 3200 B.C., about the same time as cuneiform, was known as hieroglyphics. It differed from the cuneiform writing of Mesopotamia in that it included both pictures and marks that stood for sounds. Since the Egyptian system included some written marks for sounds, it represents a mixed system intermediate between pictographic or ideographic writing and alphabetic writing.

These early writing systems used pictures or more abstract drawings to express ideas. They were fairly easy to read as long as the symbols were not too abstract. The writing communicated ideas directly. However, this was a difficult system for writers, since they had to learn a picture or symbol for each thing or idea. Pictographic and ideographic writing was replaced by alphabetic writing. An alphabetic system is more indirect. It uses letters to represent the sounds of words that, in turn, represent things or ideas. Alphabetic systems are easier than earlier systems for writers because writers have to learn only a small number of letters, and then they can combine these letters in different ways to produce any word they want to write. The limitation of alphabetic writing is that it can be understood only by a reader who speaks that language.

Early Alphabets

The Egyptian writing system combined symbols that represented things with symbols that represented sounds. The first system in which all the marks represented sounds was developed in Syria around 1500 B.C. in the port city of Ugarit. The people in this important port city needed a simple system for communicating widely. This Ugaritic alphabet still used wedge-shaped cueiform symbols at first to represent the sounds because clay was readily available. However, this was a cumbersome medium for writers.

About four hundred years later, another group of traders, the Phoenicians, introduced a smooth, paperlike substance made from the papyrus plant, for writing. Because they used papyrus rather than clay tablets, they were able to produce lines instead of the triangles that resulted from pressing sticks into clay. This linear writing made it easier to develop different letters, and they introduced an alphabet with only twenty-two letters. This Phoenician writing system used letters to represent consonant sounds, but it did not include vowels.

Some current writing systems, such as Arabic and Hebrew, still use only consonants, although currently in these writing systems, vowels are represented by placing diacritics, various small marks, over the consonants. While vowels differentiate many words, like *sit*, *set*, and *sat*, the letters representing vowels are not as important as those representing consonants. Most English speakers have trouble reading a sentence in which the consonants are deleted, such as "_ _ i_ i_ _ _ oo _ a _ ou _ _ i _ _ ui _ _ _ i _ _," even when blanks are inserted to show the missing letters. On the other hand, most readers can decipher the same sentence with the vowels deleted: "Th _ s _s _ b_ _k _b _ _ t l _ ng_ _ st _ cs."

Greek and Latin Alphabets

The Greeks developed an alphabet that included both consonants and vowels. They used the Phoenician system as a base. Some of the letters of the Phoenician alphabet represented sounds that were not part of Greek, so the Greeks used those letters to represent vowel sounds. Then they added more letters to represent sounds in Greek not present in the Phoenician language. The result was the first true alphabet. Now each sound was represented by a letter. The English word *alphabet* comes from the first two letters of the Greek writing system, alpha and beta. The Greek alphabet contained twenty-four letters.

The Romans based their alphabet on the Greek. They added letters such as *v*, *x*, and *y* to represent sounds in Latin that did not occur in Greek. The Roman alphabet is the most widely used alphabet in the world. The alphabet used for writing English is based on the Roman alphabet.

Additional Writing Systems

The Cyrillic alphabet is also a variation of the Greek alphabet. It was developed by Saint Cyril, who converted the Slavs to Christianity. It includes characters to represent Slavic sounds not found in Greek and is used today in Russia, the Ukraine, Serbia, and Bulgaria. Other widely used writing systems include Arabic and Hebrew, made up of consonants and diacritics for vowels. Japanese uses several different writing systems, and one of them is syllabic, that is, letters represent syllables rather than individual sounds. The Dvanagari alphabet, a major alphabet of India, is partly syllabic and also has symbols representing individual sounds.

English language learners whose first language is written in a non-Roman alphabet need to learn the Roman system as used by English speakers. Some alphabets, such as the Arabic system, are completely different from English. Others, such as Cyrillic, are based on the same system as the Roman alphabet and share some characters. However, a Russian learning English has to learn that P represents the sound of /p/, not the sound of /r/ as it does in Russian. Even English learners who use the Roman script in their first language have to learn different sound values for English. For example, *h* is silent in Spanish and *j* has a sound closer to the sound represented by the English letter *h*. An Italian speaker would need to learn that *chi* is /čiy/, not /kiy/, and *ci* is /siy/ or /sı/, not /čiy/.

The Development of English Spelling

Modern English spelling developed over time. In the following sections, we trace changes in spelling and pronunciation through three historical periods— Old English, Middle English, and Modern English—as well as changes effected by Noah Webster in America. After conventional spellings were established, the pronunciation of words, particularly the vowels, continued to change. An examination of these changes helps us understand our present spelling system. An excellent source for additional information about the development of all facets of the English language is Baugh and Cable's A *History of the English Language* (1976).

Old English

The Old English period dates from about 450 to 1100. During this time, the Roman alphabet was introduced to the Anglo-Saxons by Irish missionaries in the fifth century to write Old English (Tompkins and Yaden 1986). This alphabet was much like the Modern English alphabet, but Old English did not use the letters *j*, *k*, *v*, or *w* and used *q* and *z* rarely. In addition, Old English used other letters to represent sounds in the language. These included æ (called an *ash*); ð (the barred *d*) for both voiced and voiceless "th"; a kind of *z*, the *yogh*, written as ʒ, which represented the /g/ sound; and two other symbols for *th* and *w*.

During the Old English period, some sounds were spelled differently than they are in Modern English. For example, the /š/ sound was spelled *sc*, so *ship* was spelled *scip*. Both /k/ and /č/ were spelled with the letter *c*. Thus, the word *folk* was spelled *folc* and *child* was spelled *cild*. In addition, the vowel sound /ı/ was spelled with either *i* or *y*. This accounts for variations in Modern English like *gypsy* and *gipsy*. However, in Modern English, *y* is seldom used to represent the sound of /ı/, although there are a few words, like *gym*, in which it is. The letters *u* and *v* were interchangeable, and scribes put two *us* together to form the *w* (Tompkins and Yaden 1986).

Also during this period, the sound of /k/ was pronounced in words like *knee* (written as *cneo*), and the letter *f* represented both the /f/ and /v/ sounds, the voiceless and voiced labiodental fricatives. These two sounds were allophones of /f/. The phoneme was pronounced [f] at the beginning or end of a word and [v] in the middle. Modern English uses *f* and *v* to represent these two sounds, which are now two phonemes. The historical development of *f* and *v* spellings helps account for the alteration in the plurals of words ending in *f* or *fe*, like *thief* and *thieves* and *wife* and *wives*. The current spelling represents the sounds made during the Old English period.

Middle English

The Norman conquest of England in 1066 brought great changes to the language and signaled the beginning of the Middle English period, which dates from about 1100 to 1500. Many words were added from French and Latin. In addition, Norman scribes introduced a number of changes in the spelling of English words. For example, they replaced *cw* with *qu*, so Old English *cwen* became Middle English *queen*. Many words spelled with *o* in Old English were spelled with *u* in Middle English, especially when the *u* was followed by a letter with a similar shape, such as *m, n,* or *u*. Thus, Old English *cumin* was written *come* in Middle English (Tompkins and Yaden 1986). The Norman scribes also substituted *ou* for *u* to make English spelling more like French spelling. The Old English word *hus* was written as *hous* in Middle English.

In Old English the letter *h* represented two sounds. In Middle English these two sounds were replaced by one guttural sound spelled with *gh*. Modern English keeps this spelling in words like *cough* and *laugh*, although the letters are now pronounced as /f/. The letter *v* was used in many French loan words. However, *u* and *v* were interchangeable during this time to represent either the vowel sound or the consonant sound. Shakespeare spelled *universal* as *vniuersall*, for example. It wasn't until late in the eighteenth century that the current practice of using *u* to represent the vowel sound and *v* to represent the consonant sound was established.

Other changes during the Middle English period included replacing the Old English yogh, ʒ, with the French letter *g*; changing *hw* spellings, which represented the actual sequence of sounds, to *wh* (the transcription of a word like *where* begins with /hw/ because the sound of /h/ occurs before the sound of /w/); beginning to use *v* for the sound previously written with *f* (*driven*); and using *k* and *ch* for the two sounds spelled with *c* in Old English (*folk* for *folc* and *child* for *cild*).

Modern English

English spelling has continued to change during the Modern English period, which extends from about 1500 to the present time. However, a number of forces combined to stabilize spelling. William Caxton established the first printing press in England in 1476, but Caxton and other early printers were businessmen and were not concerned with consistent spellings. In fact, they brought Dutch typesetters to work in England, and these Dutch workers are thought to have introduced some spellings, like the *h* in *ghost*. Over time, though, the publishing industry employed people who had formerly worked as scribes and who had learned spelling conventions. At the same time, several prominent spelling reformers called for consistency in spelling. As more books were produced with consistent spellings, these spellings became the norm.

Although spellings were becoming fixed, for the most part, during the early part of the Modern English period, changes in spellings continued to be introduced. Many Greek and Latin words entered English during this period. Some Anglo-Saxon words were thought to have been derived from these Greek and Latin words, and their spellings were changed to more closely resemble what scholars thought were their roots. This process is referred to as *false etymology* because the word histories were not accurate. Nevertheless, spellings were changed to make it appear that the English words were derived from Latin or Greek. For example, a *b* was added to *debt* and *doubt* to mirror the Latin spellings *debitum* and *dubitare*. In the same way, a *c* was added to *scissors* because scholars thought the Anglo-Saxon word had come from the Latin word *sciendere*, meaning "to cut." Similarly, an *l* was added to *faute* to make *fault* like the Latin word *falsus*. Other spellings were changed so that the words would be spelled similarly to other Old English words. For example, an *l* was added to *could* to make it analogous with *should* and *would*, which were spelled with an *l* in Old English. The *l* was not pronounced by the end of the sixteenth century in any of the words, but writers wanted all three auxiliaries to be spelled alike.

Conventional spellings of many words came to be established by the end of the eighteenth century. Books such as Samuel Johnson's *Dictionary of the English Language*, published in 1755, with its more than forty thousand entries and thousands of quotations, helped fix many spellings. However, changes in pronunciation during this same time resulted in variation between sounds and spellings in current English. The major change, which occurred during the 1500s, is referred to as the Great Vowel Shift. During this period, a complex series of changes occurred in the pronunciation of the vowels. The long vowels were pronounced at a higher point in the mouth. In Middle English the vowel in a word like *feet* was pronounced more like the vowel sound in *fate*. By 1500, *feet* had developed its current pronunciation. In addition, high vowels became diphthongs and moved to a lower position. A word like *town* was once pronounced more like *tune*. The /uw/ became /aw/.

The series of changes in pronunciation came after spelling was fixed. As a result, some current spellings do not match well with pronunciations. For example, spellings of pairs of related words like *divine* and *divinity* and *extreme* and *extremity* reflect a period before the Great Vowel Shift when the second syllable of each of these words was pronounced with the same vowel sound as the first syllable. Thus, in *divine*, the current pronunciation of the second vowel sound is /ay/, but earlier it was pronounced /ɪ/, the same sound as the *i* in the first syllable.

Linguists can reconstruct the early pronunciations of words like *divine* by examining rhyming texts. For example, at one time the words *good* and *food* rhymed. A mealtime blessing shows this:

> God is great, God is good,
> Let us thank Him for our food

The rhyme shows that at one time these words were pronounced alike. However, the vowel shift affected the two words differently, and now they do not rhyme. The reconstruction of early languages, including the pronunciation, is the focus of historical linguistics. This work is complex, but historical linguists have worked backward from present languages to re-create earlier languages.

The Great Vowel Shift was gradual, and by the time it was completed, many spellings of vowel sounds no longer corresponded to their pronunciations. Other changes in vowels included final, unstressed vowels, especially *e* becoming silent. During Middle English, the *e* in a word like *come* was pronounced as a schwa, but in Modern English these *es* are not pronounced at all. Unstressed vowels in the middle of words were reduced to a schwa, and vowels followed by *d*, *th*, and *f* were shortened. This explains spellings of words like *bread*, *breath*, and *deaf* (Tompkins and Yaden 1986). However, not all words now spelled with *ea* followed by *d*, *th*, or *f* were shortened, as shown by words like *mead*, *heath*, and *leaf*.

In addition to changes in the pronunciation of vowels, consonant sounds were simplified. Combinations that were formerly pronounced as blends were reduced to single sounds. The letters *gh*, which at one time were pronounced as two sounds, came to be pronounced as /f/ at the end of words like *laugh*. The initial consonants of *kn*, *gn*, and *wr* were no longer pronounced. In addition, the *b* was no longer pronounced in words like *bomb*, the *n* became silent in *mn* combinations like *hymn*, and the *l* was not pronounced in *lk* combinations like *talk*. Even though the pronunciation changed, the spelling stayed the same. All these changes in pronunciation added to the split between sounds and spellings.

American English Spelling

Noah Webster was a patriot who wanted to create a uniquely American English language, different from the language of England. He also wanted to reform spelling by simplifying it. Webster was very influential, and several of the reforms he advocated were put into effect. The changes came as the result of the wide use of his *American Spelling Book*. This was the first spelling textbook published in America. It was widely used in the public schools and set the standard for American spellings. Eventually, Webster's spelling book sold more than seventy million copies.

Most Americans can recognize British spellings. American spelling, thanks to Webster, differs in several ways. Words spelled with *our* in England are spelled *or* in America (*favour, favor*). British words ending with *re* are spelled *er* in American English (*centre, center*). However, American spelling accepts *readers theatre*. Some establishments (Pointe Centre) maintain *re* spellings to add what the owners hope will be regarded as a touch of class.

Other changes included the substitution of *se* for *ce* (*defence, defense*), the shift from *x* to *ct* in words like *connection*, the change from *ise* to *ize* (*recognise, recognize*), and the dropping of *k* in words like *music*. Some of Webster's ideas did not take hold. He wanted to simplify some spellings, for example, changing *bread* to *bred* and *give* to *giv*. He also wanted the spellings to reflect American English pronunciation in words like *wimmen*. Even though not all of his reforms were accepted, Webster had a profound influence on American English spelling.

Making Sense of the American English Spelling System

The historical overview we have provided helps explain why American English spelling does not correspond to the pronunciation of some words. After conventional spellings were established, pronunciation continued to change. Most current proposals for spelling reform are humorous, not serious. It would be nearly impossible to change the way words are spelled. Who would go back and change all the books and other print materials? Even if there were a strong move to change spelling, whose dialect would prevail? The changes might seem logical at first glance, but they would be nearly impossible to put into effect.

What many reformers don't realize is that the current system is a good compromise. Writing systems are designed to serve two different groups of people: writers and readers. Changes that would make writing easier would make reading more difficult, and changes that would make reading easier would make writing harder. Most reforms are aimed at simplifying the task of spelling words by making spellings more closely correspond to sounds. That is, the reforms favor writers. But most people read a great deal more than they write, so these changes would not really be beneficial.

Current alphabetic writing systems do spell most words like they sound. However, there are exceptions. Some of these exceptions are the result of the kinds of historical forces we described in the previous sections. Other exceptions reflect the fact that written language is designed to convey meanings, not just sounds. These exceptions make writing more difficult, but they make reading easier. For example, languages have homonyms, words that sound the same but are spelled differently, like *great* and *grate*. If both these words were spelled the same, writers wouldn't have to remember which spelling goes with which meaning, but readers would have to use context cues to figure out which meaning the writer intended. The variations in spellings of homonyms signal important meanings to a reader that would be lost if all words that sound the same were spelled the same way. Of course, there are still homographic homonyms like *bat* and *bear*. Do the letters *bat* refer to the animal or the stick used in baseball? Does *bear* mean an animal or the action of carrying a heavy burden or giving birth? In these cases, readers need to use context to figure out the meaning.

English has many homonyms that are spelled differently. Consider this sentence from Smith (1985): "Eye sea too feat inn hour rheum" (p. 56). If this sentence is read aloud, a listener can make sense of it, but the sentence is quite difficult to read. American English spelling, which uses different spellings for homonyms, gives readers visual cues to the meaning. If reading is seen as a process of recoding written language into oral language to identify words, then these alternate spellings might be seen as a hindrance. However, if reading is seen as a process of constructing meaning, then these visual cues serve an important function.

Some writers have used homonyms as the basis for books for young readers. Fred Gwynne, for example, has written books like *The King Who Rained* (1988b) and *A Chocolate Moose for Dinner* (1988a) that are very entertaining. The cover illustrations portray the literal meaning of the title of each book. These books can be used for discussions of literal and nonliteral meanings. In oral English, "the king /reynd/" has two possible meanings. English language learners often have difficultly understanding jokes based on homonyms, and these books can be the basis for a discussion of homonyms in English. In addition, Marvin Terban has written *Eight Ate: A Feast of Homonym Riddles* (1982). The answer to the riddle on each page contains a homonym. For example, one page asks, "What is a smelly chicken?" The answer, of course, is "A foul fowl" (p. 9). Young readers enjoy making up their own homonym riddles based on Terban's model.

In addition to homonyms, English has pairs of related words like *medicine* and *medical* in which the same letter, *c*, is used to represent two different sounds, /s/ and /k/. Some reformers have suggested eliminating the letter *c* and using *s* and *k* to represent the two sounds. This would result in the spellings *medisin* and *medikal*. This change would result in a more consistent representation of sounds (easier to write) but would remove the visual connection between these related words (harder for readers to construct meaning). Other reformers have suggested eliminating silent letters like the *g* in *sign*. Readers would then lose the connection between the related words *sign* and *signal*. Many words with silent letters are related to other words in which the letter is pronounced, such as *bomb* and *bombard*.

Linguists have developed a system of recording the sounds of a language. In Chapter 3 we explained how phonemic transcription can be used to write any word. Linguists who use phonemic or phonetic transcription are interested in recording and analyzing oral language. They need a writing system that has a one-to-one correspondence between sounds and the marks in the writing system. A system of transcription serves a linguist's purposes very well. However, trying to change American English spelling to be more like a system of phonemic transcription would not be useful because when people read, they are not simply interested in the sounds of the language. They want to get at the meanings the writing conveys.

The Logic of the American English Spelling System

Contrary to popular belief, American English spelling does make sense. To understand spelling, it is necessary to realize that it is a complex system, much like American education. Attempts to change a system generally are not successful. Consider schools. School systems attempt to balance the needs of several different groups—students, teachers, administrators, parents, community members, and politicians, to name a few. Any proposal to change the system comes under scrutiny by each of these groups. A change that might be good for teachers might not be considered beneficial for students. Anyone who wants to reform schools needs to take into account the concerns and needs of all the different groups involved. Most reforms fail because only certain groups benefit, usually at the expense of other groups. Reformers who want to change spelling so that each word is spelled the way it sounds fail to recognize that other forces besides sound shape spelling. Two other forces are analogy and etymology (Cummings 1988).

The strongest demand on the spelling system is the phonetic demand to spell a given sound consistently. Every time a phoneme occurs, it should be spelled the same way. A second demand comes from analogy. Words that come from the same root and share the same meaning should be spelled the same way. This is the semantic demand. Finally, there is the demand that words should reflect their historical backgrounds. This is the etymological demand, a force that keeps spellings constant across time and across languages. Because of this demand, some spellings reflect the way words were pronounced in earlier periods and others reflect the spelling of the language from which they were borrowed. Figure 5–1 summarizes the demands on the spelling system.

Most words are spelled the way they sound. Even though critics point to the many exceptions, they are still exceptions. Children who spell words the way they sound get many words right. However, spellings signal meanings, not just sounds. English has many words that sound the same but have different meanings. Alternate ways of spelling a sound allow writers to show meanings through their spellings. Readers can assign the correct meaning to *flour* and *flower* because writers

Force	Demand	Example
phonetic	spell words the way they sound	sit
semantic	spell words alike that share the same meaning	hymn hymnal
etymological	spell words to reflect their origins	one (Old English) kangaroo (Australian)

Figure 5–1. Forces that shape English spelling

spell the two words differently. Even though alternate spellings of a sound introduce complexity into the system, the benefits to a reader of getting a meaning clue from the spelling outweigh the difficulty for a writer of remembering which spelling goes with which meaning.

The spelling system also allows writers to show the connections between words that share meanings. By using the same letters to spell words that sound different but mean the same, writers signal the meaning link to readers. Both *crumb* and *crumble* are written with a *b* to signal the meaning connection between the words.

Finally, some spellings reflect earlier stages of English. Some common words, such as *are* and *some*, retain their spellings even though their pronunciations have changed over time. Other words have kept the spellings of their countries of origin. In a word like *machine*, the French spelling of *ch* for the /š/ sound is kept even though the digraph *ch* usually is pronounced /č/ in English words. Most spellings that strike readers as unusual are the result of retaining foreign spellings of borrowed words.

A study of word histories can help students make sense of many spellings. An excellent book for upper-elementary- through high-school-age students is *The Journey of English*, by Donna Brook (1998). This beautifully illustrated book traces the history of the English language. Included in the book are interesting facts about English words. For example, the unusual spelling of *Wednesday* becomes clearer when students learn that the day was named after the Norse god Woden. *Woden's day* became the modern *Wednesday*. In another example, the /š/ sound is spelled *su* in a few English words. One of these is *sugar*, which was borrowed from a language of India. This book provides an accurate and reader-friendly history of the English language.

Students often enjoy studying about the history of words. A number of reference books are available for word study in most libraries. One well-known book is Partidge's *Origins: A Short Etymological Dictionary of Modern English* (1983). If students check more than one reference book, they may find different information about particular words. Tracing word histories is complicated, and students should understand that some etymologies may not be accurate. The Internet is a good source for information about words as long as students realize that they need to check more than one site. Figure 5–2 lists the addresses for several useful sites.

When teachers talk with students about spelling and help students understand how the system works, students become better spellers. The history of alphabetic writing, the history of English spelling, and the history of individual words are all interesting topics for a language arts or English class. Teachers can

Website	Comment
www.yourdictionary.com	a good dictionary site
www.m-w.com	the Merriam Webster dictionary site, which has lots of games as well as useful information
www.allwords.com	an online dictionary with a multilingual search
www.wordsmith.org	emails you a word a day with historical information
www.takeourword.com	has lots of interesting tidbits about words
www.wordcentral.com	information on word histories and vocabulary and a good dictionary resource for younger students
www.wordwithyou.com	contains word histories
www.wordorigins.org/index.htm	more word histories
www.cal.org/ericcll	an especially good site for academic documents related to language
www.darkwing.uoregon.edu/~delancey/links/linglinks.html	lots about language, even a linguistics olympics

Figure 5–2. Word studies websites

also involve students in linguistic investigations into the spelling system by taking a scientific approach to teaching spelling rules.

Spelling Rules

Research has shown that when students read and write extensively, they acquire a subconscious knowledge of possible spellings in a language. Readers, for example, know that *glark* is a possible English spelling, but *tlark* is not. This knowledge of possible combinations of letters is called *graphotactic knowledge*. It is this acquired knowledge of graphotactics that makes it possible for readers to unscramble words in puzzles or jumbles that often appear in daily newspapers or books of word games. For example, consider the following series of letters that make up a word: *garin*.

Most readers can figure out the solution to this jumble fairly quickly as *grain*. In the process of solving the jumble, readers might try ending the word with *ing*. They might try starting with *in*. However, while readers would attempt some combinations, they would never consider others, such as starting with *ng* or even *ai* because that would leave too many consonants to end the word. The five letters of *garin* have 120 possible permutations, but no jumble solver ever goes through all 120. Instead, readers rely on their subconscious graphotactic knowledge to solve the puzzle quickly.

Six-letter combinations are more difficult, but most readers can solve them as well. Consider the following letters: *ueatcp*. What word do these letters form? Adding just one letter raises the number of possible combinations from 120 to 720, so the six-letter words present six times as many possibilities. However, most readers can solve them. This set of letters presents a greater challenge because it is a compound, and in compounds, some unusual combinations of letters occur. That's what makes this jumble more difficult. But, as you may have figured out, the word is *teacup*.

Word games help students become aware of graphotactics. *Sit on a Potato Pan, Otis!* (1991) is Jon Agee's third book of palindromes. Palindromes are phrases that read the same backward and forward. The first palindrome is reputed to have been "Madam, I'm Adam." Agee includes complicated and clever palindromes accompanied by cartoons. In one, a child holds up a protest sign in the kitchen as her father cooks a meal. The sign reads, "Revile liver!" Palindromes are rare because the combinations of letters that can spell words left to right seldom spell them right to left. English graphotactics governs possible combinations of letters. However, Agee is very creative. An unusually long palindrome included in his book is "A man, a plan, a cat, a bar, a cap, a mall, a ball, a map, a car, a bat, a canal: panama."

The ability to recognize combinations of letters as possible English words develops as the result of reading. Even though extensive reading improves graphotactic knowledge, that knowledge doesn't automatically translate into superior spelling ability. Some students who are avid readers still misspell some words (Hughes and Searle 1997). The expectation for perfect spelling may be unreasonable. In some schools teachers pay more attention to correct spelling and good handwriting than to the quality of writers' ideas or the effectiveness of their writing. Parents and others expect students to spell with nearly 100 percent accuracy. However, traditional approaches to teaching spelling usually meet with little success. Students study their list of words during the week, pass the test on Friday, and still misspell the words the next time they write a composition.

A better approach to improving students' spelling is to give them strategies and resources. Young writers often simply need time to figure the system out. Their writing reflects the developmental stages that all writers go through (Freeman and Freeman 1996). However, older students can be taught to edit their writing, using dictionaries or other tools. Many students now use word processing programs that automatically correct many misspellings and feature spell checkers to catch others. Students still have to proofread carefully because spell checks don't catch misspellings that result in real words.

Two things, above all else, seem to help students become better at spelling. First, they need to be doing writing that they want others to read. When students produce writing they are proud of, they want to present it in the best possible form. Second, students need to understand that the spelling system is logical and does follow rules. Many poor spellers think that good spellers just memorize all the words. It does appear that good spellers develop some sort of visual image of a correct spelling. But the best spellers approach spelling as a problem-solving activity, not as a memorization task.

To help students investigate how the spelling system works, teachers can involve them in activities in which they collect words and try to make generalizations about the spellings. In doing this, teachers and students take a scientific approach to spelling. Even if students don't come up with a rule that works every time, the process of collecting words, looking for spelling patterns, and trying to state generalizations helps students become more conscious of correct spellings.

Investigating Vowels: The Spellings of /ey/

Sometimes teachers hesitate to take a problem-solving approach to spelling because they, themselves, have never thought about spelling in this way. However, if teachers investigate spellings with their students, everyone gains valuable

aCe	ai	ea	a	ay
rate	air	steak	mayor	day
plane	rail	great	agent	
fare	train	break	basic	away
create	aid		acorn	stay

Figure 5–3. Spellings of /ey/

insights. Mike, for example, involved his fifth graders in several spelling studies. In one, he had students work in pairs to look through books and write down all the words that contained the /ey/ sound. Once they had a list of words, they divided the words into different spellings. The words each pair found were combined into a class list, and students added to the list over several days. Figure 5–3 lists some of the words with /ey/ students might find. The words are divided by their spelling patterns. For words with a silent *e*, the pattern is written as *aCe*. The C represents any consonant letter.

In spelling books different spellings of a sound are often mixed in the same lesson. This only causes confusion. Once students learn that there can be different spellings for a sound, they have to develop some way of deciding which spelling to use. For that reason, it helps to group similar spellings together as shown in Figure 5–3 and then to try to make generalizations about the conditions under which each spelling occurs.

In studying oral language, linguists try to find what are called *conditioning environments* for the phenomenon they are studying. For example, when linguists study the allophones of phonemes, they try to find the conditioning environment for each allophone. In studying the various allophones of /t/, for example, a linguist would note that each allophone occurs in a different environment. The flapped [D] comes between two vowels when the first vowel is stressed. None of the other allophones of /t/ occur in this environment. Linguists refer to this phenomenon as *complementary distribution*. Each allophone appears in a different environment. If two different allophones could occur in the same environment, the distribution would be overlapping, not complementary.

If each spelling occurred in a different environment, it would be possible to make some generalizations. For example, if the sound of /ey/ was always spelled *ai* at the beginning of a word, students could learn that generalization. However, when it comes to spellings, most are not in complementary distribution. Since there are pairs like *pain* and *pane*, it appears that various spellings are possible in the same environment, in this case between /p/ and /n/. These spellings are in overlapping

aCe	ai	ea
stake		steak
grate		great
brake		break
plane	plain	
fare	fair	
pare	pair	

Figure 5–4. Homonyms with /ey/

distribution. Knowing that the sound of /ey/ comes between two consonants like /p/ and /n/ does not allow a student to predict the right spelling of a word.

Despite this overlap, students can benefit from studying patterns and trying to make generalizations. For example, students might notice that when /ey/ is followed by a consonant in a syllable, the possible spellings are *aCe*, *ai*, and *ea*. In addition, students might discover that the number of words that spell /ey/ with *ea* is quite small. A good class activity would be for students to develop a list of homonyms that have one of these three spellings of /ey/. Figure 5–4 lists some words taken from Figure 5–3 that could start such a list. Students could add words over time.

The process of creating a list like the one in Figure 5–4 helps bring the spellings of these words to conscious awareness. As students look for words to add to the list, they become more aware of the conventional spellings of words that make the /ey/ sound.

Although the first three spellings on Figure 5–3 are in overlapping distribution with one another, they appear to be in complementary distribution with the last two spellings. In other words, if a consonant follows in the same syllable, the sound /ey/ is spelled as *aCe*, *ai*, or *ea*, but it is never spelled with *a* or *ay*. In a word like *mayor*, the sound of /ey/ is spelled with *a*, and the *y* represents a consonant sound that begins the second syllable. The *a* spelling can begin (*agent*) or end a syllable (*mayor*). The *ay* spelling begins a syllable only in the voting word *aye*. It most often ends a word (*may*) although it can also end a syllable (*mayhem*), especially in a compound word (*maybe*). In contrast, *ai* with the sound of /ey/ does not end a word.

Students might find more examples of /ey/ spellings with time. For example, the family of *aste* words (*chaste*, *haste*, *paste*, *taste*) doesn't follow the usual pattern because there are two consonants between the *a* and the *e*. Apparently, the *e* still signals that the vowel is long. And *tasty* or *hasty* doesn't have the *e*, but the vowel is still pronounced with the /ey/ sound by analogy with *haste* and *taste*. Some students might also find borrowed words with other spellings of /ey/, such as the French *et* that occurs in *filet* and *croquet* or the word *opaque*, borrowing the French *que* instead of the more common English spelling, *ke*. When students make these discoveries, a teacher who encourages such investigations can only say, "¡Olé!"

As students and teachers investigate spelling patterns like this one, they often find more examples and exceptions over time. What is important is that the process of collecting words, categorizing the words, and trying to make generalizations helps students approach spelling as a problem-solving activity, and many students spell more words conventionally after participating in these investigations. Mike found that his fifth-grade students' spelling improved as a result of their involvement in investigations like this. Instead of trying to memorize words, his students began to take an interest in finding patterns and making generalizations about different spellings of a sound.

Investigating Consonants: The Spellings of /k/

Vowel patterns in English are quite complex. Especially for the long vowels, there are usually several possible spellings. Consonants show less variation. For example, the /b/ phoneme is usually spelled with a *b* or *bb*. Nevertheless, some consonants are also complex and would provide interesting possibilities for investigation. One such consonant is /k/. This phoneme has several possible spellings.

A teacher might begin a unit of study on the spellings of /k/ by asking the class to brainstorm all the ways /k/ can be spelled. Then students could work in small groups and look through different texts to try to find additional examples of /k/ spellings to add to the class list. Figure 5–5 lists several of the possible /k/ spellings.

Spelling	Example	Spelling	Example
c	cat	kh	khaki
k	kite	x	fox
ck	tack	cc	accord
ch	chemistry	cq	acquire
q	queen	kk	bookkeeper
que	unique		

Figure 5–5. Spellings of /k/

The teacher could have students look up words with some of the less common spellings to find out about their histories using reference books or some of the Internet sites listed in Figure 5–2. The three common spellings of /k/ are *c*, *k*, and *ck*. The other spellings are much less common.

Students would find, for example, that words in which *ch* represents /k/ come from Greek. They could compile a list of these Greek borrowings. Some students might know that the letter *chi*, which appears in different sorority and fraternity names, is a Greek letter pronounced /kay/ and written with an X in the Greek alphabet. When words with the sound represented by the Greek X were brought into the Roman alphabet, the sound was spelled with *ch*. Modern English words with Greek roots retain this spelling. Many of these words, such as *chloride* and *character*, appear in the vocabularies of science and drama.

In the same way, students would learn that *q* and *que* words come from French. Words with *q* entered English during the Norman period when French scribes replaced the English *cw* with *qu*. The spelling of *qu* for /kw/ is one of the most consistent spellings in English. The *que* spelling comes at the end of words borrowed from French. The *kh* spelling of *khaki* reflects its foreign origin as well. This word comes from Urdu and is one of several words borrowed into English from Indian languages.

The letter *x* is unusual because it represents two consonant phonemes, /ks/, in words like *fox*, which would be transcribed /faks/. English has very few words that start with *x*, and most of these are borrowed words or proper names like *Xerox*. When English words are spelled with an initial *x*, the *x* is pronounced /z/ because English words do not begin with the /ks/ sound. Students might also notice that in some words, like *exit* and *exact*, the *x* can have either a /ks/ sound or a /gz/ sound, depending on the dialect of the speaker. The phoneme pair differs only in voicing. Both /k/ and /g/ are velar stops, and /s/ and /z/ are alveolar fricatives, so the variation between /ks/ and /gz/ represents a variation in voicing.

In words like *account* and *acquaint*, the prefix ends with a /k/ sound and the root begins with a /k/. This results in /k/ being spelled *cc* or *cq*. Students might say that there are two /k/ sounds in these words. Each word has two syllables, and the words are divided between the prefix and the root (ac-count, ac-quaint). However, the syllable division in writing does not reflect the phonological reality. Linguists transcribe these words as /əkawnt/ and /əkweynt/ because speakers pronounce only one /k/ sound. The syllable split for the oral language is /ə kawnt/ and /ə kweynt/.

The spelling with *cc* or *cq* for /k/ reflects the morphology of the words, not the phonology. These spellings help readers see that these words have two meaningful parts, or morphemes. Each word has a prefix and a base. Even in compound words like *bookkeeper*, only one /k/ is pronounced. Although English allows double-consonant spellings, English does not have any words in which a consonant sound is doubled. *Bookkeeper* is an interesting word because it is the only

Syllables Starting with *c*	Syllables Starting with *k*
carrot	keep
cost	kite
cut	unkempt
climb	
crib	
record	
decade	

Figure 5–6. Syllables starting with /k/

English word with three double-letter spellings in a row. The *kk* represents another possible spelling of /k/, although it appears in only this word.

Most common /k/ spellings   Once students have examined the less common spellings, they could make generalizations about the most common spellings: *c*, *k*, and *ck*. The *ck* spelling occurs only at the end of a word. The *c* and *k* spellings can occur anywhere. A good activity to begin to investigate the letter-sound correspondences with /k/ would be for students to list a number of words with syllables that begin with the /k/ sound that are spelled with either *c* or *k* and then try to find a pattern. Figure 5–6 lists some possible words.

If students collect words in which the /k/ sound is spelled with *c* or *k*, they discover a regular pattern. The *c* spelling is always followed by one of the vowels, *a*, *o*, or *u*, or a consonant. The *k* spelling is always followed by *e* or *i*. There are very few exceptions to this pattern, all of them involving *k*. For example, words like *kangaroo*, *koala*, and *kudu* begin with *k* followed by *a*, *o*, or *u*, and *krait* has the *kr* combination, but a little investigation shows that these are all borrowed words.

Why is this pattern so consistent? Students usually recognize that in words like *cent* and *city*, the *c* has an /s/ sound. In other words, when readers see the combination *ce* or *ci*, they pronounce the *c* as /s/. The only way to signal the /k/ sound when the following vowel is *e* or *i* is to use a *k*. Students could make the following generalization:

The /k/ sound is spelled with *c* when a consonant or one of the vowels *a*, *o*, or *u* follows, and it is spelled with a *k* when an *e* or an *i* follows.

As students find exceptions to this rule, they can investigate the history of those words.

Words Ending in *ck*	Words Ending in *k*	Words Ending in *c*
pack	peek	panic
check	break	maniac
stick	soak	
rock	park	
duck	milk	

Figure 5–7. Words ending with /k/

The spelling pattern for /k/ at the end of a syllable or word is slightly more complex. The sound has three common spellings, *ck*, *k*, and *c*. Figure 5–7 lists words with these spellings.

Only a few words spell the /k/ sound at the end of a word with a *c*. Most of these have the suffix *-ic*, although a few words in English end with *-ac*. The spellings *ck* and *k* are much more common. If students collect a number of these words, they can begin to see a pattern. If the last sound before the /k/ is a consonant, the *k* spelling is always used to avoid having three consonants in a row. English words never end in *rck* or *lck*, for example.

Students have to look more closely to decide about spellings in which the /k/ sound is preceded by a vowel. The examples in Figure 5–7 suggest that the /k/ sound is spelled with a *ck* when the preceding vowel sound is short and with *k* when the vowel sound is long. Thus, /pæk/ is spelled with *ck* and /piyk/ is spelled with a *k*. This works for all the long and short vowel sounds except for /u/, a short vowel that is spelled *oo* in a word like *book*. This spelling is an exception to the short vowel–long vowel generalization. However, the *oo* spelling of many words was pronounced as a long sound, /uw/, during an earlier period. Some of these, such as *food*, retain the /uw/ pronunciation, but many others are pronounced with a short /u/ sound. Before the Great Vowel Shift, the spelling pattern was consistent, but the shift in pronunciation introduced this exception.

Since short vowels in English are generally spelled with one letter and long vowels are usually spelled with two letters, another way to describe the pattern of /k/ spellings at the end of a word would be to say that *ck* is used when the vowel sound is spelled with one letter, and *k* is used when the vowel sound is spelled with two letters. To understand this way of stating the generalization, students would need to count silent *e* as one of the two vowels. The sound of /k/ is spelled with *k* in words like *make*, *spoke*, and *fluke*. If a silent *e* follows, the *ck* spelling is not used. English has no words like *macke* or *spocke*. As long as students count the silent *e* as one of the two vowels, the two-vowel generalization works very well.

Two possible ways to state the generalization about final /k/ spellings are these:

> Spell the final /k/ sound of a word or syllable with *ck* if the preceding vowel is short, and spell the sound with *k* if a consonant precedes /k/ or if the vowel is long. The exception to this rule is words with *oo* like *book*.

Or

> Spell the final /k/ sound of a word or syllable with *ck* if there is only one vowel and with *k* if there are two vowels. Count a final silent *e* as one of the two vowels.

The spellings of /k/ are complex. However, some patterns are quite consistent. It is not so important that students learn every possible /k/ spelling. What is important is for students to begin to take a scientific approach to investigating English spellings. By collecting words, sorting them into categories, and then trying to find patterns they can state as generalizations, students bring to conscious awareness aspects of the English spelling system. They start to see spelling as systematic, not just a collection of letters to be memorized. Students who approach spelling as a logical system do much better than those who try to memorize each word. In addition, students who take a scientific approach begin to develop some of the ways of thinking that all scientists take when studying interesting phenomena. This approach is much more intriguing than the usual practice of studying a list of words for the Friday spelling quiz.

Investigating Spelling Rules: Silent e and Consonant Doubling

In addition to looking at the spellings of particular consonant and vowel phonemes, students can benefit from investigating spelling rules. Often, spelling rules are taught directly. Teachers provide the rule and give students practice in using it. Students may learn a rule and yet have trouble applying it. For example, a teacher might present the rule for changing *y* to *i*, and students may be able to recite or write the rule. However, these same students might still spell a word like *monkeys* as *monkies*. They have learned the rule, but they have not acquired it.

To help students acquire spelling rules, teachers can have them use the scientific approach described earlier. The students collect words, categorize them, and then attempt to formulate a hypothesis to account for their data. This hypothesis becomes their working rule, which can be modified whenever new data are discovered.

Two rules that are frequently taught are what Cummings (1988) calls *procedural rules*. These are rules that involve changes in spelling when adding a suffix to a root word. Two useful procedural rules are the rule for dropping a silent *e* when adding a suffix and the rule for doubling a final consonant when adding a suffix. Both of these rules are very helpful because students can't hear a silent *e* or a double consonant, so they need some other way to decide when to drop an *e* or double a consonant.

The silent *e* rule Complex English words consist of a root word and prefixes, suffixes, or both. Procedural rules govern the way words are spelled when prefixes or suffixes are added to a root. The silent *e* rule governs whether a final silent *e* is retained or dropped. For example, in the word *hope* + *ing*, the *e* is deleted (*hoping*), but in the word *hope* + *ful*, the *e* is retained (*hopeful*). Teachers could simply give students a rule for dropping the *e*, such as "Drop the *e* if the suffix starts with a vowel, and keep the *e* if the suffix starts with a consonant." However, even students who learn the rule may have difficulty applying it as they write because they have simply memorized a formula; they haven't constructed an internal rule. To help students construct rules, teachers can involve them in linguistic investigations of the type we described earlier with the spellings of /ey/ and /k/. A number of steps are involved in helping students develop a rule for the silent *e*.

The first step is to help students visualize complex words as being made up of a root and a prefix or suffix. It is hard for students to understand a rule about dropping an *e* if they don't picture the root word as having an *e* to start with. That is, students have to realize that *hoping* had a root word with an *e* that was dropped to form the complex word. Unless students grasp the basic concept of complex words, the *e* rule will not make sense to them. A teacher might begin, then, by presenting a series of words like *hoping* and having students work in pairs or small groups to figure out the parts these words consist of. Thus, the students would break a word like *hoping* into *hope* + *ing*. Teachers could either give students a list of words to work on or ask students to examine a page from a textbook and list complex words and then identify their component parts.

Once students understand that some words are complex, the teacher can move to the second step. During this step, students collect words ending in a silent *e*. It is important to give some examples to be sure that students don't include words like *be* in which the *e* is pronounced. Figure 5–8 lists a few words that end in silent *e*. If students work in pairs to compile lists of words, they can combine their results to make a more extensive class list.

The next step is to ask students to try to figure out why some words have a silent *e*. Most students would conclude from looking at the list that a silent *e* usually signals that the preceding vowel has a long sound. This is the case for the words listed in the first column in Figure 5–8. A teacher might point out that

lake	edge	love
recede	chance	toe
bike	clothe	avalanche
rope	tease	one
tube	glue	definite

Figure 5–8. Words ending in silent *e*

English has only a few words like *recede* in which the final *e* indicates that the preceding *e* is long. It is more common to spell the sound with a double *e*, as in *street*.

Although the main function of silent *e* is to mark long vowels, the silent *e* plays other roles as well. As students collect words with silent *e*, they can discover these other roles. Like scientists, they will revise their original hypothesis—silent *e* marks long vowels—in light of counterexamples.

Some students might discover a second role for the silent *e*. In words like *chance* and *edge*, the *e* serves to signal the pronunciation of a preceding *c* or *g*. When *c* or *g* ends a word, it is pronounced as /k/ or /g/, but when an *e* follows, the pronunciation changes to /s/ or /ǰ/. Many of the apparent exceptions to the "marks a long vowel" rule can be accounted for by adding something like "and gives *c* and *g* a soft sound." With this addition, many words can be accounted for, but there are still some holdouts.

This might be a good time for teachers to discuss words that end in *le*, like *nibble*. These *le* words shouldn't be considered exceptions to the rule. The *e* in these words does represent a vowel sound that is pronounced. The transcription for *nibble* is /nibəl/. Some reformers, such as Webster, wanted to change all *le* spellings in American English to *el* to make them more consistent. Although Webster succeeded in changing *re* in words like *centre* to *er*, he failed with *le*. Of course, English also has words like *nickel* that put the *e* at the point in the word where it is pronounced.

Other final *e*s are silent. There are a few pairs of words in English, like *cloth* and *clothe* and *bath* and *bathe*, in which the *e* not only signals a long vowel sound but also indicates the pronunciation of the *th* digraph. When an *e* follows, the *th* receives the voiced sound, so it is pronounced /ð/, not /θ/. As a result, *cloth* is pronounced /klaθ/ and *clothe* is pronounced /klowð/. This use of *e* affects only a small number of words, but it does so consistently.

Even excluding *th*, *le*, and the words with *g* or *c*, students will find other words that end in a silent *e* that don't seem to follow the rule. For example, many

English words end in *ve*, such as *love* and *give*. The *e* doesn't mark a long vowel in these words. Instead, the *e* serves a different function. Earlier, we discussed graphotactics, possible English spelling combinations. One feature of English is that words don't end in *v*. No one decreed that "English words shall not end in *v*." But this is a feature of Modern English. In a word like *give*, the *e* serves to prevent the word from ending in *v*. The same is true for words with *u* like *glue*. Words that do end in *u*, such as *kudu*, must be borrowed words that retained their original spelling. In addition, English spelling either adds an *e* after *z* as in *gauze* or doubles the *z* as in *buzz* so English words don't end in a single *z*.

A final silent *e* also keeps certain words from ending in a single *s*. Usually, a final *s* signals that the word is plural (*boys*), possessive (*boy's*), or present-tense (*runs*). Readers expect that in words ending in *s*, the *s* signals one of these functions. The added *e* helps avoid confusion. Readers know that *teas* is the plural for *tea*, but *tease* is not a plural. English words can also double the final *s* to prevent confusion, as in *mess*.

In English, some words are called *content words* and some are *function words*. The content words are the nouns, verbs, adjectives, and adverbs that carry the primary meanings. They are the words people include in telegrams. The function words are conjunctions, prepositions, and other words that connect and relate the content words. In general, function words are short and content words are long. In some cases, as with *toe*, an *e* has been added to a short content word so that it has at least three letters. Another feature of English graphotactics is that content words have this minimal length.

Students may find other words ending with silent *e*. Many are borrowed, like *avalanche*, in which the French spelling is retained. Others, like *one* and *come*, reflect the Old English spellings. During the Old English period these final *es* were pronounced. The pronunciation has changed, but the spelling has stayed the same. Finally, English has certain suffixes, including *-ile*, *-ine*, *-ate*, and *-ite*, in which the first vowel is not stressed. In a word like *engine*, the *i* has a reduced sound, /i/, and the *e* is simply part of the suffix. It does not signal a long vowel. In some cases, words ending in these suffixes have two possible pronunciations. For example, if *approximate* is an adjective (This is the approximate cost), the vowel is short, but if it is a verb (Can you approximate the answer?), the vowel is long. In many cases, though, words ending in these suffixes contain a silent *e* that does not follow the "marks a long vowel" rule.

Students are not apt to come up with all these uses of silent *e*, but if they can find words that are exceptions, they can look at the word history or any other fact that might explain why the exception exists. In some cases, a teacher can supply this information. Figure 5–9 lists the uses of silent *e* at the end of words. This list is based on Cummings (1988).

Reason for Final, Silent *e*	Example
marks preceding long vowel	make
marks soft *g* or *c*	edge, chance
marks voiced *th*	clothe
avoids final *v, u, z, s*	give, glue, gauze, tease
avoids two-letter content words	toe
appears in borrowed words	avalanche
appears in Old English words	one, come
appears in words with certain suffixes	engine, definite

Figure 5–9. Functions of final, silent *e*

Once students understand some of the reasons for silent *es*, they can make sense out of the rule for dropping the *e*. The primary function of a silent *e* is to signal that a preceding vowel is long. This is one instance of a general pattern of English graphotactics. In a series of letters VCV (vowel, consonant, vowel) in which the first vowel is stressed, that vowel is pronounced with a long sound. In a word like *hope*, the *e* provides the needed vowel to complete the VCV string of letters. Readers know that *hop* is pronounced /hap/ and *hope* is pronounced /howp/, and the difference in pronunciation is shown in the spelling by the *e*.

What happens when a word like *hope* becomes part of a longer, complex word? In *hoping* the *e* is dropped, but in *hopeful* it is retained. This can be explained by considering the VCV pattern. In *hoping* the letter *i* serves the same function as the *e* in *hope*. It provides the vowel needed for the VCV pattern and signals that the *o* has a long sound. The spelling ensures that *hope* and *hoping* sound alike, and this helps signal the meaning connection between the words. On the other hand, in *hopeful* the suffix starts with a consonant, so the *e* is retained to keep the long vowel sound. If the *e* were dropped, the word would be pronounced /hapfəl/, with a short vowel sound, /a/, and the sound connection between *hope* and *hopeful* would be lost. Because the suffix starts with a consonant, the *e* is still needed to signal that the *o* has a long vowel sound. At this point, students could state a rule for silent *e* as follows:

Drop the silent *e* if the suffix starts with a vowel. Keep the *e* if the suffix starts with a consonant.

If students understand why the *e* was part of the root word, they can better comprehend the rule for dropping the *e*. They can also understand the addition they need to make to the rule. Silent *e* also keeps *c* and *g* soft. Words keep the *e* after *c* or *g* if the suffix starts with a consonant (*enhancement*) but also when the suffix starts with *a*, *o*, or *u* (*peaceable*, *courageous*) because when *c* or *g* is followed by one of these letters, the sound is /k/ or /g/ as in *cake*, *go*, and *cut*. On the other hand, if the following letter is *i* or *y*, the *c* or *g* keeps the soft sound (*racy*, *raging*) and the silent *e* can be dropped. The revised rule can be stated:

> Drop a final, silent *e* if the suffix starts with a vowel. Keep the *e* if the suffix starts with a consonant. If the letter before the *e* is *c* or *g*, also keep the *e* if the suffix starts with *a*, *o*, or *u*.

This rule works quite consistently. The only exceptions are words ending in *ee*, such as *agreeing*, or *oe*, as in *shoeing*. In these cases the *e* is retained even though the suffix starts with a vowel. A word like *shoeing* uses the *e* to maintain a visual connection to the root word *shoe* that would be lost with a spelling like *shoing*. The *e* is dropped before a suffix starting with a consonant in *argument*, *awful*, *duly*, and *truly*. Most students don't recognize *awful* as a complex word with *awe* as its base. *Truly* is often misspelled, probably because it is an exception to the rule. Finally, in words ending in *dge*, the *e* is dropped before adding *-ment* as in *judgment*. The combination *dg* seems to signal that the *g* has a /j/ sound, so the *e* is not really needed.

All this sounds quite complicated. It might seem easier to simply give students the rule for dropping a final silent *e* and then point out the few exceptions. However, involving students in determining why the *e* was there in the first place helps them make sense of the rule. It also raises awareness of how words are spelled. As they try to figure out the reasons for silent *e*, students look closely at words, talk about them, and write them, and all these activities contribute to their constructing an internal spelling rule. Perhaps more importantly, students can begin to see that language can be studied from a scientific perspective. This is what linguists do.

The consonant doubling rule   A second spelling rule that students can investigate governs doubling final consonants before adding a suffix. For example, for the word *hop*, the *p* is doubled to spell *hopping*, but with *load*, the final *d* is not doubled for *loaded*. Again, teachers might plan some activities to ensure that students understand that a word like *hopped* is a complex word formed by adding a suffix to a base word (*hop* + *ed*). Once students have that concept, they can begin their investigation.

A good way to start to study the doubling rule would be to give students a list of words such as those shown in Figure 5–10 and have them work in pairs or small groups to try to come up with a rule for doubling a final consonant before adding a

Words That Double Final Consonants	Words That Don't Double Final Consonants
hopped	soaked
conferred	parked
occurrence	conference (confer + ence)
running	foxes
batted	magnetic (magnet + ic)
quitting	solidify (solid + ify)

Figure 5–10. Words for the doubling rule

suffix. In this case, a teacher might simply want to say that final consonants are never doubled before a suffix that starts with a consonant. Students almost never misspell a word like *sad* + *ly* as *saddly*. Their knowledge of possible spellings, their graphotactic knowledge, would rule *saddly* out as a possible English spelling. However, if the suffix starts with a vowel, some words double the final consonant and others do not.

Most students realize fairly quickly that the final consonant is doubled for all the words in the first column so that the vowel sound is kept short. If the *p* in *hop* were not doubled before adding *ed*, the word would be spelled *hoped*, and the sound connection between *hop* and *hopped* would be lost. A tentative rule could be stated as follows:

> Double a final consonant before adding a suffix starting with a vowel to preserve a short vowel sound.

In studying the silent *e*, students discover that the string of letters VCV with the first vowel stressed signals that the first vowel has a long sound. Thus, in a word like *hope*, the *e* completes the VCV pattern and signals that the vowel in this word is pronounced as /ow/. Long vowels can also be spelled with two vowel letters, as in *beat*. Short vowels, on the other hand, have a CVC or a CVCC pattern. Short vowels are followed by a single consonant at the end of a word (*hop*) or by two consonants in the middle of a word (*hopped*). Doubling a final consonant before adding a suffix starting with a vowel ensures that the short sound is retained.

The words in the first column of Figure 5–10 have a root word with a short vowel. In each case, the final consonant is doubled to keep the vowel sound short. An apparent exception is the word *quitting*. In this word the final *t* of the root word *quit* is preceded by two letters, *u* and *i*, that normally represent vowel sounds. This would produce a pattern of VVC. Two vowel letters together usually indicate a long vowel, like the *oa* in *soak*. However, when *u* follows *q*, the *u* represents a consonant sound, /w/. This word would be transcribed as /kwɪt/. The rule has to do with the sound of the vowel, not the spelling. Letters like *u* can represent either a vowel or a consonant sound. Since the vowel /ɪ/ has a short sound in the base word, /kwɪt/, the final consonant is doubled to preserve that sound.

The final consonant of the base word is not doubled in the second column. A word like *soak* has a long vowel sound, not a short sound, so there is no necessity to double the *k* to keep a short sound. The other words have short vowels even though the final consonant is not doubled. *Parked* already has two consonants, so there is no need to double the *k*. What about *conference*? In the base word, *confer*, the second syllable is stressed. However, when the suffix *-ence* is added, the stress shifts to the first syllable, and the second syllable has a reduced vowel, /ə/. The word is transcribed as /kánfərəns/. The change in stress ensures that the vowel sound is not long, so there is no need to double the final *r*. In contrast, in a word like *conferred*, the stress stays on the *fer*, so the *r* is doubled to prevent the preceding *e* from having a long vowel sound.

The letter *x* is transcribed as /ks/ or /gz/. Since *x* already has two consonant sounds, the vowel that precedes *x* stays short, even when the suffix begins with a vowel. For that reason, *x* is never doubled. The last two words, *magnetic* and *solidify*, have suffixes that shorten the preceding vowel. Because *-ic* and *-ify* always serve to keep the vowel in the root word short, there is no need to double the final consonant.

One difference between American and British English spelling is based on doubling final consonants. Americans spell *traveled* and *focused* without doubling the final consonant. British English has *travelled* and *focussed*. Americans who read British novels might have trouble remembering the American spelling. However, the American spelling follows the rule. There is no need to double the *l* or *s* because the stress is on the first syllable, so the vowel in the second syllable is not pronounced with a long sound.

Careful examination of words like the ones in Figure 5–10 can lead students to revise their statement of the rule for doubling final consonants. A good statement of the rule would be

> Double a final consonant to keep the vowel sound short in words in which the base ends in CVC, the stress stays on the final vowel of the root word, and the suffix starts with a vowel.

There are few exceptions to this rule. The final consonant is not doubled in *combatant* and *guitarist*, even though the stress stays on the final vowel and the suffix starts with a vowel. The final consonant is doubled in *personnel* and *questionnaire* with suffixes that begin with a vowel, even though the stress is on the suffix rather than the root. Both of these words were borrowed from French and retain the original spelling. Despite exceptions like these, the doubling rule is a useful one because it applies in so many situations.

Conclusion

People have used writing for centuries. The earliest systems were pictographic or ideographic. Written marks represented objects and ideas directly. Such systems were difficult for writers because each word was represented by a different mark, and writers had to remember many different symbols. Later writing systems used marks to represent the sounds of words in oral language. The earliest systems had letters only for the consonant sounds. The introduction of letters for both consonants and vowels first occurred in Greek writing. The alphabet we use to write this book developed over many years and is based on the Latin alphabet.

Many people have called for spelling reforms. They would like every word to be spelled the way it sounds. They consider the current spelling system illogical or even crazy. However, writing systems serve both readers and writers. Changing the system so that words are all spelled the way they sound would make writing easier but reading more difficult. Constantly changing spellings to reflect current pronunciation would be an impossible task, as would determining whose pronunciation to follow. The current system is a good compromise. It is indeed a system, reflecting the demand to spell words as they sound, the demand to spell words alike that are related in meaning, and the demand to spell borrowed words to reflect their origins.

A study of the history of writing and of individual words is interesting. In addition, students can investigate the current system and make generalizations to account for the way different sounds are spelled. They can also study certain rules, such as deleting a final silent *e* and doubling a final consonant. These rules are based on patterns of spelling, or graphotactics, that signal how vowel sounds are pronounced. The effect of both rules is to maintain the sounds of vowels when adding suffixes to base words. Keeping the sound connection helps establish the meaning link between related words. When students investigate spellings, they not only become better spellers but also learn the skills of science and begin to approach language the way linguists do.

Applications

1. This chapter outlines the history of writing development. Have students carry out research on a particular type of writing, such as Egyptian hieroglyphics, and prepare a more detailed report on that particular writing system. Students might work in groups on different systems and create a class report.

2. Some of the differences between British and American English spelling are listed in this chapter. Look at books published in England and compile a more complete list of differences.

3. The websites listed in Figure 5–2 contain interesting information on word histories (etymologies). Visit one or more of these websites and create a list of interesting words with their histories. Bring these to class to share.

4. Cummings states that three forces shape the spelling system: phonetic, semantic, and etymological. Find words that clearly reflect the effects of each of these three forces and create your own chart, like the one below:

Phonetic Demand	Semantic Demand	Etymological Demand
pin	bomb/bombard	avalanche
sat	hymn/hymnal	kangaroo

The words in the first column would be spelled as they sound. The words in the second column would be pairs in which one word is not spelled the way it sounds but has a spelling connection to a semantically related word. The words in the third column would reflect spellings of the language from which they were borrowed. Individual charts could be combined to create a class chart.

5. Many calls for spelling reforms are clever and humorous. For example, Jessica Davidson starts her poem "I Never Will Learn to Read English Aloud" with the lines:

> I never will learn to read English aloud.
> There's mowed, towed, and rowed, and then there's
>   allowed.
> And once I had finally learned to say move,
> I met love, shove, and dove, and what did it prove?
> It proves I'll never discover the coves
> Where the treasure was found, nor the stoves nor the
>   groves.

Davidson's poem contains homonyms (*aloud, allowed*) and homographs, words with the same spelling but different pronunciations and meanings. Working in pairs or small groups, write a poem like Davidson's.

6. Homonym riddles like those in Terban's book can help students become aware that words that sound the same may be spelled differently. Have

students work in groups to write homonym riddles of their own and then try these out with classmates.

7. Carry out an investigation of the different spellings of a phoneme similar to the investigations described in this chapter for /ey/ and /k/. Most long vowels have alternate spellings. A consonant phoneme with many spellings is /š/. Following the model in this chapter, collect words for a long vowel or the consonant phoneme /š/. Categorize the words, and develop generalizations about the spelling patterns.

8. In English, the /č/ sound at the end of a word can be spelled *ch* or *tch*, as in *rich* and *watch*. Similarly, the /ǰ/ sound can be spelled *ge* or *dge*, as in *cage* and *badge*. Make a list of words with these alternate spellings to try to determine a rule for when to use each one. Is there any consistent pattern, or does the variation seem to be random?

9. When the letter *c* is followed by *a, o,* or *u,* it has a /k/ sound, and when it is followed by *e, i,* or *y,* it has an /s/ sound. What about the letter *g* at the beginning of a word? When does it have a /g/ sound and when does it have a /ǰ/ sound? The pattern here isn't as consistent as the pattern for *c.* Make a list of words and then come up with a generalization. Consider words like *gin* and *girl.* Look up words that appear to be exceptions to try to discover why they don't follow the usual pattern.

6

A Linguistic Perspective on Phonics

- *How does phonics fit into each of the two views of reading?*
- *What is the difference between phonics and graphophonics?*
- *What are some alternatives to traditional phonics?*
- *What is the linguistic basis for phonics?*

People have strong feelings about phonics. However, the term *phonics* means different things to different people. It may refer to sound-letter correspondences or to a method or program for teaching reading. A variety of approaches have been taken to teaching phonics. *Put Reading First*, the document that summarizes the research from the National Reading Panel, lists six variations on phonics instruction. These are summarized in Figure 6–1.

The authors of *Put Reading First* state, "Phonics instruction teaches children the relationships between the letters (graphemes) of written language and the individual sounds (phonemes) of spoken language" (Armbruster and Osborn 2001, p. 12). These authors also point out that although there are different approaches, the goal of phonics instruction is to help children develop the alphabetic principle. When children develop the alphabetic principle, they come to understand that there are relationships between the letters of written language and the individual sounds of oral language. Children learn that each letter represents one of the sounds in a word.

Phonics fits into a sequence of skills that constitute a word recognition view of reading. This sequence involves learning

1. that words are made up of individual sounds (phonemic awareness)
2. the names of letters
3. the sounds associated with each letter
4. the correspondences between sounds and letters (phonics)

130

Name of Method	Description Have students:
synthetic	convert letters to sounds and blend sounds to form words
analytic	analyze letter-sound correspondences in known words
analogy-based	use knowledge of word families to pronounce new words
spelling	segment words into phonemes and then write words with the sounds
embedded	learn letter-sound correspondences in the process of reading
onset-rime	connect sounds of onsets and rimes to the letters used to spell them

Figure 6–1. Approaches to phonics instruction

Students can use phonics rules to recode words from written to oral form. They then can then match the sounds associated with written marks to words in their oral vocabulary.

Systematic, Explicit Phonics

Proponents of phonics claim that any failures in phonics instruction have come either because students did not have the prerequisite knowledge to learn phonics rules or because the phonics instruction was not explicit and systematic. The prerequisites include the first two items in the previous list: phonemic awareness and the names of letters. Without phonemic awareness, children cannot be expected to understand phonics rules. Until children conceptualize words as being made up of phonemes, they cannot make sense of rules that connect phonemes to letters. In addition, children need to know the names of the letters and the sounds they represent. Only then can phonics instruction make sense. Even then, the instruction must be logical and systematic.

Those who advocate for phonics instruction insist that it be systematic and explicit. *Put Reading First* highlights this statement: "Systematic and explicit phonics instruction is more effective than non-systematic or no phonics instruction" (p. 13).

The authors go on to explain, "The hallmark of programs of systematic phonics instruction is the direct teaching of a set of letter-sound relationships in a clearly defined sequence. The set includes the major sound-spelling relationships of both consonants and vowels" (p. 13). Explicit teaching involves stating rules clearly, providing examples, and giving students practice in applying the rules. This approach is contrasted with implicit phonics, in which students discover the rules in the process of decoding words.

Other writers define the terms *systematic* and *explicit* more broadly. In their article "Phonics Instruction: Beyond the Debate," Villaume and Brabham (2003) discuss different views of these terms as posted on listservs and other electronic sites. *Explicit* can refer to instruction for teachers. That is, reading programs can provide scripted directions for teachers to follow. In contrast, other reading programs provide suggestions, but they do not give step-by-step directions for each lesson. *Explicit* more commonly refers to instruction for students. Used this way, *explicit* instruction is synonymous with *direct* instruction. The term *explicit* can also refer to student knowledge. Students have explicit knowledge if they clearly understand the alphabetic principle. This explicit knowledge may come as the result of a variety of approaches to teaching phonics. Explicit knowledge in this sense is the same as metalinguistic knowledge.

Villaume and Brabham also distinguish among different meanings of the term *systematic*. Most often, *systematic* refers to a sequenced progression of lessons. Usually, the sequence is based on the lessons in the reading program a school has adopted. However, *systematic* could refer to a set of activities and materials. "Logically, effective phonics instruction features systematic activities and materials that are designed so that teachers can introduce a targeted letter-sound correspondence" (Villaume and Brabham 2003, p. 481). After introducing the correspondence, the teacher involves students with activities and materials that reinforce the rule. In this sense, *systematic* refers to the way the teacher presents the rule and involves students in follow-up activities. *Systematic* can also refer to student knowledge. Villaume and Brabham comment, "Every primary-grade teacher intends for phonics instruction to assist students in developing understandings of the alphabetic principle that are explicit (i.e. fully developed and well formulated) and systematic (i.e. orderly and coordinated)" (p. 481).

Generally, the terms *explicit* and *systematic* refer to the approach the teacher takes. However, the goal of any instruction is for students to develop a clear understanding of the concepts being taught. Their knowledge should be explicit (that is, clear) and systematic (organized). In this respect, it is not surprising that the National Reading Panel found that explicit, systematic instruction was superior to instruction that was not clear or organized.

The authors of *Put Reading First* make several claims for the benefits of phonics instruction, based on the scientific studies reviewed by the National Reading Panel. Among these claims are the following:

- Systematic and explicit phonics instruction significantly improves kindergarten and first-grade children's word recognition and spelling.
- Systematic and explicit phonics instruction significantly improves children's reading comprehension.
- Systematic and explicit phonics instruction is effective for children from various social and economic levels.
- Systematic and explicit phonics instruction is particularly beneficial for children who are having difficulty learning to read and who are at risk for developing future reading problems. (pp. 14–15)

Problems with Phonics from a Linguistic Perspective

The studies reviewed by the National Reading Panel were empirical studies of the effects of phonics instruction on students' reading. Other studies taken from a linguistic perspective have investigated phonics more directly. One study attempted to determine the number of phonics rules that would be needed to account for the sound-letter correspondences in a set of words. This study, combined with research results from eye movement studies, suggests that readers make only limited use of phonics generalizations during reading. The second study looked at the usefulness of commonly taught phonics rules. Data from these studies provide evidence that can help teachers evaluate claims for the value of teaching phonics.

The Southwest Regional Laboratory Study

One of the problems in trying to determine the sequence of rules to teach is that there are too many rules. Smith (1971) reports on a study that attempted to determine how many rules there are. The researchers (Berdiansky, Cronnell, et al. 1969) analyzed 6,092 one- and two-syllable words taken from school reading materials designed for six- to nine-year-olds. These words represented a good sample of what children this age are expected to read.

The analysis of these 6,092 words was rather complex. The researchers transcribed the words and established the correspondence between the letters and the sounds. Figure 6–2 shows how several words would be analyzed using their method.

Rather than trying to associate each letter with a phoneme, the researchers used grapheme units. These included digraphs like *th* and double letters like *bb*. Then for each phoneme, they listed all the grapheme units used to spell that sound. For example, /p/ could be spelled *p* or *pp* and /ey/ could be spelled with

cat ↑↑↑ kæt	quick ↑↑↑↑ kwɪk	think ↑↑↑↑ θɪŋk	street ↑↑↑↑↑ striyt	made ↑↑↑ meyd

Figure 6–2. Sound-letter correspondences

a, ea, aCe (as in *made*), and so on. Once the results for all 6,092 words were analyzed in this way, the researchers had to decide what constituted a phonics rule. They decided that if a phoneme was spelled a certain way at least ten times in the data, they would call it a rule, and if there were fewer than ten instances of the letter-sound correspondence, they would call it an exception. So, for example, since /p/ was spelled with a *p* more than ten times, one of the rules was /p/ = *p*.

By using this thorough procedure, the researchers were able to determine the number of rules and exceptions that would be needed to account for the sound-letter correspondences in these one- and two-syllable words in materials designed for six- to nine-year-olds. They found that there were 211 correspondences, 83 for the consonants and another 128 for the vowels. Of these correspondences, 166 qualified as rules, and the other 45 were listed as exceptions. This means that to recode these words relying entirely on phonics, the six- to nine-year-old readers would need to know 211 correspondences. As they read, they would have to decide, in each case, whether to use one of the 166 rules or one of the 45 exceptions. As this study shows, this approach is simply not feasible. A linguistic analysis shows that there are too many phonics rules and too many exceptions for any set of rules a teacher might choose to teach to be useful.

Based on studies such as this one, Smith (1973) has written extensively about the limitations of phonics rules for recognizing words. He points out that although reading in English goes from left to right, readers need to look to the end of a word to get the information needed to make decisions about how to pronounce individual letters. Smith points out, for example, that if a word begins with the letters *ho*, there are eleven possible pronunciations, as shown in the following words: *hot, hope, hook, hoot, house, hoist, horse, horizon, honey, hour,* and *honest.* Readers need to see the whole word to decide which of these eleven pronunciations of *ho* is the right one.

To take another example, if a word begins with *c*, readers don't know if the *c* is pronounced /s/ or /k/ until they reach the second letter. If the second letter is *i*, readers know that the *c* has an /s/ sound, but now they don't know the pronunciation of the *i*. What if the next letter is *t*? Readers know to pronounce this letter as /t/, but they still don't know how to pronounce the *i*. If the last letter is *e*, the *i* has a long sound (*cite*), but if the last letter is *y*, the *i* has a short sound (*city*). In fact, although readers know that *t* is /t/, they don't know which allophone of /t/ to pronounce until they see the whole word. In *cite* the allophone is [ʔt], but in *city* it is [D]. Until readers see the whole word, they can't determine the pronunciation of the individual letters.

Smith goes on to show that readers need to consider longer stretches of text in order to determine how to pronounce a word. For example, how should *read* be pronounced? Is it /riyd/ or /rɛd/? The answer depends on whether the sentence is in present or past tense. Many English words are spelled the same but pronounced differently in different contexts. For example, *wind* can be /wɪnd/ or /waynd/. Smith argues that evidence from linguistic analyses shows that sounding out words by moving from left to right one letter at a time is simply not what readers actually do.

In light of extensive evidence from linguistics, Smith claims that the idea that words can be recognized by sounding out seems obvious but is false (Smith 2003). He refers to the idea that words can be sounded out as the "Just So" story. He explains, "I call it the Just So story—Just Sound Out, and you can read. But the Just So story is false. This isn't just my opinion: it has to be false logically and linguistically" (p. 256). Smith goes on to say, "Just So may seem obvious, just as it is obvious that the earth is flat, the sun travels round the earth, and flying machines will take off only if they flap their wings like birds. Obvious, but false" (p. 256). Many people who have never taught and have never studied language claim that phonics is the best way to teach reading, but linguistic evidence suggests that this popular belief is not based on real scientific evidence.

Evidence from Eye Movement Research

Smith claims that readers do not recode words by going from left to right letter by letter. Readers have to know what the whole word is to assign phonemic values to individual letters. In many cases, they have to understand the whole sentence before they can pronounce individual words. Otherwise, they won't know if a series of letters like *permit* is pronounced as /pərmít/, a verb, or /pérmɨt/, a noun.

Evidence from eye movement research (Paulson and Freeman 2003) supports Smith's assertion. Researchers have studied how readers' eyes move as they scan a text. Eye movement research, carried out over the last one hundred years, has become more sophisticated as new technology has developed. In early studies, readers had to wear a harness or actually bite down on a bar as they read so that their head wouldn't move. Current technology uses a laser beam that reflects off a reader's eye and does not hinder head movement, so the reading is quite natural. The text is projected on a computer screen, and the eye movements can be tracked with great accuracy.

Although readers have the sensation that their eyes sweep smoothly across the page as they read, the eye actually moves in a series of jumps called *saccades*. Each time the eye stops, or *fixates*, information is sent to the brain. When the eye is moving, no information is recorded. However, the brain fills in the gaps between fixations to produce the perception that the movement is continuous. The brain operates in the same way during reading as it does when someone watches a movie. The series of frames that flash by are perceived as one continuous action, not as a series of still pictures. In fact, the brain works this way all the time. As people look around a room, their eyes make a series of fixations, but people sense a continuous motion, not a series of snapshots.

Eye-tracking equipment can record exactly where on the page the eye fixates during reading. At each fixation, an oval area that covers five or six letters is in clear focus. This is called the *foveal area*. A larger area, of thirty to forty spaces around the fixation point, is in peripheral vision. This area is called the *parafovea*. Current software can also determine the length of each fixation.

Eye movement research shows that readers do not fixate words one letter at a time moving from left to right. In fact, readers do not fixate each word in a text. As Paulson and Freeman (2003) report, research over the last one hundred years has been very consistent in reporting that readers fixate between 60 and 80 percent of the words in a text. This is true of both proficient and struggling readers. It is true of readers reading in their first language and in a second language. This finding has been remarkably consistent.

Studies of eye movement support a sociopsycholinguistic view of reading. However, some writers have misinterpreted eye movement studies, and proponents of phonics have used this secondary reporting to buttress their claims that readers' eyes fixate each letter. For example, Grabe (1991) writes, "Recent research on eye movements in reading has demonstrated that fluent readers read most words on a page . . . The point is that we typically do not guess or sample texts, nor is reading an appoximative skill. Rather, reading is a very precise and very rapid skill" (p. 376). Similarly, Adams (1994) claims that "skillful readers visually process virtually every letter of every word as they read; this is true whether they are reading isolated words or meaningful, connected text" (p. 841).

Paulson and Freeman (2003) show that Grabe and Adams misinterpreted the original research they cite. Eye movement research findings have been very consistent over a long period of time in showing that only about two-thirds of the words in a text are sampled. The eyes don't fixate each letter of each word. In addition, the original research shows that during reading, the brain directs the eyes to gather needed information. Paulson and Freeman carried out studies that replicated earlier investigations that showed that readers fixate the important content words much more frequently than the less important function words like prepositions and conjunctions. Readers predict what they will see and fixate just enough to confirm these predictions as they sample text. This is the claim of those who hold a sociopsycholinguistic view of reading, and the claim is borne out by eye movement data.

The Clymer Study

Those who advocate for phonics acknowledge that there are many sound-letter correspondences, but they claim that just a few basic rules can account for the correspondences in most words. A review of basal reading programs shows that the rules that are presented are not in the linguistic form of "pronounce *p* as /p/." Instead, they are more general statements, such as "When a vowel is in the middle of a one-syllable word, the vowel is short" and "When words end with silent *e*, the preceding *a* or *i* is long."

Students could investigate these patterns, as we suggested in Chapter 5, but in classes where phonics is taught explicitly and systematically, students are told the rule. Then they practice with a set of words. They show mastery of the rule by completing a quiz or test that measures their ability to mark vowels with long or short sounds, for example.

An important question is "How often do these commonly taught phonics rules work?" This is the question Clymer (1963) investigated. Clymer was teaching in an elementary school, and as he presented different phonics generalizations from a list he had been given, one of his students, Kenneth, kept finding exceptions to each generalization. Clymer's experience with Kenneth led him to undertake a research project.

Clymer began by reviewing four widely used sets of basal readers. He found a total of 121 phonics generalizations in these readers. He notes that different series included different sets of rules and introduced them in different sequences. He states, "Of the 50 different vowel generalizations, only 11 were common to all four series" (p. 253). In addition, even when the same rule appeared, it came in a different sequence and a different grade level. Clymer's review showed that across reading series, there is no consistency in which rules are taught or when they are taught. Instruction in this respect is not systematic.

In order for phonics instruction to be systematic, lessons should be logically ordered. However, there is no research base for any particular order of phonics lessons. The lessons could follow almost any sequence. For example, the first lessons could be on vowels and later lessons could focus on consonants. The consonant lessons could begin with stops and then move to fricatives and so on. But this is not what usually happens. Instead, teachers follow the sequence of lessons in the teachers guide. Lessons in current guides follow lessons in previous guides. The sequence seems to follow tradition rather than any linguistic principles.

Some linguistic factors come into account in choosing the sequence of phonics rules to present. For example, it is not possible to produce an oral stop consonant in isolation. The sound of phonemes like /p/ or /g/ occurs when the sound is released into the following vowel. For that reason, nasals like /m/ or fricatives like /s/ are usually introduced first. The stop consonants are combined with vowels and presented as syllables. But none of this is based on any systematic sequence.

Clymer chose forty-five generalizations to examine. He comments, "The selection of these was somewhat arbitrary. The main criterion was to ask, 'Is the generalization stated specifically enough so that it can be said to aid or hinder in the pronunciation of a particular word?'" (p. 254). Once he had chosen the generalizations, Clymer selected a set of words to test them against. He made a composite list of all the words introduced in the four basic reading series and added words from the Gates Reading Vocabulary list. This gave him about twenty-six hundred words. He checked the pronunciation of each word, giving it a phonetic spelling based on Webster's New Collegiate Dictionary. Then he tested each generalization against all the words in his list.

The results of Clymer's study showed that many commonly taught rules work only some of the time, although there is considerable variation. For example, the rule "Words having double e usually have the long e sound" works 98 percent of the time. In Clymer's sample, there were 85 words, like *seem*, that followed the rule and the only exceptions were two instances of the word *been*. On the other hand, the rule "When there are two vowels side by side, the long sound of the first one is heard and the second is usually silent" works only 45 percent of the time. This rule, popularly expressed as "When two vowels go walking, the first one does the talking," applies to many words. Clymer found 309 words, like *bead*, that followed the rule but 377 others, like *chief*, that do not. Since the rule works less than half the time, it is not useful to teach it.

What about the short vowel or silent e rules mentioned earlier? Clymer found that the vowel in the middle of a one-syllable word is short 62 percent of the time. The silent e rule works only 60 percent of the time. Clymer's study is important because it looked at words young readers frequently encounter. Using those words, Clymer evaluated the phonics rules listed in four basal reading programs. The results show that many rules simply do not work often enough to be useful to readers trying to use phonics to identify words.

Phonics and Graphophonics

Those who hold a word recognition view of reading point to the importance of phonics. In contrast, those who take a sociopsycholinguistic view claim that traditional phonics instruction is not useful. They argue that readers acquire a knowledge

Phonics	Graphophonics
conscious: learned as the result of direct, systematic, explicit teaching	subconscious: acquired in the process of reading
the primary source of information used in decoding words	one of three sources of information used in constructing meaning
a prerequisite for reading that develops through practice with decodable texts	a result of reading that develops through engagement with texts that have characteristics that support reading
can be tested independently of meaningful reading	can be assessed only in the context of meaningful reading

Figure 6–3. Phonics and graphophonics

of graphophonics as they read. Phonics rules are generalizations about sound-letter correspondences. Graphophonics knowledge includes subconscious knowledge of phonology, orthography, and the relationships between phonology and orthography. Phonics is often confused with graphophonics. However, there are some important differences between the two. These are summarized in Figure 6–3.

Conscious or Subconscious

The first difference between phonics and graphophonics is that phonics knowledge is conscious, but graphophonic knowledge is subconscious. Phonics rules are learned and become conscious knowledge. Students can recite phonics rules, such as "When two vowels go walking, the first one does the talking." Graphophonics, in contrast, is subconscious knowledge that is acquired as people read. It is this knowledge that allows a reader to pronounce the final s in *pleks* with the sound of /s/ and the final s in *plems* with a /z/ sound. Readers can do this even though they can't state the rule for the pronunciation of s in these words.

Krashen (2003) claims that learned rules can be used to monitor output. However, it is acquisition that builds basic language competence. It is difficult to apply learned rules during speaking because use of the monitor requires knowledge of the rules, time, and attention to language forms, not meaning. Often when speakers monitor too much, their speech becomes halting. It is not possible to think about what one says and how one is saying it at the same time. A speaker who starts to think about whether the upcoming verb should be in simple past or past perfect will probably lose track of her message.

In the same way, during reading, readers rely primarily on subconscious graphophonic knowledge as one of three cueing systems to construct meaning. Attempting to use conscious knowledge of phonics during this process interrupts meaning construction. Students who spend time trying to recode words overload short-term memory and forget what the sentence or paragraph meant up to that point. Many struggling readers focus too much on phonics. They may be able to pronounce each word, but their comprehension is minimal. Monitoring reading by using phonics knowledge is not a good reading strategy.

Linguists study phonological rules that govern the pronunciation of phonemes. People who have acquired a language don't need to learn these rules in order to pronounce words. They have already internalized the rules. It is only when they study linguistics that students become consciously aware of phonological rules. In the sections that follow, we consider two rules and how these rules contribute to readers' graphophonic knowledge. We also discuss the phenomenon of reduced vowels in longer English words.

Phonological rules: Coarticulation A common phenomenon in languages is the coarticulation of phonemes. *Coarticulation* occurs when two phonemes are produced or articulated in the same place in the mouth. Coarticulation is an example of assimilation, when one sound becomes similar to another sound. A good example of coarticulation in English is nasal assimilation.

Earlier we explained that English has three nasal stops: /m/, /n/, and /ŋ/. In addition, English has three pairs of oral stop consonants, /p/ and /b/, /t/ and /d/, and /k/ and /g/. Figure 6–4 shows the place of articulation for the oral and nasal stop consonants.

As Figure 6–4 shows, English has a biliabial nasal, /m/, and a pair of bilabial stops, /p/ and /b/. English has an alveolar nasal, /n/, and a pair of alveolar stops, /t/ and /d/. And English has a velar nasal, /ŋ/, and two velar stops, /k/ and /g/. Now consider the following words: /læmp/, /æmbər/, /hɪnt/, /bænd/, /θæŋk/, and /fɪŋgər/. In each word, a nasal precedes an oral stop consonant. For example, in /læmp/ the /m/ precedes /p/. A careful analysis of the other words in which nasals

Place of Articulation	Nasal Stop	Oral Stop
bilabial	m	p, b
alveolar	n	t, d
velar	ŋ	k, g

Figure 6–4. Nasal and stop consonants

140

precede stops shows that the nasal and the stop are always produced in the same place in the mouth. The /m/ and /p/ in /læmp/ are both biliabials. English phonotactics restricts the possible combinations of nasal and oral stops. There are no words, for example, in which /m/ is followed by /t/ or /k/, at least when the two sounds occur in the same syllable, and often across syllables. This generalization can be stated as a phonological rule: Whenever a nasal stop precedes an oral stop within a syllable, the two stops will have the same place of articulation.

Coarticulation of nasal and oral stops is an example of assimilation. The two sounds become like one another in a certain way. In this case, they are produced in the same place in the mouth. To produce an /m/, for example, a speaker blocks the air with the lips and allows air to pass through the nasal cavity. To make a /p/ or /b/, the speaker blocks the air with the lips and also blocks off the flow of air through the nose. To make the /mp/ sound in /læmp/, then, the speaker stops the air at the lips, allowing air to pass out of the nose, and then blocks air from entering the nasal cavity. The mouth is already in position to make a /p/ and that is the sound that is produced when air is first blocked from passing through the nose and then released at the end of the word. It is easy to test this process by making an /m/, stopping the /m/ sound, and then opening the mouth. The result is /p/ or /b/.

This rule operates very consistently. The word /pʌmpkɨn/ (*pumpkin*) follows the rule for coarticulation. However, many English speakers say /pʌŋkɨn/ rather than /pʌmpkɨn/ in casual speech. What is interesting is that this variation also follows the rule because when the second /p/ is deleted, a /k/ follows the nasal, so the nasal changes from /m/ to /ŋ/. Another word with two possible pronunciations is /ɪnpʌt/. This is a compound word, and the two stops are in different syllables. In the word, an /n/ is followed by a /p/. Even though the nasal and the stop are in two different syllables, most speakers follow the rule for coarticulation and pronounce this word as /ɪmput/ so that /m/ precedes /p/.

The tendency to pronounce an oral stop after a nasal accounts for the pronunciation of words like *warmth*, *something*, and *symphony*. Even though no oral stop follows the nasal in these words, speakers often insert one. All three are commonly pronounced as though they had a /p/ sound after the /m/. In the case of *symphony*, the presence of the letter *p* makes the /p/ insertion even more likely. Children often spell words like these with a *p* and they may identify an extra phoneme in a word like *warmth*. On the other hand, since the nasal and the oral stops are produced at the same point in the mouth, young children learning to spell often omit the nasal. They might write *wind* as *wid*. This spelling is not as inaccurate as it may seem, since the vowel picks up the nasal sound in a word like this. A linguist could represent the word as [wĩd]. The diacritic over the [ĩ] indicates a nasalized vowel.

The orthographic representation of the sounds of nasals preceding stops is complicated by the fact that there are three nasal phonemes but only two graphemes that usually represent nasals. There is no letter to represent /ŋ/. Usually, this phoneme is spelled *ng*, as in *ring*. However, when a velar stop follows, a /k/ or /g/ as in /θɪŋk/ or /fɪŋgər/, the sound is spelled with an *n*. The words are spelled *think* and *finger*, not *thingk* and *fingger*. In *finger*, the *g* represents the /g/ sound in the second syllable. Words with *ng* spellings can have either an /ŋ/ or an /ŋg/ pronunciation. A town near where we used to live is named *Sanger*. Until we talked with locals, we didn't know that the *ng* was pronounced like the sounds of *ng* in *anger*, not those in *singer*.

As children acquire English, they acquire phonological rules such as nasal coarticulation. These rules form part of their graphophonic knowledge. Knowing that nasals and following oral stops are coarticulated is part of a child's subconscious phonotactic knowledge. Then, as they learn to read, children develop graphotactic knowledge. This is their subconscious knowledge of how letters go together. They also learn the relationship between phonology and orthography. Graphophonics is the acquired subconscious knowledge of all three components: phonology, orthography, and the connections between the two systems. These relationships are complex and must be acquired. They can't easily be captured by phonics generalizations.

Morphophonemic rules: Plural   In addition to rules governing coarticulation, such as nasal assimilation, other rules account for the pronunciation of certain morphemes. These are called *morphophonemic rules* because they are phonological rules that apply to specific morphemes. Morphemes are the smallest units of meaning in a word. For example, in a word like *trees*, *tree* is a morpheme, and so is *s*. The *s* carries the meaning of plural. In Chapter 7 we discuss morphemes in more detail. In this chapter, we describe one rule that explains the pronunciation of the plural morpheme, usually spelled *s* or *es*.

Although there are two spellings of the plural morpheme, there are three pronunciations: /s/ as in *cats*, /z/ as in *dogs*, and /ɨz/ as in *bushes*. Given a new word, like *glark*, a person who has acquired English knows that the plural will have the sound of /s/, not /z/ or /ɨz/. Native speakers would agree with this pronunciation even though *glark* is a made-up word that nobody could have heard before. The reason for this agreement is that in the process of acquiring a language, a person acquires morphophonemic rules, such as the rule for plurals. Knowledge of the rule is subconscious. Linguistic analysis brings this subconscious knowledge to a conscious level. How does this rule work?

To discover the rule for the plural morpheme, linguists collect a number of words and for each, they decide on the pronunciation of the plural morpheme.

mats	ships	shelves	rugs	watches
plays	dramas	beds	foxes	cabs
baths	cells	roses	cars	tacks
buses	lashes	cliffs	mazes	judges

Figure 6–5. Plurals

The words in Figure 6–5 provide a small sample. Look at each word and decide whether the plural is pronounced /s/, /z/, or /ɨz/.

The second step a linguist would use to discover the rule for the plural would be to transcribe the words and group together all the words with each of the three endings. Figure 6–6 shows how the words from Figure 6–5 would be categorized.

The third step, a more difficult one, would be to try to determine the environment that conditions each of the plural forms. Assimilation is a very common phonological process. In this process, one sound shares some features with a sound next to it. That is, one sound assimilates to become more like a nearby sound. In this case, since the plural is at the end of the word, no other phoneme follows, so it must be the preceding phoneme that determines whether the plural is /s/, /z/, or /ɨz/. The phonemes that precede the /s/ plural are /t/, /θ/, /p/, /f/, and /k/, and those that precede /z/ are /ey/, /ə/, /l/, /v/, /d/, /g/, /r/, and /b/. What do the words in each of these groups have in common that makes them different from the other group?

/s/	/z/	/ɨz/
mæts	pleyz	bʌsɨz
bæθs	draməz	rowzɨz
šɪps	sɛlz	læšɨz
klɪfs	šɛlvz	faksɨz
tæks	bɛdz	meyzɨz
	rʌgz	wačɨz
	karz	ǰʌǰɨz
	kæbz	

Figure 6–6. Transcription of plurals

Both groups include consonants, so the plural is not conditioned by whether a consonant or a vowel precedes it. Both groups have stops and fricatives, so it does not appear that the manner of articulation causes the change. Both groups have sounds produced at the same place as well. For example, both /p/ and /b/ are bilabials, so the place of articulation must not be the cause (as it was with nasal assimilation). The only consistent difference between these two groups can be seen by considering the difference between /p/ and /b/ or between /f/ and /v/. In each case, these phonemes are pairs in which one is voiced and one is voiceless. A careful examination of the two groups of phonemes shows that all the phonemes associated with /s/ are voiceless and all the phonemes associated with /z/ are voiced.

At this point a linguist could say that when the preceding phoneme is voiceless, the plural is /s/, and when the preceding phoneme is voiced, the plural is /z/. This would describe what is going on, but it wouldn't explain the phenomenon. Why is /s/ associated with preceding voiceless sounds and /z/ with preceding voiced sounds? The answer lies in the difference between /s/ and /z/. The only difference between these alveolar fricatives is that /s/ is voiceless and /z/ is voiced. At this point, it becomes clear that the plural rule is an assimilation rule. The plural assimilates in voicing with the preceding phoneme. Both sounds are either voiceless or voiced. If the vocal cords are not vibrating at the end of the word, they don't start vibrating for the plural. If they are vibrating to produce a voiced sound, they continue vibrating during the plural.

This helps explain the words in the first two columns, but what about the words in the third column? The phonemes preceding /ɨz/ are /s/, /š/, /z/, /č/, and /ǰ/. The list includes both voiceless and voiced sounds. However, what all these phonemes have in common is that they have a sound quite similar to the sound of /s/ or /z/. It would be hard to distinguish between the singular and plural of these words if the plural simply involved the addition of /s/ or /z/. How could someone decide if /bʌss/ or /meyzz/ meant one bus or maze or two? Drawing out the sound of the /s/ at the end of *bus* would not signal plural very clearly. For that reason, English adds a sound, /ɨ/, between the end of the word and the plural morpheme. This is a process called *epenthesis*, inserting a sound into a word. Since the added sound is a vowel and all vowels are voiced, then the plural is /z/, which follows the general rule.

This linguistic analysis would lead a linguist to a rule for the pronunciation of the plural morpheme. The rule could be stated as "If the base word ends in a sound like /s/ or /z/, the plural is /ɨz/. In all other cases, the plural is /s/ if the base ends in a voiceless sound and /z/ if it ends in a voiced sound." In other words, the plural morpheme assimilates in voicing to the last phoneme in the base word. This complicated rule is acquired subconsciously and forms part of a native speaker's knowledge of phonology. Even though most people could not state the rule, they could apply it to any word, like *glark*, that they encounter. In fact, this same rule applies to possessives. In *Pat's*, the possessive is /s/, in *José's*, the possessive is /z/, and in *Clarise's*, the possessive is /ɨz/. In addition, the rule applies to the third-person *s* used to indicate the present tense in words like *walks* (/s/), *runs* (/z/), and *rushes* (/ɨz/).

However, since this is a morphophonemic rule, it applies to specific morphemes, not all the words that end in the sound of /s/ or /z/. There are pairs of words like *place* and *plays* and *toss* and *tease* that show that either pronunciation can occur when the phoneme is not a plural, a possessive, or a third-person *s*. In each pair, the sound that precedes the final phoneme is a voiced sound, a vowel. In *place* and *toss*, the following sound is /s/, but in *plays* and *tease*, the following sound is /z/. If this final phoneme were a plural, it would be possible to predict whether the sound would be /s/ or /z/, but in these words, it is not possible to predict the pronunciation of the final phoneme (/s/ or /z/) based on what precedes the phoneme. This is why the rule is called a morphophonemic rule. It applies only to certain morphemes, not to all the words in the language. On the other hand, the rule for nasal assimilation is a general phonological rule of English that always applies.

Morphophonemic rules such as the plural rule form part of a person's knowledge of phonology. When a person learns to read, he develops knowledge of the orthography and also begins to associate the sounds of the plural with the spellings. As in the case with nasals preceding stops, the sound-letter correspondences for the plural are complex. The *s* spelling is associated with two different sounds, /s/ and /z/. Children sometimes spell words like *plays* with a *z* because that is the sound they hear. However, as they read and are read to, they realize that the sound /z/ is sometimes spelled with an *s*. This is part of the children's graphophonic knowledge.

Reduced vowels Phonics exercises and tests, especially those that assess students' knowledge of vowels, almost always consist entirely of one-syllable words. Even though many phonics generalizations have numerous exceptions, as Clymer showed, they work more often with one-syllable words than with longer words. This is because in longer words, at least one of the syllables is unstressed. For example, in a word like *about*, the first syllable receives less emphasis than the second one. The stress falls on *bout*. In *medicine*, the second and third syllables are unstressed. In a word like *relative*, the second syllable gets less stress than the other two.

Unstressed syllables are very common in English. Linguists refer to the vowels in these syllables as reduced vowels, and they represent them with the schwa, /ə/, or the barred *i*, /ɨ/, as in /əbáwt/, /médɨsɨn/, and /rɛ́lətɨv/. Reduced vowels cause difficulty for children learning to spell English words. The first vowel sound in *about* and the second vowel in *medicine* sound the same, but one is spelled with an *a* and the other with an *i*. The schwa sound can be spelled with any of the letters that commonly represent vowel sounds. Even though the spelling varies, the sound is the same. This makes it difficult to learn to spell these words.

One strategy for spelling words with reduced vowels is to find a related word in which the vowel is stressed. For example, in *medicinal*, the second vowel is stressed and it is possible to identify the /ɪ/ sound. In *relate*, the second vowel has an /ey/ sound spelled with *a*. However, children learning to spell seldom know words like *medicinal*, so this strategy is more useful for older students or adults who are trying to refine their spellings.

The rules for stress in English are complex because English vocabulary is based on words from many different languages. Other languages have more regular stress patterns. For example, in Spanish the stress is regular, and when a word deviates from the normal pattern, an accent mark is placed over the vowel to be stressed. However, in English it is difficult to predict where the stress will fall in an unfamiliar word. Unless a person has heard a word pronounced, there is no reliable way to decide where to put the stress. Many students have difficulty pronouncing the word *anemone*. Often they put the stress on the first syllable and assume the final *e* signals a long vowel. They pronounce the word as /ǽnəmown/ rather than the conventional /ənɛ́məniy/, with the stress on the second syllable and the first and third syllables reduced. David remembers trying to pronounce *tachistoscope* during an oral exam. He wasn't sure whether the stress fell on the first syllable or the second. Fortunately, one of the professors conducting the exam provided the conventional pronunciation.

This experience helps show that there are words people can read even though they can't sound them out. Phonics rules are of little use if a person doesn't know where the stress falls. Stressed and unstressed vowels are pronounced very differently. Phonics worksheets usually contain only one-syllable words to avoid this problem. Some decodable books consist almost entirely of one-syllable words as well. However, authentic literature and content books include many long words. Conscious knowledge of phonics rules provides little help in pronouncing these words. People who acquire English acquire knowledge of how the complex stress rules work. This knowledge forms part of their phonological knowledge. When they begin to read, they develop knowledge of orthography and of the complex relationships between the sounds and the spellings. This graphophonic knowledge provides cues readers use to construct meaning as they read.

An Explanation for the Development of Graphophonics

One explanation for the development of graphophonic knowledge comes from the work of Moustafa (1997). She asks how children develop their knowledge of letter-sound correspondences. Her explanation rests on the linguistic analysis of syllables into onsets and rimes. English words like /striym/ and /pleyt/ contain syllables made up of two parts. The initial consonant phonemes constitute the *onset* of the syllable. Thus, in these two words, the onsets are /str/ and /pl/. The *rime* is the part from the vowel to the end of the syllable. For these words the rimes are /iym/ and /eyt/. In poetry, the rime is the part of the word that rhymes. Consider this poem by Marchette Chute (Prelutsky 1986, p. 53):

My Teddy Bear
A teddy bear is a faithful friend.
You can pick him up at either end.
His fur is the color of breakfast toast,
And he's always there when you need him most.

The rimes of the rhyming words in this poem would be transcribed the same even though they are spelled differently. The first couplet (*friend* and *end*) have the rime /ɛnd/, and the second couplet (*toast* and *most*) have /owst/ as the rime. In rhyming poetry like this, the onsets differ, but the rime is the same.

Although syllables can be divided into an onset and a rime, some syllables, like the word *end*, have no onset. In this word, no consonants precede the vowel, so this word has only a rime. In English, every syllable has a vowel sound, so every syllable must have a rime. Onsets and rimes refer to the sounds in words, not the spellings. In longer words with several syllables, each syllable can be divided into its onset and rime.

Moustafa summarizes a great deal of research to show how children develop graphophonic knowledge. She reports that Treiman (1985) conducted experiments that showed that children are able to divide words into onsets and rimes. Treiman played word games with eight-year-old children and with adults. She found that her subjects were able to split syllables into onsets and rimes and that they had trouble splitting syllables in any other way. The ability to split syllables up in this way seems natural and does not require instruction.

Knowledge of onsets and rimes seems to be part of the subconscious phonological knowledge speakers of English acquire. They use this knowledge to figure out new words by finding analogies with known words. Moustafa describes how Wylie and Durrell (1970) studied first-grade children. They gave them sets of letters that represent rimes in English, such as *-ack*, *-eck*, *-ick*, and *-ock*, and asked them to circle the one that says /æk/. Later, they asked children to circle the letter that says /æ/, for example. Children did much better at identifying the rimes than the individual phonemes. Wylie and Durrell's research suggests that children can identify rimes more easily than phonemes.

In addition, Moustafa reports on experiements by Goswami (1986) in which she gave children pairs of words like *hark* and *harm* and *hark* and *lark*. These words have similar sequences of letters, *har* in the first pair and *ark* in the second. She found that children who knew only one word in the pair (based on a pretest) could figure out the other word by analogy. What is interesting is that children did much better with words like *hark* and *lark* than with words like *hark* and *harm*. Even though there is only one letter difference in each sequence, in the second pair the letter sequence represents the rime /ark/, while in the first pair the similar letters *har* represent phonemes that make up the onset and part of the rime of the word. Moustafa interprets Goswami's research as showing that children use their knowledge of onsets and rimes, not their knowledge of phonemes, to recode new words by analogy.

Moustafa's work suggests that graphophonic knowledge develops as children learn new words by analogy with known words by relying on their natural ability to divide syllables into onsets and rimes. The key, then, is for children to build up a large number of known words. The more words they know, the more words they can use to make analogies. Studies have shown that children develop vocabulary more rapidly when they read than when they are taught vocabulary directly (Nagy, Anderson, et al. 1985). Moustafa cites research by Goodman (1965) that shows that children can read more words in context than in isolation and research by Kucer (1985) that shows that children can read natural text more easily than text that has been manipulated to include certain phonics patterns. All this research suggests that the best way to help children acquire graphophonic knowledge as well as knowledge of the other cueing systems is by involving them in reading engaging, authentic texts. Young children benefit from being read to and by being involved in language games, songs, and rhymes. In addition, when teachers write stories that children dictate during a language experience activity, children develop subconscious graphophonic knowledge.

Two books that provide especially rich examples of classroom practices to help students develop knowledge of how sounds correspond to letters are *Looking Closely: The Role of Phonics in One Whole Language Classroom* (Mills, O'Keefe, et al. 1992) and *Rethinking Phonics: Making the Best Teaching Decisions* (Dahl, Scharer, et al. 2001). Although both books refer to phonics in the title, the practices that are described are all activities that develop graphophonic knowledge. Evidence from linguistics, including rules for nasal assimilation and the plural, along with Moustafa's research, support the claim that readers use subconscious graphophonic knowledge rather than conscious knowledge of phonics as they read.

Most Important Cue or One of Three Cues

A second difference between phonics and graphophonics listed in Figure 6–3 is that from the word recognition perspective, phonics is seen as the most reliable way of turning written marks on a page into the sounds of the oral language, but from a sociopsycholinguistic perspective, graphophonics is considered just one of three linguistic cueing systems. Teachers who hold a word recognition view believe that students who know and apply phonics rules can recode almost any string of letters into the sounds of oral language. In Chapter 5 we reviewed the historical development of writing systems. We also showed that American English spelling is systematic. However, like all complex systems, the spelling system is not based simply on the phonetic demand to spell words the way they sound. Spelling also reflects the semantic demand to spell words that are related in meaning similarly and to spell borrowed words to reflect their origin. Because the writing system of English is not designed completely to represent sounds, knowledge of phonics does not always allow students to recode all words successfully.

We were reminded recently that phonics is not always helpful. Our daughter visited Thailand, where she bought us T-shirts. On the back is written the name of a city in Thailand she visited. The Roman alphabet rendering of the city's name is *Phuket*. The natives pronounce the word /puwkέt/, but that's not how shoppers read it at our local grocery store! Phonics was not our friend, and we decided not to wear the shirts in public anymore.

Phonics does not always benefit students, either, especially if they come to believe that the goal of reading is to pronounce words. Yvonne asks her preservice and graduate inservice teachers to conduct the Burke Interview (Goodman, Watson, et al. 1987) with both native Spanish and native English speakers in their classes. The interview is done in Spanish for native Spanish speakers and in English for native English speakers. The students' answers to the question "When you are reading and come to something you don't know, what do you do?" or "¿Qué haces cuando estás leyendoy llegas a una palabra que no conoces?" reveal some interesting information about the strategies students use when they read. Of 277 readers interviewed over two semesters, 113 (or 41 percent) said "sound it out" or "pronunicar las sílabas" (pronounce the syllables) was their first strategy. What was perhaps even more disconcerting was that an additional 62 of the 277 said they would "ask the teacher" as their first strategy. So the two most common strategies students came up with were "sound it out" and "ask the teacher." Few students mentioned a strategy such as "skip it and read on" (13) or "go back and reread" (14) or "look at the pictures" (18), all strategies that might help the students figure out meaning. Most students, instead, relied on phonics.

Teachers have often commented to us that their students who received intensive phonics instruction in lower grades struggle with reading comprehension. Even though their oral reading sounds good, these students score poorly on any measure of comprehension. Vivian's story is rather unusual. At one time, she was a firm believer in phonics. In her graduate classes she is learning about a sociopsycholinguistic view of reading. In one of her responses, this is what Vivian wrote:

> I taught kinder my first two years of teaching, and these [phonics-based] methods were drilled and practiced during language arts . . . I am now teaching second grade, and my biggest challenge has been to teach comprehension and to teach the students to be able to construct meaning when they read. Ironically, I really can't place the blame on another teacher for not teaching my second graders the foundation of how to become effective and efficient readers in the lower grades because 60 percent of my students now were the students I taught in kinder two years ago. I ask myself at least twice a day why I didn't teach them to focus on what I now have come to recognize as "constructing meaning" when they read.

Vivian is now providing the kind of instruction her students needed all along. Fortunately, she has come to understand the importance of helping students use all the cueing systems instead of relying only on phonics. Her students will benefit this year, and she will be able to help them see that reading involves making sense of texts, not just pronouncing words.

Unfortunately, when students experience reading difficulties, the first response is often "They need more phonics." Rather than realizing that an overreliance on phonics can handicap readers, teachers may think that the students are having difficulty because they didn't get enough phonics. As a result, most remediation programs for struggling readers are heavily phonics-based. Instead of blaming phonics, school personnel may blame the students for not having learned phonics. This leads to a cycle of struggling readers getting more phonics when what they need, as Vivian realized, is a focus on comprehension.

Miscue data on struggling readers confirms Vivian's experience. David asked students in his graduate reading class to choose a struggling reader and conduct a miscue analysis of that student's reading. The students were all third graders or older. Figure 6–7 lists the results in percentages for twenty-two students in the areas of graphic similarity, syntactic acceptability, and semantic acceptability (the labels in parentheses refer to the possible miscue ratings).

The first column shows the scores for graphic similarity. In other words, how much did the word the student produced look like the word on the page? To determine graphic similarity, a researcher compares each substitution a reader makes with the expected response in the text. Researchers divide words into three parts (beginning, middle, end). If two parts are the same, the similarity is high. For example, if a reader substitutes *hot* for *hat*, the two words have high similarity. If one part is the same, the similarity is some. This would be the case if the two words were *hot* and *hip*. Notice how high these troubled readers scored. Even for the lowest

Graphics (high similarity, some similarity)	Syntax (strength, partial strength, overcorrection)	Semantics (no loss, partial loss)
100	35	27
100	48	26
100	52	46
100	60	34
98	42	30
97	34	27
97	46	52
95	31	32
93	53	46
92	19	24
92	38	41
92	60	56
91	64	76
90	62	73
89	51	20
87	54	66
87	61	65
85	58	26
85	61	45
84	51	56
83	56	68
82	58	46

Figure 6–7. Miscue results

student, 82 percent of the miscues showed at least some similarity to the expected response. All these readers relied primarily on the graphophonic cueing system.

The scores in the next two columns are much lower. The second column shows the readers' use of syntax. Researchers analyze each miscue to determine whether the resulting sentence or part of the sentence with the miscue still sounds like English. If the whole sentence still sounds like English, the score is "strength" for syntax. If part of the sentence, including the miscue, sounds like English (the first half of the sentence or the last half), then the rating is "partial strength." These readers often produced sentences with no syntactic acceptability. For example, the first student on the list, who scored 100 percent on graphophonics, scored only 35 percent on syntax. This means that 65 percent of the sentences were not syntactically acceptable. Similarly, these readers scored very low on semantics. The sentences they produced did not make sense. A score of "no loss" for semantics means that the whole sentence makes sense. A score of "partial loss" means that at least part of the sentence, including the miscue, makes sense. That first reader's score on semantics was 27 percent. That means that 73 percent of the time, all or part of the sentences he produced made no sense.

It is clear, from even a quick look at these scores, why these students are struggling readers. They rely heavily on just one cueing system. Not surprisingly, these students had great difficulty in retelling the stories they read. This analysis shows that these students do not need more phonics. Rather, they need to learn to use their background knowledge and cues from syntax and semantics as well as from sounds and letters to make sense of texts.

Proponents of a word recognition view of reading claim that struggling readers like these differ from proficient readers in the way they use the cueing systems. Stanovich (1996), for example, argues that proficient readers recognize words automatically and almost effortlessly. Struggling readers, in contrast, have poor word recognition skills and rely heavily on context to predict upcoming words. As readers become more proficient at recognizing words, they depend less on the context.

Data from miscue analysis studies, like the data reported in Figure 6–7, provide quite a different picture. Struggling readers rely heavily on graphophonics to identify words and fail to use the syntactic and semantic contexts. As a result, their reading often doesn't sound like English and doesn't make sense. All the readers listed in Figure 6–7 produced miscues that looked and sounded like the words in the text the majority of the time. However, their miscues resulted in sentences that were not grammatical and didn't make sense. Further, these struggling readers were not able to retell what they had read.

Kucer and Tuten (2003) researched the claim that proficient readers recognize words automatically without the help of context. They conducted a study of the reading of twenty-four graduate students. Their results indicate that these proficient readers did make use of syntactic and semantic context and relied minimally on graphophonic cues.

Kucer and Tuten report that "approximately 87 percent of all initial miscues made sense within the previous context of the story, 94 percent maintained the previous syntactic structure of the sentence in which they were found, and 88 percent were acceptable with the previous meaning of the sentence in which they were located" (p. 288). These high percentages show that proficient readers make use of both the syntactic and semantic cues from the text as they read. When they make miscues, the miscues fit the sentence and the story to that point.

Proficient readers rely more heavily on the syntactic and semantic context than on the graphophonic cues. Kucer and Tuten considered all miscues, including omissions and insertions. They found that only 35 percent of all the miscues these proficient readers made had high graphic similarity to the text, and an additional 11 percent had some similarity. That meant that more than 50 percent of the time, these readers made miscues that didn't look or sound like the words in the text. This suggests strongly that these readers were not using advanced word recognition skills and identifying words automatically. Instead, they were constructing meaning by relying primarily on the syntactic and semantic contexts. They made only minimal use of graphophonemic information.

The results for the twenty-four proficient readers stand in sharp contrast to the analysis of the twenty-two struggling readers. Despite claims that struggling readers rely heavily on context because of their inability to recognize words automatically, the struggling readers made little use of context and relied heavily on graphophonic information. The proficient readers, on the other hand, made minimal use of graphophonic information and relied heavily on the syntactic and semantic contexts.

These two studies indicate that instruction should help students use all three linguistic cueing systems rather than relying on phonics to identify words. As Kucer and Tuten put it, "these adult readers cause us to question early reading programs that rely heavily on the teaching of graphic and sound (phonic) strategies, especially in isolation" (p. 290). Kucer and Tuten also caution that many programs that claim to offer balanced literacy instruction emphasize phonics, and yet proficient readers, like the adults in their study, actually rely more heavily on syntax and semantics than on graphophonics to predict words as they read. Vivian's experience and the research on miscue analysis help confirm that phonics instruction, even if it is explicit and systematic, is not the solution for every struggling reader.

A Prerequisite for Reading or a Result of Reading

A third difference between phonics and graphophonics is that phonics knowledge is considered a prerequisite for reading, and graphophonic knowledge is developed as the result of reading and being read to. Teachers who take a word recognition view believe that students who know their phonics rules can use them to attack words. Until students can sound words out, they cannot be expected to read. Teachers who hold a sociopsycholinguistic view believe that graphophonics is acquired in the process of reading. In fact, the only way that this subconscious knowledge can be developed is through reading and being read to. Graphophonics is a result of, not a prerequisite for, reading.

Decodable books   Most phonics programs provide students with many opportunities to practice using the phonics correspondences they have learned by reading books that contain many examples of the phonics rules. These books are referred to as *decodable books* because most of the words in each book follow patterns that students have been taught. Use of these books is based on the belief that phonics knowledge develops as students practice reading words that follow the rules they have been learning.

Some books for beginning readers provide many opportunities for students to practice a particular sound-letter correspondence. For example, lines such as "The fat cat sat on the mat" and "Dan can fan Nan" have many words with the /æ/ sound. However, there are no clear guidelines for how many words in a book must follow patterns students have been taught. In other words, there is no standard for what constitutes a decodable book. In addition, there is no research showing the benefits of using decodable books.

Books with characteristics that support reading   Teachers who take a sociopsycholinguistic view of reading believe that students develop their ability to use the linguistic cueing systems as they enagage with interesting texts. In early stages, teachers read to and with students. Later, students can begin to read independently. Teachers choose books with certain characteristics that support reading. Figure 6–8 is a checklist teachers have used to determine if a book has the characteristics that support reading. The checklist takes into account both the features of the text and the interests and background knowledge of the reader.

Alphabet books   In addition to using books that have characteristics that support reading, teachers who hold a sociopsycholinguistic view ensure that beginning readers learn the names of letters and begin to associate letters and sounds. One way they do this is by using alphabet books.

Many alphabet books for young readers focus on initial sounds. *Annie, Bea, and Chi Chi Dolores* (Maurer 1996) contains names of things associated with school activities, such as "J jumping rope," "K kicking a ball," and "L lining up." Another book for beginning readers, *ABC and You* (Fernandes 1996), has student names and characteristics on each page from Amazing Amanda to Zippity Zack.

Checklist: Characteristics of Text That Support Reading

1. Are the materials authentic? Authentic materials are written to inform or entertain, not to teach a grammar point or a letter-sound correspondence.

2. Are the materials predictable? Books are more predictable

   - when students have background knowledge of the concepts, so teachers should activate or build background
   - when they follow certain patterns (repetitive, cumulative) or include certain devices (rhyme, rhythm, alliteration)
   - when students are familiar with text structures (beginning, middle, end) (main idea, details, examples, etc.)
   - when students are familiar with text features (headings, subheadings, maps, labels, graphs, tables, indexes, etc.)

3. Is there a good text-picture match? A good match provides nonlinguistic visual cues. Is the placement of the text and pictures predictable?

4. Are the materials interesting and/or imaginative? Interesting, imaginative texts engage students.

5. Do the situations and characters in the book represent the experiences and backgrounds of the students in the class? Culturally relevant texts engage students.

Additional Considerations for Older Struggling Readers

1. Is the text limited?
2. Are the pictures, photographs, or other art appropriate for older students?
3. For content texts, are there clear labels, diagrams, graphs, maps, or other visuals?
4. Is the content age-level-appropriate?

Figure 6–8. Checklist for characteristics of text that support reading

After the teacher reads this book, students can work together to create a class alphabet book with the names of all the students. Students might discuss what characteristic to connect with each of their classmates. They would also have to decide what to do if several students' names started with the same first letter and other letters were missing. This kind of problem-solving activity promotes students' learning as they work collaboratively.

It Begins with an A (Calmenson 1993) is an unusual alphabet book that presents students with a series of riddles to solve. Each rhyming page gives clues and asks, "What is it?" For example, the *c* page reads, "This takes your picture. It starts with a C. Get ready, get set. Now smile for me!" Students enjoy solving the riddles, and groups of students can work together to create a similar book of their own with a riddle for each letter of the alphabet. Writing rhyming pages also helps students become more aware of different spellings for a given sound.

An alphabet book that encourages children to play with sounds and which can help them develop phonemic awareness is *The Disappearing Alphabet Book* (Wilbur 1997) . This playful book asks what would happen if letters of the alphabet were to disappear. For example, the *p* page reads, "How strange that the banana's slippery peel, Without its P would be a slippery EEL!" This book helps students realize that sometimes when they delete a letter from one word, they create another word. Again, students can collaborate to make a book modeled on this one. This book can also be used effectively with older students.

Teachers can use alphabet books as part of a theme study. There are alphabet books on many different topics. For example, Veronica read *The Icky Bug Alphabet Book* (Pallotta 1986a) as part of a unit on bugs (Freeman and Freeman 2000). As a follow-up activity, her first graders collected and brought in real insects. Veronica wrote the names of the insects on strips of paper and talked with her students about bugs whose names started with the same sounds and letters. Then, the students drew pictures of their bugs on the strips and hung each under the corresponding letter of the alphabet. To make an alphabet book, Veronica helped the students organize the labeled pictures into a class *Icky Bug Alphabet Book*. In the process, they discovered that not all the letters of the alphabet were included, so they had to decide what insects could be put on these pages. As they worked together, Veronica's young students became more conscious of initial letter sounds and spellings.

Francisco carried out an extensive theme study on the ocean with his third graders (Freeman and Freeman 2000). One book his students particularly enjoyed was *The Ocean Alphabet Book* (Pallotta 1986b). Each page features an ocean animal. For example, the *j* page reads, "J is for Jellyfish. Jellyfish are soft, gooey and see-through. Their dangling arms can sting if you touch them." Francisco's students used this book as a resource for group investigations into different ocean animals. At the same time, because this is an alphabet book, it provided a review of all the alphabet letters and sounds. As students looked for specific animals in the book, they also practiced their alphabetizing skills.

As their final project for the ocean unit, one group of Francisco's students decided to make their own ocean alphabet book. They followed the model of the Pallotta book. They discussed what ocean animal to put on each page. They drew pictures of their sea animals and then wrote what they had learned about each ocean creature. They read their finished book to the class. It became a favorite resource book in Francisco's classroom library.

For older students, Pallotta (1993) has written *The Extinct Alphabet Book*. Each page of this beautifully illustrated book features an animal that has become extinct. For example, students learn that *akiola* birds used to live in Hawaii but died out after they caught a disease. Classes studying an environmental theme would find this alphabet book very useful.

Another fascinating alphabet book for older students is *The Butterfly Alphabet* (1996). The author, Kjell Sandved, spent more than twenty-five years photographing butterflies whose wing patterns contained the letters of the alphabet. Each page is a close-up of one wing with the name of the butterfly, and at the end of the book, the author includes additional information about each butterfly. The text on each page is a two-line poem with the key word printed in the color of the letter on the butterfly wing that is pictured. Books such as *The Butterfly Alphabet* not only expand students' vocabulary but help them think about words that have the same ending sounds even when spelled differently. For example, for the page showing the butterfly wing that looks like the letter *n*, Sandved writes, "Butterflies enchant the hours / Sipping *nectar* from the flowers." Here, students see two spelling patterns, *ours* and *owers*, for the same sequence of phonemes. Similarly, for the page with the letter *t*, the author writes, "Nature's angels fill the skies / In *twinkling* butterfly disguise" (contrasting *ies* and *ise*). This book offers two models for a group or class alphabet book: students can write poetry for each letter around some theme or they can highlight certain words within their poems. As students create their books, they continue to develop content knowledge along with awareness of alphabet letters and different spelling patterns associated with various sounds, and they see that the rimes of words are not always spelled the same.

A culturally relevant alphabet book is Alma Flor Ada's *Gathering the Sun*, with its vivid illustrations by Simón Silva. This bilingual book has a poem in English and one in Spanish for each letter of the alphabet. The poems center on objects and events in the life of migrant farm workers. The *d* page, for example, has a poem about *duraznos* (peaches), and the *c* and *ch* pages commemorate the life of César Chavez. Ada's poetry and Silva's art help readers understand and respect the life of Hispanics whose roots come from Mexico and whose livelihood comes from the soil.

Teachers can use alphabet books such as these to help students develop an understanding of the relationships between letters and sounds. These are authentic, predictable texts that help students develop the alphabetic principle. Figure 6–9 lists the alphabet books mentioned in this section.

Ada, Alma F. 1997. *Gathering the Sun*. New York: Lothrop, Lee, and Shepard.

Calmenson, Stephanie. 1993. *It Begins with an A*. New York: Scholastic.

Fernandes, Eugenie. 1996. *ABC and You*. Boston: Houghton Mifflin.

Maurer, Donna. 1996. *Annie, Bea, and Chi Chi Dolores*. Boston: Houghton Mifflin.

Pallotta, Jerry. 1993. *The Extinct Alphabet Book*. New York: Scholastic.

———. 1986a. *The Icky Bug Alphabet Book*. New York: Scholastic.

———. 1986b. *The Ocean Alphabet Book*. New York: Trumpet.

Sandved, Kjell B. 1996. *The Butterfly Alphabet*. New York: Scholastic.

Wilbur, Richard. 1997. *The Disappearing Alphabet Book*. New York: Scholastic.

Figure 6–9. Alphabet books

Assess Independently or Assess in Context

A final distinction between phonics and graphophonics listed in Figure 6–3 is that phonics can be assessed independently of meaningful reading, but graphophonics can be assessed only during reading. Researchers and teachers can test students' knowledge of phonics by asking them to pronounce nonsense words or words the children are not likely to have seen before. It is easy to construct worksheets and quizzes to practice phonics skills and test phonics knowledge because it is conscious, learned knowledge. However, graphophonics can be assessed only in the context of reading. Using miscue analysis, researchers can evaluate readers' use of graphophonics as part of a more complete analysis of how they use linguistic cues to construct meaning.

Teachers can develop lessons to determine whether or not students can use their knowledge of letter-sound correspondences as they read. Such lessons provide insights into students' acquisition of graphophonics. Watson (1996) first developed these "determining lessons" as an alternative to worksheets and quizzes designed to measure students' knowledge of phonics. Often, students who do poorly on phonics worksheets do very well when they encounter the same words in the context of a reading passage. Determining lessons illustrate the difference between students' conscious knowledge of phonics rules and their subconscious knowledge of graphophonics.

To develop a determining lesson, a teacher begins with a phonics worksheet. Then, the teacher either creates or modifies a reading selection so that it contains many words with the same sound-letter pattern as the phonics worksheet. Students can first complete the worksheet and then read the passage. The teacher records the reading and marks any miscues. Then students' performance on the two tasks can be compared.

Directions: The vowel digraph has two sounds: short *e* and long *a*. If a word is unfamiliar, try each of the four sounds. At this time, you should be able to recognize the word. Show the sound of *ei* and *ie* on the line before each word.

Key: fi*e*ld = e   rec*ei*ve = e   *ei*ght = a   sc*ie*nce = i

1. ____ grief	15. ____ conceit	29. ____ shrieking
2. ____ deceive	16. ____ veil	30. ____ neighborhood
3. ____ conceivable	17. ____ heir	31. ____ believed
4. ____ sleigh	18. ____ leisure	32. ____ yield
5. ____ ceiling	19. ____ their	33. ____ either
6. ____ reign	20. ____ briefcase	34. ____ field
7. ____ mischievously	21. ____ seizing	35. ____ chief
8. ____ relieve	22. ____ beige	36. ____ receive
9. ____ niece	23. ____ receipt	37. ____ weigh
10. ____ shield	24. ____ neither	38. ____ vein
11. ____ scientist	25. ____ scientific	39. ____ surveillance
12. ____ height	26. ____ weird	40. ____ achieve
13. ____ eighteen	27. ____ perceived	41. ____ disbelief
14. ____ weight	28. ____ windshield	42. ____ sheik

Figure 6–10. Phonics worksheet

For example, Lucero gave one of her students, Lupita, the worksheet shown in Figure 6–10. Lupita missed twelve of the forty-two items on this worksheet.

This worksheet is designed for older students. The words are quite difficult. Even for older students, though, the worksheet may be quite confusing. The directions refer to "the vowel digraph," but the key lists two digraphs, *ie* and *ei*, as well as a third, *ie*. In a word like *science*, the two letters are in different syllables, and each one is pronounced. As a result, they do not form a digraph, two letters that make one sound. The key lists the *ie* of *science* as having a long *i* sound but the *e* represents an additional sound, /ə/. Further, *ie* is always pronounced as /iy/, and it is only *ei* that is associated with two sounds, /iy/ and /ey/. The worksheet

Each night I thought I saw a weird shape on the wall. ⓇI was

only two years old and unaware of the fear and grief attached to

the light. I believed that the "thing" would kill me if I told anyone

about it. I stared and the ceiling full of disbelief. I felt deceived ⓇBy

my own imagination. I teased myself with the fear, knowing I

               could Know
couldn't seize it. Once I knew the source of the light that crept
             2.mishieve—
             1.mi—
into my room each night, I could mischievously enjoy the fear.

Finally, one evening, during my daily surveillance, I
     Ⓡ
perceived that it was a car windshield reflecting the streetlight
               through-out ② neighbor
outside. The car came shrieking through the neighborhood and out
                      would be
onto the field. I realized the things I had believed could
            would
conceivably be wrong. I could either accept scientific reasons or

yield to my vivid imagination. Childhood events can have a big

impact on a person's life.

Figure 6–11. Lupita's reading

seems to be measuring spelling along with phonics, and that is probably why the two spelling patterns are included. Finally, there is reference to four sounds, but the key lists three sounds.

The directions here also clearly reflect a word recognition view of reading. Students are told to try each of the sounds and they "should be able to recognize the word." Many native English speakers would have trouble with a number of these words listed in isolation. English language learners would probably experience even more difficulty with this worksheet. It is not surprising that Lucero's student missed twelve words. Even if she could pronounce them, it's unlikely that she could recognize them. Following directions can also lead a student to produce the sounds of a word the student knows even though it isn't the right word. For example, Lucero's student marked *height* with an /ey/ sound. She was probably thinking of the word *hate*. In the same way, she marked *heir* with an /iy/ sound, which would produce *here* or *hear*, words she probably knew.

After Lupita completed the worksheet, Lucero asked her to read a modified version of "Lights in the Night," by Annie Dillard. Figure 6–11 shows Lupita's reading with the miscues marked. The passage contains many *ie* and *ei* words, but Lupita miscued on only two of these, one of which she corrected.

A comparison of Lupita's worksheet and her reading shows that she lacks some phonics knowledge, but she has acquired the sound-letter correspondence and it is part of her graphophonics knowledge. Despite having missed about 30 percent of the words on the worksheet, Lupita miscued on only two *ie/ei* words in the story. This lesson determined that Lupita had good control over the sound-spelling correspondences involving *ie* and *ei* even though her performance on the worksheet would have earned a low score.

Conclusion

The word recognition view of reading is based on the idea that readers must recognize words and put the meanings of words together to get to the meaning of a text. Phonics is a key for word recognition. The sociopsycholinguistic view of reading is based on the idea that readers construct meaning from text by using their background knowledge and cues from the three linguistic cueing systems. Proponents of phonics argue that phonics instruction is successful if it is explicit and systematic, and phonics has failed when it is taught unsystematically or implicitly.

Even though the terms *phonics* and *graphophonics* are often confused, they are components of very different views of reading. They differ in several ways. Phonics is conscious knowledge, but graphophonics is subconscious. Phonics is the primary source of information for identifying words, but graphophonics is one of three linguistic cueing systems. Phonics is seen as a prerequisite for reading, but graphophonics develops as students are read to and as they read. Finally, phonics can be tested independently of meaningful reading, but graphophonics can be tested only in the context of reading.

Applications

1. Clymer tested a set of phonics generalizations against the words in several reading programs. Look through a basal program or a phonics program and find several phonics generalizations that are commonly taught. Then choose a set of words, perhaps the words in the reading program used at your school. Analyze the words to see how often they follow the rules. This application could be divided up among students in a class, with each student checking a set of words against a list of generalizations the class agrees upon.

2. We describe a determining lesson in the chapter. Make up a similar lesson. Find a phonics worksheet of the type Lucero used. Then write a short passage that contains many of the words from the phonics worksheet. Have a student complete the worksheet. Then ask the student to read the passage. Record the miscues. How does the student's performance on the worksheet compare with the reading? What conclusions can you draw from this determining lesson?

3. We provided a checklist for characteristics of text that support reading (Figure 6–8). Evaluate several books using this checklist. Bring the books to class and discuss your results with classmates.

4. We listed several alphabet books in Figure 6–9. Choose a theme that you teach or that you would like to teach and find alphabet books that could support the development of that theme. Bring the list of alphabet books on the theme to class to share.

5. Smith reported on a study in which the researchers investigated the number of rules that would be necessary to account for the letter-sound correspondences in more than six thousand words. You could replicate this study on a smaller scale. To do this, choose a passage from a text that contains about one hundred different words. To select the words, begin at some point and, eliminating duplicates, take the first one hundred words. Then transcribe each word and draw a line from each phoneme to the letter or letters representing that sound in the spelling of the word as in the example in this chapter (Figure 6–2). Then transfer the results to the following chart. If students each use a different text or different parts of a text as a source of words, the results can be combined. Looking at the chart, what do you notice about the possible spellings of different phonemes? Were there some words for which it was difficult to decide how to align the sounds and the spellings?

Phonology Project: Summary of Analysis

Phoneme	Spelling	Spelling	Spelling	Spelling
stops				
p				
t				
k				
b				
d				
g				
fricatives				
f				
v				
θ				
ð				
s				
z				
š				

Phoneme	Spelling	Spelling	Spelling	Spelling
ž				
h				
affricates				
č				
ǰ				
nasals				
m				
n				
ŋ				

liquids				
l				
r				
glides				
y				
w				
vowels				
iy				

Phoneme	Spelling	Spelling	Spelling	Spelling
I				
ey				
ɛ				
æ				
ʌ				
uw				
u				
ow				
oy				
a				
ay				
aw				
ə				
ɨ				

7

English Morphology

- *How do linguists analyze words?*
- *How do new words enter a language?*

What Is a Word?

Morphology is the study of words. However, linguists find it difficult to define the term *word*. This may seem strange to anyone who can read. In most modern written languages, each word is set off from other words by a space. Even in written language, though, it is not always clear whether an item should be considered one word or two. For example, is a contraction like *isn't* a single word? Is a compound like *merry-go-round* one word or three!

When it comes to oral language, decisions about what constitutes a word become even more difficult. When linguists examine the physical speech stream, they do not find breaks between what people normally consider separate words. Consider the sentence "I should have gone." A spectrographic display of this sentence would show no breaks between the words. In addition, in casual speech, this sentence is pronounced /ay šudəv gan/. The word that is written *have* is reduced to /əv/ and attached to /šud/ to form one unit. Is *have* really a separate word here?

Like phonemes, words are perceptual units, not physical units. When people speak, they cause sound waves to travel through the air. The interpretation of speech involves perceiving these sound waves as individual words. Humans do this effortlessly in a language they have acquired, but as anyone who has listened to a foreign language realizes, it can be very difficult to pick out individual words in a new language.

The concept of word seems to be more associated with written language than spoken language. Early writers did not put spaces between what we call words. Similarly, young children don't put spaces between words even though they must perceive language as being made up of individual units in order to understand it.

166

Through exposure to written language, children begin to adopt the conventions of writing, which include putting spaces between words. These spaces make reading easier. Writingwithnospacesishardtoread. Nevertheless, it is important to recognize that the separation of written words on a page is more a convenience for readers than a reflection of a physical reality. That is one reason linguists find it difficult to define *word*.

How Words Are Formed

Another reason that linguists find it difficult to define *word* is that words can be broken down into smaller meaningful parts. These parts are called morphemes. In a word like *tree* there is just one morpheme. This word can't be divided into smaller meaningful parts. However, the word *trees* has two morphemes, *tree* and *s*. Each part of the word carries some meaning. *Tree* refers to a kind of tall plant, and *s* carries the meaning of plural.

Words like *trees* are made up of two kinds of morphemes: free morphemes and bound morphemes. *Free morphemes* are units that can stand alone as words by themselves. *Tree* is a free morpheme. *Bound morphemes* are units that must be attached or bound to a free morpheme. They cannot be written as separate words. The *s* in *trees* is a bound morpheme. Bound morphemes in English are either prefixes or suffixes. The general term *affix* refers to a prefix or a suffix. Some languages also have *infixes*, bound morphemes that are inserted into the middle of a word rather than being bound to the beginning or the end.

Affixes can be either inflectional or derivational. In English the inflectional morphemes are all suffixes. *Inflectional morphemes* add to a word without changing the part of speech. For example, an inflectional morpheme doesn't change a word from a noun to a verb or a verb to an adjective. In addition, inflectional morphemes don't change the meaning of the base word. English has only eight inflectional affixes. These include the plural *-s* and *-es* and the possessive *s* added to nouns, the *-s*, *-ing*, *-ed*, and *-en* added to verbs to show tense, such as present continuous or past, and the *-er* and *-est* added to adjectives and adverbs to show comparison.

Derivational affixes do change meaning and can be either prefixes or suffixes. When a derivational affix is added to a base word, a new word is derived. Derivational affixes may change the part of speech of the base word. For example, adding *-er* to the verb *work* produces the noun *worker*. However, not all derivational affixes change the part of speech. Adding the prefix *un-* to the verb *tie* produces another verb, *untie*. In this case, the affix *un-* changes the meaning but not the part of speech. Figure 7–1 summarizes this information about English morphology.

Free Morphemes	Bound Morphemes	
• tree	prefixes: • derivational (un-)	suffixes: • derivational (-ion) • inflectional (-s)

Figure 7–1. English morphemes

Generally speaking, derivational prefixes carry a meaning that is easier to define than those of derivational suffixes. For example, *trans-* means "across" and *un-* means "not." It is fairly easy to find a synonym for a prefix. Prefixes help readers understand the meaning of a word. If someone is *unhappy*, the person is *not happy*. Suffixes, on the other hand, tell more about the part of speech than the meaning of the word. It is hard to define a suffix like *-ion* or *-ly*. In other words, derivational prefixes and suffixes serve somewhat different functions and carry different kinds of meaning.

Both derivational and inflectional suffixes can be added to the same word. However, there is an order for these affixes when this occurs. The inflectional suffix comes last. For example, in the word *considerations*, the derivational suffix *-ion* precedes the inflectional suffix *-s*. In *worker's*, the derivational *-er* precedes the inflectional *s*.

Phonology is the study of the sounds of words. Morphology is the study of meanings. A word like *trees* has four phonemes, /t/, /r/, /iy/, and /z/, and two morphemes. There is no consistent relationship between the phonology and the morphology of a word because these are two different kinds of analyses. The long word *elephant* has only one morpheme even though it has seven phonemes.

Types of Words

English words are made up of free and bound morphemes. Words with just one free morpheme, like *tree*, are *simple words*. Words with a free morpheme and one or more bound morphemes, like *trees*, are *complex words*. Words that consist of two free morphemes, like *teacup*, are *compound words*. Figure 7–2 shows the types of words in English.

Types of Languages

Since linguists find it difficult to define *word*, it is not surprising that they also find it difficult to classify languages by the ways they combine morphemes to form words. In some languages, like Chinese, almost every word consists of just one

Simple	Complex	Compound
one free morpheme (tree, rhinoceros)	one free morpheme and one or more bound morphemes (predisposition, unwanted)	two free morphemes (hotshot, bookkeeper)

Figure 7–2. Types of English words

morpheme. Some of these are lexical morphemes that carry meaning, like *tree*, and others are grammatical morphemes that show things like plural or tense. Languages that have one morpheme per word are called *analytic*. In *analytic languages*, morphemes are not bound to one another.

Languages like Latin are classified as synthetic. *Synthetic languages* add many inflections to words. For example, in Latin *porto* is "I carry" and *portas* is "you carry." One word in Latin carries the meaning of two words in English. Spanish and French are not so heavily inflected as Latin, but they are more inflected than English. One of the difficulties linguists have in classifying languages by the way they combine morphemes is that most languages fall somewhere between the pure cases, such as purely analytic or purely synthetic.

Besides classifying languages as analytic or synthetic, linguists refer to some languages as *agglutinative* and others as *polysynthetic*. *Agglutinative languages*, like Turkish, combine many morphemes into a word. The parts are glued together. However, in this process the morphemes are not changed. In English, the plural can be *s* as in *cats*, *es* as in *bushes*, or it can involve a change like the change from *foot* to *feet*. All these variations signal plural. In an agglutinative language, the morpheme that indicates plural is always the same. It doesn't change form when it combines with other morphemes. In general, agglutinative languages have words made up of many morphemes that are combined by placing them together. The difference between a synthetic language and an agglutinative language is that in a synthetic language, morphemes may change their form.

In *polysynthetic languages*, many more inflections are added than in a synthetic language like Latin. Polysynthetic languages might be considered supersynthetic. Words are made by starting with some base and adding many affixes. Each word could be translated as a whole sentence. For polysynthetic languages, such as Navajo, a dictionary has to list morphemes, not words, because every word is made up of many morphemes and represents a whole sentence. Since there are an infinite number of possible sentences, dictionaries have to list morphemes, not words. The distinction between a word and a sentence in a language like Navajo is blurred.

Another example of a polysynthetic language is Kivunjo, a Bantu language. The Kivunjo expression *Näïkìmlyíïá* translates into the English sentence "He is eating it for her." According to Pinker (1994, pp. 127–28), this word/sentence consists of the following parts:

N   A marker indicating that this word is the focus of that point in the conversation.

ä   A subject-agreement marker. It identifies the eater as falling into Class 1 of 16 gender classes, human singular. Other classes include thin objects, animals, several humans, body parts, precise locations, and more.

ï   Present-tense marker (other tenses include today, earlier today, yesterday, no earlier than yesterday, yesterday or earlier, in the remote past, habitually, ongoing, consecutively, hypothetically, in the future, at an indeterminate time, not yet, and sometimes).

kì   An object-agreement marker indicating that the thing eaten falls into gender Class 7.

m   A benefactive marker indicating for whose benefit the action is taking place, in this case, a member of gender Class 1.

lyí   The verb "to eat."

ï   An applicative marker indicating that the verb applies an additional object ("I baked a cake" versus "I baked her a cake").

á   Tells whether this is indicative or subjunctive mood.

As this example shows, humans such as the Bantu have developed highly complex language systems. The idea that some people speak a primitive language has been dispelled by modern linguistic studies. Even though this language appears to be extremely complex, children who grow up hearing Kivunjo acquire the language just as easily as children acquire French or English.

A chapter on Kivunjo morphology would need to be a great deal longer than this chapter on English morphology. English words can contain prefixes and suffixes, but they do not carry the heavy information load a Kivunjo word carries. Further, polysynthetic languages help show why linguists find it difficult to define *word*. However, morphemes are the basic units of meaning in a language, so it is possible to describe and analyze how languages combine morphemes to produce larger units, such as words and sentences.

Types of Words and Types of Sentences

One difference between languages that are more analytic and those that are more synthetic is that analytic languages rely on the order of words to show the functions of different words in a sentence. In synthetic, polysynthetic, and agglutinative languages, on the other hand, each word carries more information, so the order of the words is less important. A good example of a language that relies on word endings to signal the functions of the different words in a sentence is Japanese. Consider the following four Japanese sentences (Farmer and Demers 1996, p. 145):

Watasi-no kodomo-ni sensei-ga sono hon-o ageta.
Sensei-ga watasi-no kodomo-ni sono hon-o ageta.
Sono hon-o sensei-ga watasi-no kodomo-ni ageta.
Sono hon-o watasi-no kodomo-ni sensei-ga ageta.

All four sentences would be translated into English as "The teacher gave that book to my child." What makes it possible for Japanese speakers or writers to express this same sentence in four different ways?

Japanese adds endings to words to indicate each word's function in the sentence. The ending *-ga* shows that the noun to which it is attached is the subject of the sentence. As long as the word for teacher, *sensei*, is marked with *-ga*, it doesn't really matter where it comes in the sentence. Wherever it is placed, the *-ga* shows it is the subject. The ending *-o* marks the direct object. In this sentence, the direct object is *hon* (book). The ending *-o* marks the word as the direct object no matter where it occurs. In addition, *-ni* marks the indirect object. In this sentence, the indirect object is "my child." Again, the word for *child* (*kodomo*) can appear anywhere because the *-ni* shows it is the indirect object.

Japanese does have a preferred sequence of words. That is, one sentence pattern is more common than the others. In addition, every sentence ends with the verb. All four of these variations end with *ageta*. Also, the words for *that* and *my* precede the nouns with which they are associated: *sono hon-o* (that book) and *watasi-no kodomo-ni* (my child). Although the position of some words in Japanese sentences is fixed, the nouns can be moved around because the word endings show how the nouns function in the sentence.

In contrast, if words are moved around in a more analytic language, like English, the meaning changes. In a sentence like "The man chased the dog," the man is the subject, the one doing the action, because *man* comes at the beginning and *dog* comes after the verb. In "The dog chased the man," *dog* is the subject because it comes first, and *man* is the object. English relies on the order of the words to signal the subject or object, not on word endings the way Japanese does. In general, languages either rely more on word endings or rely more on word order, but all languages use both endings and order to help convey meaning.

Morphology includes the study of types of morphemes and the ways morphemes are combined to form words. Morphemes make up words, but linguists find it difficult to define *word* because words are not the smallest unit of meaning, and different languages use different combinations of morphemes to form words. Words are not physical entities. However, people perceive speech as being divided into words, and they represent words as separate units in written language. Using morphological, syntactic, and semantic information, linguists can classify words into different types. This linguistic analysis contrasts with traditional approaches to studying types of words.

Traditional Approaches to Classifying Words

Most people remember identifying parts of speech. They learned that a noun is the name of a person, place, or thing and then found all the nouns on a worksheet. They learned the difference between main verbs and helping verbs. Usually, language arts texts list eight parts of speech, but sometimes there are more or fewer.

The traditional classification of words into parts of speech reflects an earlier period in history. At one time, school was conducted in Latin. When English became the language of instruction, many teachers suddenly had nothing to teach. The children already knew English, so they didn't need to be taught the language of school.

Even though children knew English, they didn't know English grammar. Schools for young children were called grammar schools because that is where grammar was taught. The teachers of English grammar were not linguists; they were former Latin teachers. As a result, they attempted to apply Latin categories to the English language. Many grammar rules reflect the influence of Latin. For example, the rule that English sentences should not end with a preposition is based on the fact that Latin does not have prepositions at the end of sentences.

In addition, Latin categories were applied to the classification of English words. Even though English has many words with Latin roots, English is a Germanic language, and trying to make English words fit Latin categories is not easy. The definitions for parts of speech found in grammar books are not good examples of scientific classification. For example, nouns are defined by what they are: names of people, places, or things. Adjectives are usually defined by what they do: modify a noun. Conjunctions join parts of sentences. Each part of speech is defined in a somewhat different way, and, as a result, students have trouble figuring out how to classify words.

In earlier times, many teachers taught English grammar simply because school was no longer conducted in Latin. Often, teachers argued that studying grammar was good mental discipline. At that time the mind was regarded as a kind of mental muscle that needed exercise to grow. Students spent hours learning or trying to learn the rules of English grammar, including the parts of speech.

Knowing the parts of speech doesn't turn a student into a better reader or writer. Weaver (1996) summarizes a number of studies, and all of them show that there is no transfer from the study of traditional grammar to improved literacy skills. This is bad news for those of us who are linguists and love grammar. Yet, it confirms views of reading and second language acquisition that claim that both oral and written language are acquired, not learned. Grammar rules, no matter how well they are learned, are difficult to apply when speaking or writing.

Despite the scientific evidence that the study of grammar does not improve reading and writing skills, schools still follow the Latin tradition and teach and test grammar. Students are expected to know whether a word is a noun or a verb. Memorizing definitions of parts of speech doesn't seem to help students. Fortunately, some creative children's authors have written books that can help children acquire many of the terms of traditional grammar. They have produced colorful, interesting books that contain many of the labels children are expected to master (see Figure 7–3).

Ruth Heller has written a series of books, one for each of the traditional parts of speech. One of her first books was *A Cache of Jewels and Other Collective Nouns* (1987). Like all her books, this one includes beautiful illustrations and catchy, rhyming language. Heller includes many collective nouns, such as *an army of ants* and *a bevy of beauties*. Young readers often remember long passages because of the rhyme. For example, the book begins, "A word that means a collection of things, like a cache of jewels for the crowns of kings . . . or a batch of bread all warm and brown, is always called a collective noun." Heller ends this first book on parts of speech with these lines:

> But nouns aren't all collective,
> and if I'm to be effective,
> I'll tell about the other nouns
> and adjectives and verbs.
> All of them are parts of speech.
> What fun!
> I'll write a book for each.

True to her word, Heller has gone on to write a book about each part of speech. *Many Luscious Lollipops* (1989) is a book about adjectives, and *Kites Sail High* (1988) is a book about verbs. Each book includes terms students are expected to know. For example, the book about adjectives includes articles, demonstratives, and proper adjectives. The book about verbs has pages on tense, mood,

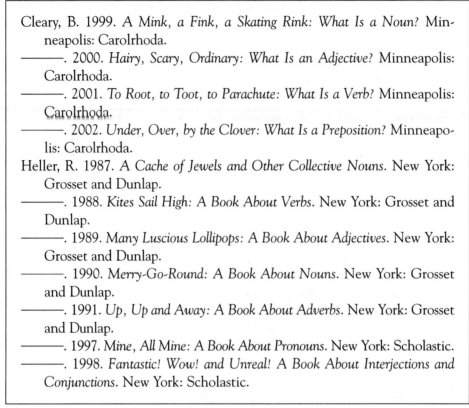

Cleary, B. 1999. *A Mink, a Fink, a Skating Rink: What Is a Noun?* Minneapolis: Carolrhoda.

———. 2000. *Hairy, Scary, Ordinary: What Is an Adjective?* Minneapolis: Carolrhoda.

———. 2001. *To Root, to Toot, to Parachute: What Is a Verb?* Minneapolis: Carolrhoda.

———. 2002. *Under, Over, by the Clover: What Is a Preposition?* Minneapolis: Carolrhoda.

Heller, R. 1987. *A Cache of Jewels and Other Collective Nouns.* New York: Grosset and Dunlap.

———. 1988. *Kites Sail High: A Book About Verbs.* New York: Grosset and Dunlap.

———. 1989. *Many Luscious Lollipops: A Book About Adjectives.* New York: Grosset and Dunlap.

———. 1990. *Merry-Go-Round: A Book About Nouns.* New York: Grosset and Dunlap.

———. 1991. *Up, Up and Away: A Book About Adverbs.* New York: Grosset and Dunlap.

———. 1997. *Mine, All Mine: A Book About Pronouns.* New York: Scholastic.

———. 1998. *Fantastic! Wow! and Unreal! A Book About Interjections and Conjunctions.* New York: Scholastic.

Figure 7–3. Children's books about parts of speech

and auxiliary verbs. The book about adverbs points out that adverbs of place always precede adverbs of time. As Heller writes:

> Before an adverb answers "When?"
> it always answers "Where?"
> This ship will sail AWAY TODAY
> It will not sail TODAY AWAY

Lines like these give both native speakers and English learners important insights into how English works.

One fifth-grade teacher reported his students' scores on a standardized language test went up dramatically after he read these books and then left them out for students to read. Students can also try to compose their own books about the parts of speech following Heller's model.

Another writer who has produced a series of books on the parts of speech is Brian Cleary. These books with cartoonlike illustrations and simple rhymes are especially appealing to young children. For example, one book is *Under, Over, by the Clover: What Is a Preposition?* (2002). This book begins, "Prepositions tell us where, like in your bed, beside the chair." Each phrase is accompanied by a colorful illustration that shows the meaning of the preposition. These books would be wonderful for English learners.

Cleary has written other books as well, including books about adjectives, nouns, and verbs. Each book follows a similar pattern. The title asks, "What is a verb (or noun or adjective)?" and the text answers the question by providing many rhyming examples. The book on verbs, for instance, is titled *To Root, to Toot, to Parachute*. It is filled with verbs: "Verbs are words like sing and dance, pray or practice, preach or prance." Cleary includes a number of unusual words that pique student interest. Figure 7–3 lists books written by Heller and Cleary. These books come in hardback or inexpensive paperback form.

Current Approaches to Classifying Words

Even though traditional, Latin-based grammar does not constitute a good scientific method for classifying words, it provides the vocabulary students need to discuss and analyze language. Without some terms like *noun* and *verb*, it would be almost impossible to talk about the kinds of words in a language. Linguists have attempted to refine the definitions of these terms, and they have added additional terms to describe English and other languages.

To classify words, linguists rely to some extent on the meanings of words. This semantic knowledge is what people use when they define a noun as a person, place, or thing, or a verb as a word that shows action. All languages seem to have words that function like nouns and other words that serve as verbs. Humans describe their world by naming objects and actions, and these categories may be part of Universal Grammar. In addition, languages have ways to modify both nouns and verbs. Adjectives serve to describe people, places, and things while adverbs provide extra information about actions. A first step in classifying a word is to use this semantic information. Additional evidence from syntax and morphology can then be used to confirm the category for the word.

Syntactic evidence comes from the position or role of the word in the sentence. Here is a sentence that follows the general pattern or word order:

The hungry linguist quickly ate a delicious sandwich before class.

Linguist comes near the beginning of the sentence and serves as the subject. Words in subject position are usually nouns or pronouns. *Ate* serves as the predicate of this sentence: it names the action. Words that serve as predicates are verbs. *Sandwich* follows the predicate and serves as the direct object of the sentence. *Class* comes after the preposition *before* and is the object of the preposition. Words like these that serve as objects are usually nouns. *Hungry* and *delicious* precede and describe nouns. Words that precede nouns are usually adjectives. *Quickly* precedes the predicate and describes the action. Words like *quickly* are adverbs. Adverbs can occur in many different positions in a sentence, but they usually come near the predicate. The position of these words in the sentence and the roles they play provide syntactic evidence for the part of speech of each.

Morphological evidence can also be used to help classify words. Both inflectional and derivational suffixes provide clues about parts of speech. For example, it is possible to add the inflectional suffix *-s* or *-es* to a noun to make it plural. This inflectional morpheme can be added only to nouns. Thus, words like *linguists* and

Part of speech	can add these inflectional suffixes	can add these derivational suffixes
noun	*-s* or *-es* (plural): *trees, bushes* *'s* (possessive): *animal's*	commence*ment* preven*tion* neat*ness* clar*ity* depend*ence* farm*er* parachut*ist*
verb	*-s* (third-person singular): He walks. *-ing* (progressive): He is walking. *-ed* (past): He walked. *-en* (past participle): He has driven.	class*ify* character*ize* evalu*ate*
adjective adverb	*-er* (comparative): *bigger/faster* *est* (superlative): *biggest/fastest*	mischiev*ous* color*ful* fest*ive* reg*al* flex*ible* quick*ly* (adverb)

Figure 7–4. Morphological evidence for parts of speech

sandwiches are probably nouns. The derivational suffix *-ly* is added to adjectives in English to make them adverbs. The *-ly* ending signals that a word like *quickly* is an adverb. Figure 7–4 lists morphological evidence that can be used to confirm that a word fits into a certain category.

Evidence from semantics, syntax, and morphology all need to be considered to determine the classification of a word because many English words can be nouns, verbs, or adjectives, depending on the sentence. For example, *table* functions as a noun in "That is a table," as a verb in "He tabled the motion," and as an adjective in "He has poor table manners."

Content words and function words   The kinds of words listed in Figure 7–4 are what linguists refer to as *content words*. These are the words that carry the main meanings in sentences. When people write a telegram, they use primarily the content words. Content words are also referred to as *open-class words*, because new words that come into English through processes like borrowing are always content words. English has four types of content words: nouns, verbs, adjectives, and adverbs.

English also has a second group of words, called *function words*. Function words serve a variety of purposes. They include determiners, quantifiers, pronouns, auxiliaries, prepositions, conjunctions, intensifiers, and particles. Some of these terms, like *preposition* and *conjunction*, are familiar. Others, like *determiners* and *intensifiers*, may be new. Figure 7–5 lists examples of some of the kinds of function words.

Determiners and quantifiers are words that precede nouns. In English every singular common noun has to be preceded by a determiner or a quantifier. An

Type	Example	Example	Example
determiners	the	this	my
quantifiers	one	every	several
pronouns	you	yourself	who
auxiliaries	is	has	might
prepositions	in	before	of
conjunctions	and	if	however
particles	up	down	around
intensifiers	rather	very	so

Figure 7–5. Types of function words

English sentence like "He bought book" doesn't sound right because it lacks a determiner or a quantifier. English speakers say, "He bought that book," or "He bought two books." There are three kinds of determiners: articles like *a*, *an*, and *the*, demonstratives like *this* and *these*, and possessives like *my* and *their*. In traditional grammar, determiners are often classified as adjectives, but they signal that a noun is coming rather than describing the noun. Content adjectives, like *green*, can take *-er* or *-est*, but these inflectional endings cannot be added to function words like determiners. Quantifiers serve much the same purpose as determiners. The difference is that they specify an amount or quantity.

Pronouns are words that are used in place of noun phrases. Pronouns replace whole phrases, not just nouns. The pronoun *her* can replace several words, not just the noun, in the sentence "I saw the sweet, elderly woman who lives down the street." A speaker would say, "I saw her," not "I saw the sweet, elderly her who lives down the street." Pronouns are considered function words because they do not carry meaning by themselves. Instead, they take their meaning from the nouns they refer to. Pronouns provide a shorthand way of referring to a series of words. There are different kinds of pronouns, including personal pronouns (*I*, *my*), indefinite pronouns (*someone*, *anything*), reflexive pronouns (*myself*, *yourself*), reciprocal pronouns (*each other*, *one another*), interrogative pronouns (*who*, *where*), possessive pronouns (*mine*, *his*), and relative pronouns (*who*, *which*).

Auxiliaries are often referred to as *helping verbs*. They are words that tell more about the tense or aspect of a verb. This group includes modal auxiliaries like *can* and *would* as well as words like *be* and *have*. English has a complex verb system. Speakers can add inflections to verbs and also use auxiliaries to express shades of meaning. "I should have been asked to go" includes three auxiliaries and the inflection *-ed* on the verb *ask*. English learners often find it difficult to master the verb system. Not only can English verb phrases contain several auxiliaries, but they occur in a fixed order. For example, a speaker would not say, "I been have should asked to go." The knowledge of the order of auxiliary verbs is acquired, not learned. It is too complex to teach and learn.

Prepositions often show place or time relationships. In "The pen is on the table," the preposition *on* shows the relationship in space between the pen and the table. In "I left after the dance," the preposition *after* shows the time relationship between the dance and the leaving. Words like *of* and *with* are also prepositions. Conjunctions also show relationships. For example, in "I read the book, and I ate dinner" the conjunction *and* connects two complete ideas. In "He ran and jumped," the conjunction joins the two verbs.

Two other kinds of function words are particles and intensifiers. Particles are little words added to verbs to make two- or three-word verbs, sometimes called *phrasal verbs*. For example, in "He ran up a big bill," the particle *up* is part of the verb phrase *ran up*. Together, the two words have a meaning that is different from a combination of the meanings of *run* and *up*. Someone who runs up a bill may do no physical exercise. The phrase means something like "charged" or "created." This *up* is not a preposition like the *up* in "He ran up a big hill." In this second sentence, *up* shows where he ran, and *up a big hill* is a prepositional phrase. Two-word verbs are very common in English. However, since the meaning has little to do with the individual meanings of the parts, English learners are often confused by two-word verbs. The problem is compounded by the fact that different particles are used in different languages. In English, a person can say, "He is married to her," while in Spanish the sentence would be "He is married with her." Finally, intensifiers are words like *very* and *somewhat* used to qualify an expression, making it stronger (He is very happy) or weaker (He is somewhat happy).

Function words provide the grammatical connections among the content words. Function words are also referred to as *closed-class words* because languages don't add new words in these categories. Generally, languages have all the conjunctions, prepositions, and so on that are needed. Even when a new function word would be useful, speakers have great difficulty accepting it. For example, in English, third-person pronouns show gender: *he, she, it*. Writing conventions require writers to avoid sexist language. In the past, *his* in a sentence like "A student should do his best work" could refer to a male or a female student. The masculine term was considered to include both males and females. However, current usage would require a writer to say, "A student should do his or her best work." The use of *his or her* seems awkward, so various alternatives have been proposed, such as *his/her* and *s/he*, but none of these alternatives has caught on. The failure to accept any word as a candidate for a new pronoun reflects the fact that pronouns, like other function words, form a closed class, and no new words are added, even when it would seem useful to do so.

Although some categories of words form closed classes, other categories are open, and new words are added to English all the time. Dictionaries keep expanding. In fact, English has one of the largest vocabularies of any of the world's languages. Words enter English in a variety of ways.

How New Words Enter a Language

"Mrs. Granger, you have so many dictionaries in this room, and that huge one especially . . . where did all those words come from?" (p. 15). Nick, the main character in Andrew Clements' delightful book, *Frindle* (1996), asks this seemingly innocent question near the end of seventh period. Nick's question is a classic example of communication that has both a direct and an indirect intent. On the surface, this seems like a straightforward question asked of a teacher who loves dictionaries. However, the real purpose of Nick's question is to sidetrack his teacher, to get her talking about dictionaries, so that she won't assign any homework.

"Several kids smiled, and a few peeked at the clock. Nick was famous for doing this, and the whole class knew what he was doing . . . Unfortunately, so did Mrs. Granger" (p. 15). Not only does Nick's ploy fail, but Mrs. Granger assigns Nick an oral report on where words come from, due the very next day. Nick gives a good report, but at the end, he asks, this time really wanting to know the answer, "I still don't really get the idea of why words all mean different things. Like, who says that d-o-g means the thing that goes 'woof' and wags its tail? Who says so?" (p. 29). Mrs. Granger's answer surprises Nick: "Who says *dog* means dog? You do, Nicholas. You and me and everyone in this class and this school and this town and this state and this country. We all agree" (p. 29).

Mrs. Granger's answer gets Nick thinking, and when his friend Janet finds a gold pen, Nick decides to act. This creative fifth grader begins calling the thing his friend found a frindle. Not only does Nick call pens frindles, but he persuades his friends to go along with his plan. If people call the thing they use to write a pen just because everyone agrees to call it a pen, then that could change if everyone started to call it something else. Nick has his friends sign an oath, "From this day on and forever, I will never use the word *PEN* again. Instead, I will use the word *FRINDLE*, and I will do everything possible so others will too" (p. 38).

The oath launches Nick's campaign to bring a new word into English. Clements' account of Nick's adventures and his battles with Mrs. Granger make wonderful reading for students in the fourth grade and higher, but the story also makes a serious point about words. The association between a word and an object is arbitrary. It is a social convention. English speakers call the writing instrument a pen simply because that is what others call it. There is no physical or logical connection between words and things, between sounds and meanings.

Frindle is an excellent book that teachers can use to lead students into an investigation of how words enter a language. Some words do enter the way *frindle* does in the story. Someone makes up a name for an object, and the name sticks. This process is called *coining*. But words enter a language in a number of ways. These include compounding, clipping, creating acronyms, blending, back-formation, and borrowing (Andrews 2001).

Usually, people coin words to label new inventions or products, not to rename existing objects the way Nick did. Many of these words start as proper nouns and then become common nouns. For example, *kleenex* began as *Kleenex*, but now the word applies to almost any brand of facial tissue. *Coke* is another example. People now use the term to apply to almost any soft drink. Many of the new words that have entered English are related to computers. Some of these, like *mouse* and

Noun + Noun	Adj. + Noun	Prep. + Prep.	Adv. + Verb	Noun + Verb
cupboard	highchair	into	downfall	sunshine
teacup	hotshot	throughout	upturn	headache

Figure 7–6. Compounds

desktop, assign new meanings to existing words. Pinker (1994) lists words like *ambimoustrous* and *depediate* as examples of words that appeared in a dictionary of computer terms. A person who is ambimoustrous can use a mouse with either hand, and if the printer cuts off the bottom of a page, it depediates it (takes away its foot). Many computer terms like these are short-lived, but others have entered the language permanently.

Earlier we discussed how compounds are formed by joining two free morphemes. English has many compound words, like *teacup* and *cupboard*. Some of these are written as one word. Other compounds, like *merry-go-round* and *son-in-law*, are hyphenated. Still others, like *sports car* and *grocery store*, are written as two words. This variation in spacing reveals an ambiguity. Dictionaries are not consistent in recording the preferred spellings of compounds. Although English spelling of compounds is not consistent, many new words are created by joining existing words. Almost any part of speech can be joined with almost any other part. Figure 7–6 lists several examples of compounds. The list could easily be expanded.

Compounds are easily confused with noun phrases consisting of an adjective and a noun. For example, the words *high* and *chair* can be combined to refer to a child's seat or a seat that is tall. Usually, a highchair is a seat for a baby, and a high chair is an unusually tall chair. The compound *highchair* is pronounced with the stress on the adjective, *high*, and the noun phrase *high chair* is pronounced with stress on the noun, *chair*. Words like *toothbrush* and *haircut* must be compounds, not noun phrases, because people brush more than one tooth and cut more than one hair. The usual rules for plural are suspended in a compound.

Both clippings and acronyms are abbreviated forms of words. Clipping occurs when a word is shortened. *Mathematics* becomes *math* and *gasoline* becomes *gas*. Some names of college courses are clipped. *Economy* may be referred to as *econ* and *educational psychology* as *ed psych*. Both *cab* and *taxi* are clipped forms of *taxicab*.

Acronyms are words made up of the first letters of several words. *Acro* is Greek for "high," so acronyms are "high names," names made up of the tall (capital) first letters. Some acronyms, like *scuba* (self-contained underwater breathing apparatus), are pronounced as words. In other cases, like *VIP*, each letter name is pronounced. This is usually the case for colleges and universities. People say each letter of *UCLA*. They don't pronounce it /yuwklə/. Part of learning a new field of study is learning the acronyms. Students of second language acquisition learn about LEP and FEP students, BICS and CALP, L2 and SLA. All these acronyms may make students feel as though they are studying a foreign language.

A few words in English are blends created by combining two words. Examples are *brunch* (*breakfast* + *lunch*), *smog* (*smoke* + *fog*), and motel (*motor* + *hotel*). A newer blend is *spork*, that utensil cafeterias pass out when they can't decide whether to give students a spoon or a fork. The writer Lewis Carroll created a number of blends, like *slithy* and *chortled*, in his poem at the end of *Through the Looking Glass* (1981).

Back-formation is a process that has resulted in many new words being added to English. At one time, English had the nouns *peddler* and *beggar* but did not have the verbs *peddle* and *beg*. However, English has many pairs like *teacher* and *teach* and *worker* and *work*. These pairs were formed by adding *-er* to the verb to make a noun. Even though there was no verb *peddle* or *beg*, people assumed that *peddler* must have been formed from *peddle* and *beggar* must have been formed from *beg*. When they created *peddle* and *beg*, they followed the usual rule, but in reverse. Rather than going from the verb to the noun (*teach* → *teacher*), they went from the noun to the verb (*peddler* → *peddle*). That is why the process is called back-formation.

English speakers regularly create verbs from nouns using back-formation. Often, this simply involves using the same word for both parts of speech without changing the ending. Almost any noun in English can become a verb through this process. For example, someone can *head* a committee, *table* a motion, and *email* a friend. Recently we were told to *expense* an organization. Maybe *expense* will replace *bill*, another word produced by back-formation.

Even though they are spelled the same, many two-syllable words are pronounced differently depending on whether they function as nouns or verbs. For example, *permit* with the stress on the first syllable is a noun. Shift the stress to the last syllable and it becomes a verb. This is the general pattern. Nouns like *convict* and *subject* change into verbs when the stress shifts to the second syllable.

Many English words were borrowed from other languages. The term *borrow* is probably not accurate. The process is closer to plagiarism. English gets a word like *boutique* from French. However, the French still have the word. Now English speakers have it, too. Both groups claim ownership. So this isn't the usual process people think of as borrowing. Nevertheless, this is the term linguists use. In some cases, the spelling of the borrowed word is changed to reflect the English spelling pattern. *Duet* is the English spelling of the Italian word *duetto*.

Because English has borrowed words from many different languages, the English vocabulary is very large. Sometimes it is difficult to know where a word came from. The word *yen* started out as a Chinese word and then was borrowed into

Chinese	Greek	Dutch	Persian	Italian
tea	acme	golf	lilac	granite
yen	acrobat	brandy	jasmine	piano
chow	tantalize	yacht	paradise	duet
Spanish	**German**	**French**	**African**	**American Indian**
cargo	frankfurter	dime	chigger	skunk
mosquito	sauerkraut	cent	okra	moose
alligator	hamburger	prairie	yam	chipmunk
Polynesian	**Japanese**	**Russian**	**Australian**	**Yiddish**
taboo	kimono	ruble	kangaroo	bagel
tattoo	tycoon	vodka	boomerang	kosher
Slavic	**Malay**	**Bengali**	**Turkish**	**Bantu**
vampire	amuck	bungalow	yogurt	zebra

Figure 7–7. Borrowed words

Japanese. Eventually, it became an English word. Did English borrow *yen* from Chinese or Japanese? The answer is often not clear. Figure 7–7 lists the origins of a number of English words.

The labels African and American Indian include words that could have come from a number of different languages. Figure 7–7 is just a small sample of the many words that have been borrowed into English.

Word Formation Rules

Even though the processes described in the preceding section account for many of the new words that enter English every year, one of the richest sources of new words is the morphological process of derivation. Many English words are formed by combining a free morpheme with a derivational affix. Earlier we explained that *teacher* is derived by adding *-er* to the verb *teach*. This is an example of a general pattern. When the suffix *-er* is added to a verb, a new noun is created. English has many *-er* words—*preacher*, *baker*, and *singer*, to name just three.

Base Word	Derivational Affix	Sound Change	Category Change	Meaning Change
teach	er	add /ər/	verb to noun	one who teaches

Figure 7–8. Word formation rule for *-er* suffix

Words like *teacher* are formed by a process that includes a change in sound, in part of speech, or category, and in meaning. Each word that is formed following this pattern undergoes the same sound change, the same category change, and the same meaning change. Figure 7–8 shows the pattern for the formation of *-er* words like *teacher*.

Linguists refer to patterns like these as *word formation rules*. These rules are descriptions of regular processes in the language. Every word that follows this rule undergoes the same sound change (add /ər/), the same category change (verb to noun), and the same meaning change. Linguists express the meaning change generally for this rule as "one who Xes." The X represents the meaning of the verb. So a teacher is one who teaches, and a singer is one who sings. Word formation rules like this help people figure out new words. For example, a reader might assume that the nonsense word *glarker* must refer to a person who *glarks*, whatever that is.

New words follow the pattern. A xeroxer is a person who makes copies, and an emailer is probably someone who sends many emails. This is a very productive rule because it applies to many verbs in English. However, the rule is blocked when a noun meaning "someone who Xes" is already associated with a verb. For example, a cooker is not a person who cooks and a sailer is not someone who sails. Since English has the nouns *cook* and *sailor*, the word formation rule cannot be applied. What is interesting is that people assign new meanings to words like *cooker* and *sailer*. A cooker is probably a cooking utensil, not a person, and a sailer might be a Frisbee throw or a baseball pitch that catches some wind, as a thing that sails.

Adding a derivational suffix like *-er* usually results in a word with a different part of speech than the base word. To take a second, very productive word formation rule, *-ly* can be added to adjectives to form adverbs. Thus, English has words like *quickly*, *slowly*, and *laboriously*. The *-ly* suffix can be added to many different adjectives. In each case, the pattern is the same. The sound change is the addition of /liy/, the category change is from adjective to adverb, and the meaning of the new word is "in an X manner." If someone does something quickly, she does it in a quick manner. When a reader encounters a new word, like the nonsense word *trebly*, he can assume that this must mean in a treb manner. People can

Base Word	Derivational Affix	Sound Change	Category Change	Meaning Change
happy	un	add /ən/	adjective to adjective	not happy

Figure 7–9. Word formation rule for *un-* prefix

determine the probable meaning of the new word by analogy with other words that follow the same pattern.

Not all *-ly* words are the result of this word formation rule. For example, *homely* does not mean "in a home manner." The reason *homely* doesn't fit this rule is that *home* is a noun. The same is true of *friendly*. These words result from a different word formation rule, one in which *-ly* is added to nouns like *friend* and *home* to create adjectives. The sound change is the same, but the category and meaning changes are different.

New words can also be derived by adding prefixes to base words. For example, *un-* can be added to adjectives to form words like *unhappy* and *unusual*. Figure 7–9 shows the pattern for this word formation rule.

Prefixes don't change the part of speech of a word. Although linguists refer to a category change, there is no change with a prefix. The rule simply lists the base as an adjective and the derived word as an adjective. The meaning change could be expressed simply as "not X." This would account for any word formed by this rule.

English contains some *un-* words, like *uncouth*, that at first appear to have been formed by this rule. However, although the word *uncouth* occurs fairly often, the base word *couth* is much less common. It would seem odd to many people to be referred to as *couth* (although it would be a positive remark). In the same way, the word *unkempt* occurs more frequently than *kempt*. If a colleague remarked that he was pleased that his formerly disheveled friend now looked *kempt*, I would have to stop and think about what that meant.

The words *couth* and *kempt* both appear in dictionaries. It may be that they are the result of backformation in the same way that *peddlar* and *beggar* are. That is, the language may have had *uncouth* and *unkempt* first and then, by analogy, people formed the words *couth* and *kempt*. Or these words may have been formed by the usual word formation rule for adding the *un-* prefix. Only a historical analysis could determine the processs.

In other cases, only the negative has entered the language. Your remarks can be *uncalled for* but it would seem strange to say, "I found his remarks to be called for." English has a number of words that express the negative for which there is no positive alternative. Someone can be disconsolate, but not consolate. A speech can be impromptu, but not promptu. And a person can be nonchalant, but not chalant. These gaps reflect the fact that the lexicon of a language is not completely regular. For this reason, linguists find it difficult to develop a theory of morphology that applies consistently to all the words that make up the lexicon.

Words like *untie* follow a different rule than words like *unhappy*, even though the same prefix is involved. In this case, the *un-* has been added to a verb. Although the sound change is the same, the category would be expressed as verb to verb. In other words, this rule starts with verbs and creates new verbs. The meaning change is also different. To untie one's shoes is not the same as to not tie one's shoes. Added to verbs, *un-* has a meaning something like "to reverse the action of X." It is possible to *undo* only some action that was completed previously. Thus, a person can *unlock* or *unwind*. Some actions don't seem to be reversible. We don't *unplay* a game or *unwrite* a paper. The word used to describe reversible actions is *irreversible*, not *unreversible*. More than one prefix can be used to express the negative meaning.

Word formation rules account for many of the words in the lexicon of English. Speakers of English create these words by analogy with known words. People also understand many new words by analogy. If someone knows what the nonsense verb *braf* means, she knows that a brafer must be a person who brafs. Knowing one word can open up the meanings of many other words formed by adding derivational affixes.

A problem with word formation rules is that there are often different derivational affixes that can be used to achieve the same effect, just as *un-* and *ir-* can both signify the negative. A colleague recently used the word *humbleness* to describe a quality of a mutual friend. We understood what he meant, but English already has the word *humility*, so the rule for forming new words by adding *-ness* to the base does not work for *humble*. Despite these problems, word formation rules are used by many speakers of a language to create and understand new words.

Conclusion

Morphology is the study of words. A morpheme is the smallest meaningful unit or part of a word. Words are made up of free and bound morphemes. Linguists analyze words by their structure. Simple words have one free morpheme. Complex words combine free and bound morphemes. Compound words consist of two or more free morphemes.

Languages differ in the kinds of words they contain. English has only a limited number of inflectional affixes, so it is considered more of an analytic language than a synthetic language. Like other analytic languages, English relies more on the order of words in a sentence than on word endings to signal the role of each word in the sentence.

Traditional methods of classifying words are not scientifically based, but morphological information can be used, along with syntactic and semantic information, to determine whether a word is a certain type of content word, such as a noun or a verb. English also contains many types of function words.

Words enter a language in a number of ways. Some are coined and others are borrowed. Many new words are formed by adding derivational affixes to roots. These word formation rules follow regular patterns. English has a large vocabulary because English borrows words regularly and because many new words are created through word formation rules.

Applications

1. Although about 60 percent of the words in an English dictionary have Latin or Greek roots, many words in a text are function words or simple content words. Take a passage of one hundred consecutive words. Working in pairs, classify each word by placing it on a chart similar to the one that follows. All the function words go in the rightmost column. If a word is repeated, list it each time it appears. An example of each type of word is shown in the sample chart to help you get started.

	Simple	**Complex**	**Compound**	**Function**
Nouns	boy	boys	toothbrush	the
				through
Verbs	go	prioritize		
Adjectives	green	unsatisfactory		
Adverbs	fast	slowly		

Now analyze your results by answering the following questions:

What percent of the words are function words?
What percent are simple words?
What percent are complex words with inflectional suffixes?
What percent are complex words with derivational suffixes?
What percent are compound words?

If each pair of students takes a different passage, the class results will provide a good sample of what students typically read. The class members could discuss their findings. What percent of words in running text have meanings that can be determined by structural analysis? That is, how many of these words are compound words or complex words with derivational affixes?

2. Two-word verbs like *run across* in the sentence "I ran across an old friend" can be difficult for English learners. Many English verbs combine with the particle *up* to form a two-word verb. List at least one hundred *up* words. Be careful to distinguish between cases when *up* is a particle (He ran up a big bill) and when it is a preposition (He ran up a big hill). Two-word verbs have a meaning that is different from the meanings of the individual parts. To *look up* a word has nothing to do with the direction *up*. Create a composite *up* chart and add words over time. It is easier to come up with *up* words than you may realize.

3. Word formation rules are general patterns that follow the same sound change, category change, and meaning change. Following the examples in this chapter, investigate a word formation rule. You might use a prefix like *de-* or *trans-* or a suffix like *-ize* or *-ity*. Collect several words that follow this pattern and then describe the sound change, category change, and meaning change. Try to find additional words that appear to fit the pattern but are not the same as the other words in some way.

8

Implications from Morphology for Teaching Reading and Teaching a Second Language

- *How do readers make use of their knowledge of word parts as they read?*
- *What is the best way to increase vocabulary?*
- *What does it mean to know a word?*
- *How can teachers help English learners acquire academic vocabulary?*

Reading and Morphology

Insights from linguistic studies of morphology can inform reading instruction. In Chapter 2 we introduced two views of reading. Two differences between the word recognition view and the sociopsycholinguistic view relate specifically to morphology. These are differences in knowledge of parts of words and differences in teaching of vocabulary.

Teachers who adopt a word recognition view of reading encourage students to use phonics to help them identify words. Some words, like *of* and *one*, do not follow phonics rules, and they are taught as sight words. It is difficult to apply phonics rules for longer words, but these words can sometimes be identified by looking for the meaningful parts, or morphemes, that make up the words. This process is referred to as *structural analysis* and is often explained to students as looking for the little words inside the big words. Knowledge of morphology can help teachers evaluate the usefulness of using structural analysis for word recognition.

Teachers who take a sociopsycholinguistic view engage students in structural analysis in the process of studying language from a scientific, linguistic perspective. Students might try to develop word formation rules like the rule for *-er* or the rule for *un-* described in Chapter 7. In the process, students may learn new vocabulary and gain insights into how language works. They may even apply some of this knowledge as they read. However, the focus is on learning about language, not on using structural analysis to figure out new words.

Difficulties in Applying Structural Analysis During Reading

The writers of *Put Reading First* (Armbruster and Osborn 2001) state, "Knowing some common prefixes and suffixes (affixes), base words, and root words can help students learn the meanings of many new words" (p. 38). Students can figure out the meaning of a word like *transportation* if they recognize that this word is made up of a prefix, a root, and a suffix, and if they know that *port* means "to carry," *trans-* means "across," and *-ion* means "state or condition of." Thus, *transportation* means something like "the state of carrying across."

The *Put Reading First* authors also comment that "learning suffixes can be more challenging than learning prefixes. This is because some suffixes have more abstract meanings than do prefixes" (p. 38). As we discussed earlier, many derivational suffixes signal the part of speech of a word. The suffix *-ion* attaches to verbs to create nouns. Knowing that a word is a noun can help a reader make sense of a sentence, but it may not provide a strong clue for the meaning of a particular word. In general, it is difficult to define a suffix. Even though we can define *-ion* as a "state or condition," that definition is not too helpful in determing the meaning of a word like *transportation*.

There are several other difficulties in using knowledge of word parts to recognize words. These include recognizing the parts in words, learning the meanings of the word parts, and combining the meanings of the parts to discover the meaning of a word. Knowledge of word parts may be helpful during a vocabulary test. Knowing that *port* means "carry," for example, could help a student pick the right synonym out of a list of four answers. But this knowledge is more difficult to apply during the reading of connected text.

Recognizing word parts   In some cases, it is fairly easy to divide a word into its meaningful parts, or morphemes. For example, a word like *transportation* has three morphemes that might give someone clues to the meaning of the whole word. The root is *port*, the prefix is *trans-*, and the suffix is *-ion*. These three parts are fairly easy to recognize. However, it is not always so easy to recognize word parts.

At times, big words contain little words, but the little words aren't actually meaningful morphemes. For example, students might notice the word *hot* in the word *hotel*. In this case, the little word offers no clue to the meaning of the longer word. Since *hotel* has only one morpheme, there are no smaller meaningful parts that can be used as clues to word meaning. Or, to take another example, a student could spot *quit* in the word *mosquito*, but this is just a coincidence. There is no relationship between the meanings of *mosquito* and *quit*.

Sometimes, words are made up of meaningful parts, but it is difficult to decide which part of the word is a prefix and which part is the root. For example, the word *cognate* is made up of the prefix *co-*, which means "with," and the root *gnatus*, meaning "to be born." Cognates are words like *comply* and *reply* that come from the same root, or are "born together." However, if a student doesn't know the meaning of *cognate* and is trying to use structural analysis to figure out the meaning, there would be other ways to divide this word. One common root is *cogn*, meaning "to know," and the suffix *-ate*, meaning "to make." Thus, *cognate* could mean "to make known." The student might know a word like *recognize* and assume that *recognize* and *cognate* are related in meaning. However, the words have different roots. The root of *cognate* is *gnatus* and the root of *recognize* is *cogn*.

The word *cognate* illustrates a second problem in recognizing word parts. The prefix is *co-*, meaning "with." However, this prefix is difficult to identify because the word is pronounced /kag neyt/, not /kow neyt/. The *g* attaches to the first syllable and is pronounced as /g/ rather than being seen as part of the second syllable, where it would be silent, like the *g* in *gnaw*. This is a case where the phonology and the morphology don't match. Part of the root is pronounced as part of the prefix.

In addition, this prefix, like many other prefixes in English, changes its spelling depending on the first sound in the root word. The prefix *con-* may be spelled *co-*, *con-*, *com-*, *col-*, or *cor-*. Usually, *co-* occurs when the root starts with a vowel, as in *coauthor* and *coexist*. *Con-* is the most common spelling of the prefix, but it changes to *com-* usually when the root begins with a bilabial, as in *commingle*, *combine*, and *comport*. However, it also changes to *com-* in a word like *comfort*. When the root starts with *l*, the prefix changes to *col-*, as in *collate* and *colleague*. Finally, the prefix changes to *cor-* before roots starting with *r*, as in *correct* and *correlate*.

These variations in spelling make it difficult for students to recognize the prefix as the one they studied. On the other hand, students undertaking a linguistic investigation could come to understand these variations as examples of a common process of assimilation that occurs frequently in all languages. The final sound of the prefix assimilates to the first sound of the root, and the current spellings reflect this process. Knowing that *con-* means "with" can help students understand complex words, but only if they can recognize that the prefix of each word is one of the variants of *con-*.

Some prefixes are even more difficult to recognize than *con-*. One of the most complicated prefixes is *ad-*, a prefix that means "to," "toward," or "near." An analysis of this prefix using a large dictionary yields the data shown in Figure 8–1.

In addition to these changes, scribes added a *d* to *avance* because they thought this word came from Latin and originally had a *d*. As a result, *advance* looks like it has the *ad-* prefix when it really doesn't. Even if a student recognized one of these variations, it would still be hard to use this knowledge to figure out the word meaning. For example, how does the meaning of *ad-* as "to," "toward," or "near"

No Assimilation Before	Assimilates Before Other Consonants	Assimilates to *a* Before Two Consonants
d: ad + dition = addition	ad + breviate = abbreviate	ad + scend = ascend
h: ad + here = adhere	ad + cent = accent	ad + spire = aspire
j: ad + judicate = adjudicate	ad + firm = affirm	ad + stound = astound
m: ad + mit = admit	ad + gressive = aggressive	
v: ad + verb = adverb	ad + literation = alliteration	
vowels: ad + opt = adopt	ad + nounce = announce ad + pear = appear ad + tempt = attempt ad + quit = acquit ad + range = arrange ad + sist = assist	

Figure 8–1. Assimilation of *ad-* prefix

apply in a word like *adopt* or *assist*? This example shows that prefixes may be difficult to recognize, and even if a student recognizes the prefix, the meaning it carries may not unlock the meaning of the entire word.

Suffixes undergo fewer changes than prefixes. However, the *-ion* suffix can trigger changes in the root word, as shown in Figure 8–2. When added to most words that end in *s* or *t*, no change occurs. However, for some words that end in *t*, like *invert*, the *t* changes to *s* before *-ion* is added. Similarly, words that end in the sound of /d/, such as *evade*, change the *d* to *s* before adding *-ion*. Other words, like *imagine* or *organize*, add *-ation*. There are also more complex cases, such as the way *redeem* changes to *redemption* and *revolt* becomes either *revolution* or *revulsion*.

The situation is further complicated by the fact that in some cases, the last phoneme of the base or root word becomes the first phoneme of the suffix. In both *prevention* and *repression*, for example, the last phoneme of the base, /t/ or /s/, is pronounced as the first phoneme of the suffix. Here again, there is a split between

Root or Base	Word
prevent	prevention
repress	repression
invert	inversion
evade	evasion
imagine	imagination
redeem	redemption
revolt	revolution/ revulsion

Figure 8–2. Changes caused by the *-ion* suffix

the morphology and the phonology. The morphological analysis of *prevention* is *prevent* + *ion*, but the phonological analysis would be /priy vɛn šən/. The syllables of the spoken word don't match the morphemes that make up the word. Using knowledge of word parts in cases like these does not help students pronounce words.

Structural analysis as an aid to understanding words during reading is complicated by the difficulty caused by variations in spellings of word parts. In addition, part of a root word may be pronounced as part of a prefix or a suffix. This makes it more difficult for students to recognize the parts of a word. Even advanced students often fail to notice the word *image* in *imagination* because the spelling and pronunciation of the base changes with the addition of the suffix.

Learning the meanings of word parts Once they recognize that a word is composed of separate parts, students may have little difficulty figuring out the meanings of some word parts. They can easily remember that *port* means "carry" because many English words, like *transport* and *portage*, use this root. Those who favor a word recognition view claim that students can apply their knowledge of a few roots to many words.

However, other roots are more difficult than *port*. About 60 percent of English words have Latin or Greek roots, but most students don't know Latin or Greek. They have to learn the meaning of the root and then use that knowledge to figure out the meaning of words built on that root. In some cases, it would be easier for them to learn the meaning of the whole word directly than to learn the meanings of the parts.

In a word like *transmission*, the root *mis* means "send." The root is also spelled *mit*, as in *transmit*. This root appears in a number of English words, but students seldom know its meaning. On the other hand, a word like *knowledge* contains the base *know*. A base is an English word, and students are more apt to recognize bases than roots. They can use their knowledge of English to figure out complex words without having to learn the meaning of Greek or Latin roots. A word like *creation*, with the base *create*, is easier to figure out than a word like *prediction*, with the root *dict*, meaning "said."

Generally, the meanings of prefixes are easier to learn than the meanings of roots. However, prefixes may have more than one meaning. *Ad-*, for example, means "to," "toward," or "near." These meanings are related, but not identical. *Re-* can mean "back," as in *regress* (*gress* means "go"), or "again," as in *regret* (*gret* is a Scandanavian root meaning "weep"). Even *in-* can mean either "in" (*inside*) or "not" (*incorrect*). In some cases, it may be better to say that two prefixes, like the two *in-* prefixes, are homographic homonyms. They sound and are spelled the same, but they are really different prefixes. However, the fact that there are two *in-* prefixes makes it more difficult for students to use their knowledge of prefixes to figure out the meanings of words beginning with *in-*.

Suffixes, as we have noted, serve primarily to indicate the part of speech. They do carry a meaning, but the meaning is somewhat abstract. The suffix *-ly* indicates the manner in which something is done (if it is added to an adjective, like *quick*, not if it is added to a noun, like *friend*). The suffix *-ize* could be defined as "to make," so *to realize* is "to make real," and *to finalize* is "to make final." Of course, *to institutionalize* does not mean "to make an institution." The suffix *-ize* usually means "to make" only if it is added to adjectives like *real* and *final*, and it usually has a different meaning when added to nouns like *institution*.

Students may find it difficult to pick out the parts of complex words. Once they identify the parts, they need to assign the correct meaning to each part. However, even knowing the meanings of the parts does not always ensure that students can figure out the meaning of the whole word.

Combining meanings of word parts to determine the meaning of a word
Structural analysis is a process of building up from small parts to the whole. This morphological process is similar in concept to the phonological process of using the smallest sound units, the phonemes, to figure out the pronunciation of a word. The problem is that the meaning of the whole is often more than the sum of the meanings of the parts. When someone knows the meaning of the whole, the meanings of the parts can make sense. However, going from whole to part is easier than going from part to whole. Trying to put the

Prefix	Root	Suffix
re: back, again	cogn: know	ize: to make
con: with	bene: good	ion: state or condition
un: not	dic(t): say	al: relation to
de: down, from	greg: flock	ate: to make
	capit: head	able: able to

Figure 8–3. Word parts

meanings of the parts together to come up with the meaning of the whole is a much more difficult task.

Figure 8–3 lists the meanings of some common prefixes, roots, and suffixes. These parts can be combined to produce words such as the following:

con + greg + ation + al = relation to the state or condition of being with the flock

un + re + cogn + ize + able = not able to make known again

bene + dict + ion = the condition of saying something good

de + capit + ate = to make the head go from

The meanings of these words do seem to be at least roughly a combination of the meanings of the parts. In the case of *congregational*, one would need to use the metaphorical meaning of the church group as a flock. But, in general, there is a relation between the meanings of the parts and the meaning of the whole. Readers who already understand what *congregational* means can see the relationship between the meaning of the whole words and the meanings of the parts.

However, if a word is unknown to a student, the student must try to use knowledge of the parts to determine the meaning of the whole word. This task is more difficult than the task faced by the person who already knows the word and is attempting to understand the relationship between the whole and the parts. The real question is "Do the meanings of the parts provide the necessary information to determine the meaning of the whole?" One way to test this is to try to use these word parts to figure out meanings of less familiar words. We invite readers to use the meanings of the morphemes listed in Figure 8–3 to determine the meanings of these words: (1) *capitation*, (2) *capitular*, (3) *cognomen*, (4) *beneficiate*, and (5) *benefice*. We have chosen words that we think will not be familiar to most readers so that they can experience what a student experiences in trying to use word parts to figure out meanings. The task is formidable. *Capit* means "head" and

-ion is defined as "state or condition of." So what is *capitation*? Each of these words presents a similar challenge. However, we are not trying to frustrate readers, just put them in the same position that many students face when they try to use the meanings of word parts to figure out the meanings of words. We list the dictionary definitions of the five words here:

capitation: a direct, uniform tax imposed upon each person
capitular: of or relating to an ecclesiastical chapter
cognomen: surname or nickname
beneficiate: to prepare iron for smelting
benefice: an ecclesiastical office to which revenue for an endowment is attached

Most people find it difficult to use word parts to define these words. However, if a person knows, for example, that *capit* means "head," they might make the connection with a kind of "head tax." Without knowing the meaning of *capitation*, it is much more difficult to make the link between the word part meanings and the word meaning. This exercise is designed to help readers experience what students often feel. Word parts make perfect sense—if the person already knows the meaning of the complete word. Otherwise, they are not too helpful.

Recognizing the parts of a complex word, learning the meanings of word parts, and combining the meanings of the parts to determine the meaning of the whole are all difficult. As a result, structural analysis has limited value for readers. The reader's task is further complicated by the fact that the pronunciation of words is not always based on the morphology. Part of a prefix may be pronounced as part of the root. In addition, when students pause during reading to apply knowledge of word parts, they may lose the sense of the whole sentence. The focus on the meaning of an individual word can distract the reader from constructing the meaning of the text. Linguistic investigations into how words are formed can be interesting and rewarding for students, but attempting to use structural analysis to determine word meanings can be an exercise in frustration.

Vocabulary and Reading

A second difference between the word recognition view and the sociopsycholinguistic view that relates to morphology is the approach to vocabulary. Teachers who take a word recognition view often preteach vocabulary that they think students may not know. In contrast, teachers who take a sociopsycholinguistic view recognize the importance of building background knowledge for reading, and they also engage students in extensive reading so that they can acquire word meanings as they encounter words in context.

Preteaching vocabulary or building background knowledge There is an important difference between preteaching vocabulary items and building background for reading. Teachers face certain problems in trying to preteach vocabulary. For one thing, it is difficult to decide on which words to teach. Some students know most of the words a teacher might choose, while other students may not know any of them. It is very difficult to choose the particular set of words that most students are ready to learn.

Further, even though research studies stress the importance of extended instruction, most preteaching activities are brief. Often, students are asked to find dictionary definitions of words and to write sentences using the words. Teachers who have asked students to look up words know the problems that can result. The definitions students choose are often not the definitions that fit the story context.

Frequently, sentences that students write reflect a limited understanding of how words are used. We remember helping our daughter with a vocabulary assignment. We told her that *condolences* means saying you are sorry or expressing sympathy to someone who is having some trouble. The sentence our daughter wrote was "The girl said her condolences to her friend at the funeral." Teachers often get these kinds of sentences. The student has the right meaning but produces a sentence that doesn't sound natural. In English, one can *express* condolences, *send* condolences, and probably even *email* condolences. But for some reason, one can't simply *say* condolences. Students need to see a word in context to develop a sense of how the word is used, not just learn a definition.

In some cases, students may learn the definition of a word without understanding the concept the word represents. The authors of *Put Reading First* (Armbruster and Osborn 2001) point out that "extended instruction that promotes active engagement with vocabulary improves word learning" (p. 36). Similarly, Droop and Verhoeven (2003) write, "Numerous encounters with a word in many different contexts should be provided as students who encounter a word in a variety of activities and different contexts develop a more accurate understanding of its meaning and use" (p. 101). Students do need extended instruction, but the focus should be on concept development, not just word learning.

Effective teachers involve students in activities that help them build concepts. A word can be a label for a complex concept, and there is a danger of students learning the labels without fully developing the concepts if too much emphasis is put on word learning. Freire (Freire and Macedo 1987) expresses this well when he writes: "Reading does not consist merely of decoding the written word or language; rather, it is preceded by and intertwined with knowledge of the world. Language and reality are dynamically interconnected" (p. 29). Teachers help students develop their knowledge of the world by engaging them in activities that build concepts along with the vocabulary used to express those concepts. This is different from choosing specific words to preteach.

Droop and Verhoeven (2003) comment, "Teachers must recognize that the context of textbooks is not equally familiar to all children. The conduct of such prereading activities as discussion of the content of a story, provision of background information, building a common experience, and explanation of difficult lexical items can, therefore, be recommended" (p. 101). These are good suggestions because the focus is on building background, not just on learning words. However, these authors then add, "For second language readers, vocabulary knowledge appears to be an extremely important factor. Extensive vocabulary training thus appears to be crucial for efficient second language reading comprehension" (p. 101). They don't specify what they mean by "extensive vocabulary training," but their focus here shifts from building background to learning words. Teachers who take a sociopsycholinguistic perspective on reading keep the focus on concept development rather than on having students learn vocabulary items.

Activities designed to build concepts can help students comprehend a text. For example, in the story *Space Pet* (Clarke 1957), the crew members in a space station are alerted to a problem with their air supply system when a pet canary faints because of a lack of oxygen. Students reading this story may have difficulty with the word *oxygen*. However, simply preteaching this word by having students define *oxygen* or having them write a sentence using the word does not build the background they need. Instead, students need to understand why canaries are used to monitor oxygen levels in places like coal mines and space stations. Just knowing the meaning of the word *oxygen* will not be sufficient for students to comprehend this aspect of the story. In fact, a series of interrelated concepts are involved here, including differences in oxygen demands for birds and people. Teachers who take a sociopsycholinguistic view of reading plan activities to help students build the concepts needed as background for reading, rather than choosing a list of words like *oxygen* to preteach.

A good approach to helping students build both the concepts and the vocabulary they need to read texts is what Hoyt (2002) refers to as *frontloading*. She explains, "To improve understanding and scaffold vocabulary in informational texts, I always attempt to frontload vocabulary and concepts so the reading is fully supported by understanding. My goal is to provide rich dialogue and experiences using the vocabulary of the text before reading" (p. 104). Frontloading involves learning about something, talking about it, wondering about it, and then reading and writing about it. Hoyt gives as an example a lesson on magnets. Before having students read an article on magnets, she brings some magnets into the classroom and engages students in discussion and experimentation. What can magnets pick up? She then asks students for some words they have used to talk about magnets, and she lists them on chart paper. Next, she demonstrates how polarization works by using bar magnets and adds words like *polarization* and *North Pole* to the list. She then has students write what they know about magnets using some of the words from the chart as a resource. All these activities serve to frontload the concepts and vocabulary students need to read an article about magnets. In her book, Hoyt lists a number of other specific prereading activities she uses to prepare students to read informational texts. All of them involve helping students develop concepts and the related vocabulary prior to reading.

Developing vocabulary through reading   Frontloading and other prereading activities designed to help students build background stand in contrast to exercises that focus on the words themselves. One of the biggest problems with extensive vocabulary training is that time spent on vocabulary exercises is time taken away from reading. Students acquire vocabulary as they read. Teachers who take a sociopsycholinguistic view of reading provide time for students to read because they believe that extensive reading is the best way for students to develop their vocabulary. A number of studies support programs like sustained silent reading (SSR) because students see words many times as they read, and repeated encounters with words leads to acquisition. Students acquire many more words through reading than they could possibly learn as the result of direct teaching of vocabulary.

Vocabulary size   The best evidence that vocabulary is acquired rather than learned comes from studies of vocabulary size. Researchers find it difficult to determine the average size of the vocabulary of a group of people, such as high school graduates or adults. A key problem is determining what to count as a word. For example, while most researchers would agree that *walk* and *walking*, *walks*, and *walked*, the inflected forms of the verb, should be counted as just one word, it is more difficult to decide about derivationally related words such as *tie* and *untie* and *consider* and *consideration*. Some researchers attempt to measure vocabulary size by counting the number of derivationally related word families a person knows. Further, if someone knows that a fork is an instrument for eating and also a division in the road, does the person know two words or just one? Many words like *fork* have metaphorical extensions. A chicken is a bird, but the term can also apply to a cowardly person. Researchers have to make some difficult decisions about just what they will count as a word.

Once researchers have determined what units to count, they can't simply ask people to list all the words they know. The usual procedure of estimating vocabulary size is to randomly select a sample of words from a dictionary and test people on their knowledge of these words. This is usually done with a multiple-choice test of synonyms. Dictionaries vary considerably in size, but a large dictionary might have about 450,000 words. A researcher takes a random sample of words from the dictionary and tests subjects on their knowledge of these words. The percentage of words that a person gets right, after correcting for guessing, is then applied to the total number of words in the dictionary to produce an estimate of vocabulary size.

Different studies of vocabulary size have produced very different results. Seashore and Eckerson (1940) estimated that adults know about 156,000 words. A later study by Lorge and Chall (1963) revised the figure all the way down to 40,000 words. More recently, Pinker (1994) estimated that the number is closer to 60,000 words. He bases his estimate on a very thorough study by Nagy and his colleagues (1985). These researchers decided that the average adult knows at least 45,000 words. Pinker points out that "this is an underestimate because proper names, numbers, foreign words, acronyms, and many common undecomposable compounds were excluded . . . If they had been included, the average high school graduate would probably be credited with something like 60,000 words . . . and superior students, because they read more, would probably merit a figure twice that high" (p. 150).

If the average high school graduate knows 60,000 different words, the student must have acquired, not learned, most of this vocabulary. In schools students might study 20 words a week. During a school year of thirty-six weeks, a student would study about 720 words. Even if there were no weeks when this study was interrupted, and even if a student learned all 20 words each week, the total would still be too small to account for the average 60,000 words most graduates know. Learning 720 words a year for twelve years would add up to only 8,640 words, less than 15 percent of the average high school graduate's vocabulary.

The low number of words learned through direct teaching contrasts sharply with words acquired as children develop oral language and as they read. Miller and Gildea (1987) estimated that young children between the ages of four and six pick up an average of fourteen new words per day. At that rate, a child would acquire more than five thousand words per year. This number is more in line with Pinker's estimate of sixty thousand words.

Studies of vocabulary development through reading give further support to the claim that most vocabulary is acquired. Anderson and Nagy (1992) carried out a series of studies on how children acquire words during reading. They found, for example, that there is about a one in twenty chance that a student will acquire a new word from seeing it in context. This number is an average and varies depending on the kind of text the student is reading. If students see a word more often, they are more likely to acquire the word. Anderson and Nagy report that the average fifth grader reads for about twenty-five minutes a day. They comment, "This number is certainly lower than would be desired, but it translates into about a million words of text covered in a year" (p. 46). If even 2 percent of the words were unfamiliar, students would encounter twenty thousand new words in a year.

If they acquired one out of every twenty, then they would acquire at least one thousand words a year.

These authors go on to say, "An avid reader might spend an hour or two a day reading, and thus cover four or more times as much text. The rate of learning from context for self-selected text is likely to be closer to one unfamiliar word in ten than one in twenty. For children who do a fair amount of independent reading, then, natural learning could easily lead to the acquisition of five to ten thousand words a year, and thus account for the bulk of their annual vocabulary growth" (p. 46).

Two other studies lend support to the argument that most vocabulary is acquired in the process of reading. A study carried out with adult speakers of English and college students learning English as a second language (Saragi, Nation, et al. 1978) showed that both groups were able to define many new vocabulary words just from reading a novel. Subjects read *A Clockwork Orange* (Burgess 1986), which contains words in a made-up language that the students could not have known before reading. The novel comes with a glossary, but subjects were given copies of the novel without the glossary. After they read the novel, they were given a multiple-choice test on 90 of the 241 made-up words. Scores ranged from 50 percent to 96 percent right, with an average score of 76 percent. This means that subjects, on the average, acquired more than 183 new words simply by reading the book.

Additional evidence for the positive effect of reading on vocabulary growth comes from research conducted by Elley (1998), who has introduced book flood programs in several third world countries including Fiji, Singapore, Sri Lanka, and South Africa. In each case, he secured funds to buy large numbers of books and trained teachers in methods of shared book reading. Elley reports remarkable gains in all aspects of reading for students in these programs, including students learning English as a foreign language.

In one study, for example, teachers read a high-interest story to the students three times during a seven-day period. For one group, teachers simply read the story. For a second group, the teachers paused in the story to define key words in ways that did not interrupt the reading and carried out other activities consistent with effective shared reading. Students were given pre- and posttests on words from the stories. The group that simply heard the stories had an average gain on the vocabulary test of 15 percent. However, the group that experienced shared reading gained 40 percent. For example, 57 percent of the students knew the meaning of *dingy* in the pretest, and 88 percent knew it on the posttest, a gain of 31 percent for that item. The 40 percent gain represents the average for the students in the shared book group. This study, and others by Elley, shows how much vocabulary students gain when teachers read to them.

Nagy, Anderson, and Herman (1985) found that picking up words from reading is ten times faster than learning words through intensive vocabulary instruction.

However, they also suggest that some vocabulary study can be useful. They encourage teachers to help students develop a sense of what they call *word consciousness*. "We believe that the goal of instruction should be to develop what one lexiphile has termed word consciousness. Encounters with words should be playful, so as to provide curiosity and an interest in word study" (Anderson and Nagy 1992, p. 46). This is also the approach we would advocate, especially if students approach word study from a linguistic perspective. By the way, Anderson and Nagy inserted the word *lexiphile* on purpose. It's a word they made up, but they note that most readers can figure out the meaning from the context. It also helps if the reader can associate *lexiphile* with other words that contain *lex*, meaning "word," such as *lexical* and *lexicon*, and *phile*, meaning "love." *Philadelphia* means "the city of brotherly love." One goal of teaching should be to turn students into lexiphiles.

A delightful book that details how children can increase their interest in words is *Miss Alaineus: A Vocabulary Disaster* (Fraiser 2000). This children's literature book is based on activities that are part of the curriculum at schools in Minnesota and Florida. In this story, Sage, a fifth grader, gets sick and stays home on Tuesday, vocabulary day. She calls her friend, who quickly gives her the fifteen vocabulary words to be learned during the week. As Sage writes, "I had to scribble them quickly because her mom was calling her to the car. 'The last one's Miss Alaineus!' Starr yelled. 'I gotta go.'"

The vocabulary words that Mrs. Page, Sage's teacher, gives each week are all related to a theme. The students are asked to look up each word in the dictionary and write a definition. Sage, like many good students, already knows some words. As she writes, "I already know the words, so I try to make the definitions sound like I looked them up." Sage has no trouble with the first fourteen words on the list, but she thinks the last word is odd. Then, she remembers studying other words, like *pasteurization*, based on a person's name, so she decides Miss Alaineus must also be someone whose name has become a word, an eponym.

Sage remembers that when she was young she thought that Miss Alaineus had something to do with the drawer in the kitchen where odds and ends were kept. Then one day at the grocery story, her mother had told Sage to wait while she picked up some Miss Alaineus things. One thing she bought was a box of spaghetti. On the box was a picture of a beautiful woman with her long hair tumbling down, like strands of spaghetti. Sage concluded that the woman on the spaghetti box must be Miss Alaineus, so she writes her definition: "Miss Alaineus: the woman on green spaghetti boxes whose hair is the color of uncooked pasta and turns into spaghetti at the ends."

On Monday, when Sage returns to school, the students line up for a vocabulary test. Naturally, Sage, who usually lives up to her name, gets Miss Alaineus, and her definition, given confidently, leaves all her classmates and her teacher "one huge giggling, laughing, falling-down mass." Other kids start calling Sage "Miss Alaineus." Fortunately, Sage finds a way to redeem herself at the end of the story.

Reading this book could lead to discussion of how people form their ideas of what words mean. In addition, the book has many clever details that could raise students' awareness of words. Throughout the book, Sage defines words as she writes. The story starts with "None of this would have happened if it wasn't for Forest. Forest is not a thicket of trees. Forest is a boy." At Sage's school, students participate in a vocabulary parade. They dress up to illustrate their favorite word. For example, one student dresses up as a sheep to exemplify *sheepish*, and another comes strung with lights for *electric*. The book includes a letter that a school or teacher could send to parents explaining the vocabulary parade.

Sage and the other students are asked to write a sentence that contains three interesting words for each letter of the alphabet. The pages in this book are labeled with letters rather than being numbered, and on each page is Sage's sentence for that letter. These sentences are designed to tell the teacher "something about your daily activities." Sage's *a* page reads, "I have a feeling this *awesome ailment* will cause me great *agony* soon." Even the end pages contain a word hunt for words from Sage's dictionary. Every aspect of this book is designed to pique students' interest in words, to raise their word consciousness.

What Does It Mean to Know a Word?

As *Miss Alaineus* shows, it is important for students to develop a thorough understanding of words. One of the benefits of acquiring vocabulary through reading is that students develop a more complete understanding than the superficial knowledge gained by memorizing a definition. Knowing a word involves much more than knowing a synonym for the word or a short definition, as our daughter's experience with *condolences* shows. From a linguistic perspective, knowing a word involves having phonological, morphological, syntactic, semantic, and pragmatic information. This information can come only through seeing or hearing the word in a variety of natural contexts.

Phonological information Although a person may be able to recognize a word during reading without being able to pronounce it, being able to recognize a word in oral language and being able to pronounce the word constitute part of knowing a word. Some words, such as names in Russian novels or words with odd pronunciations like *anemone*, may be in a person's reading and writing vocabulary but not in his listening or speaking vocabulary.

Morphological information Knowing a word means knowing the inflectional and derivational affixes it combines with to produce complex words. For example, knowing a verb means knowing whether the past is regular, like *walked*, or irregular, like *went*. Knowing an adjective might mean knowing if the comparative takes *-er*, as in *bigger*, or *more*, as in *more difficult*. Words also differ in the derivational affixes they take. The adjective *humble* becomes *humility* as a noun, not *humbleness*, but *cheerful* does add *-ness* to form *cheerfulness*, and there is no word *cheerfulity*.

Syntactic information   Part of knowing a word is knowing how it functions in a sentence. A word like *blessed* can be a verb (The priest blessed the couple) or an adjective (It was a blessed event). If a word is a verb, it is necessary to know whether or not it takes an object. A verb like *go* does not take an object, but a verb like *chase* needs one. It is fine to say, "I will go," but not, "I will chase."

Semantic information   When someone talks about knowing a word, she usually means that she can define the word or give a synonym. This is semantic information. However, semantics also refers to extended or metaphorical meanings of words. For example, *tiger* can refer to a person who goes after what he wants aggressively, and this is part of the meaning of the word. Semantics also involves knowing other words related to the word and the level of generality of the different words. *Cook,* for instance, is a general word, and related, more specific words include *bake, roast,* and *broil.*

Pragmatic information   Pragmatics refers to the real-world use of a word. Knowing a word involves knowing the contexts in which it is appropriate to use the word. A word like *dude* could be used in informal contexts while the same person might be referred to as *sir* in a more formal situation. English learners often have difficulty in learning the level of formality of words, and this can lead to situations in which they offend someone unintentionally.

When one considers all that is involved in knowing a word, it is clear that simple classroom exercises such as asking students to write a dictionary definition and asking them to use a word in a sentence will not adequately develop vocabulary. On the other hand, when students see and hear a word in a variety of contexts, they build a subconscious understanding of that word. Extensive reading is the best way for students to build a rich vocabulary.

Second Language Teaching and Morphology

Morphological concepts also are important in understanding second language acquisition and teaching. First, Krashen's Natural Order hypothesis is based on morpheme studies. Even though language is very complex, it is possible to observe the order in which different common inflectional morphemes appear in an English learner's speech or writing. Second, English learners need to develop academic vocabulary to succeed in school. Much academic vocabulary consists of words with Latin or Greek roots and derivational morphology. Teachers who understand morphology are better prepared to help English learners develop academic vocabulary.

The Natural Order Hypothesis

Krashen's (2003) theory of second language acquisition, described in Chapter 2, includes the Natural Order hypothesis. This hypothesis maintains that people acquire components of a second language in a natural order. This hypothesis was based on Krashen's analysis of data from studies of the order of acquisition of morphemes. Some morphemes appear in an English learner's speech before others. Figure 8–4 lists the order of morpheme acquisition.

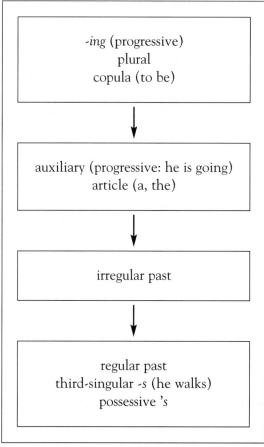

Figure 8–4. Average order of acquisition of grammatical morphemes

The order of acquisition is the same for both children and adults from different language backgrounds. For example, Spanish speakers and Chinese speakers acquire English morphemes in this same sequence. The order of acquisition for English as a second language is similar to that of English as a first language. The bound morphemes, the inflectional endings, are acquired in the same order. However, native English speakers acquire auxiliaries and forms of the verb *to be* (the copula) later than English learners.

Morphemes within each box may differ in their order of acquisition, but items in the top box are generally acquired before those in the second box, and so on. This ordering helps account for patterns teachers often observe. For example, even though the plural and the third-person singular are both -*s*, the plural -*s* appears in speech much sooner than the -*s* in a sentence such as "He likes to eat pizza."

This order holds for natural learning contexts in which people are acquiring English. Teachers may attempt to teach certain bound morphemes, such as the past-tense -*ed*, before students are ready to acquire them. This will result in a temporary ability to add -*ed* to verbs on an exercise in class. However, students can't fully incorporate the form into their speech or writing until they acquire it. Direct teaching doesn't change the order of acquisition. Language is complex, and students are acquiring phonology and syntax at the same time that they are acquiring morphology, so this list of morphemes can't be turned into a teaching sequence. Even so, it is helpful for teachers to be aware of the natural order so that they can support students' English development.

Academic Language

One of the major tasks for English language learners in school settings is to acquire academic English. Cummins (2000) distinguishes between academic language and conversational language. Conversational English is the language of everyday conversation. In conversational settings, language is embedded in a rich context. People talk about things they can see or touch. They use tone of voice and gestures to help convey meanings. Topics for discussion are not cognitively demanding. Instead, people talk about familiar things, such as the weather and recent events, so English learners can draw on background knowledge to help construct meaning. Conversational language extends to written forms ranging from environmental print, such as a McDonald's logo, to an email message. This written language is also cognitively undemanding and is often supported by visual clues to the meaning. English learners acquire conversational English in about two years. They are exposed to a great deal of conversational language both in and outside of school.

In contrast, academic language is generally more cognitively demanding. When English learners study new concepts in science or social studies, they are coping with both new ideas and new vocabulary used to express those ideas. Not only is the cognitive demand greater, but there is often less contextual support. Students may have to listen to lectures with no visual aids or read textbook chapters that include few helpful pictures or diagrams. Academic English takes much longer to acquire, at least five years. In part, the longer time reflects the fact that students are exposed to less academic language than conversational language. Academic language is used almost exclusively in school settings. In addition, much of the input from academic language may not be comprehensible, and only comprehensible input leads to language acquisition.

The distinction between cognitively demanding, context-reduced academic language and cognitively undemanding, context-embedded conversational language is an important one. Many students who appear to speak and understand English quite well still struggle in reading academic texts or passing standardized assessments. This is because they have acquired conversational English but lack academic English. One difference between these two registers of English is in the vocabulary. A review of the history of the English language shows that conversational and academic English vocabulary have different roots.

The Development of Academic English

Over time, English has borrowed words from a number of different sources. The academic language register of English, which includes words used in academic texts and discussions, includes many words from Greek and Latin. The everyday vocabulary of English comes from a number of other sources. A brief review of the history of the English language shows how words that form the vocabularies of both conversational and academic English entered at different times (Tompkins and Yaden 1986).

The Romans occupied Britain from A.D. 43 to 410, and during this time a few Latin words, such as *camp* and *port*, were borrowed into Celtic. During the Old English period, from about 450 to 1100, the Angles and Saxons invaded Britain and drove the Celts into the northern and western areas. The mixture of Germanic tribes spoke Englisc. Few words from Old English remain. Some of these are basic words such as *child, hand, foot, mother*, and *sun*. These words form part of the conversational English register. The Englisc speakers borrowed some words from the Celts, such as *Britain, cradle, London*, and *babe*, including words the Celts had borrowed from Latin.

Additional Latin words were borrowed directly into Englisc through contact between Roman soldiers and traders and the Germanic tribes in England and also on the continent. Missionaries who reintroduced Christianity to Britain in 597 brought in religious Latin words like *angel, disciple, hymn*, and *priest*. In 787, the Vikings invaded from the north and ruled England for three centuries. The

Old English	Norman-French
steer	beef
sheep	mutton
calf	veal
pig	pork
deer	venison

Figure 8–5. Old English and Norman-French words

Vikings contributed pronouns, including *they*, *their*, and *them*, and many everyday words, like *husband*, *low*, *ugly*, and *window*.

In 1066 the Norman-French invaded England and ruled for three centuries, contributing many words to English, such as *army*, *navy*, *peace*, and *stomach*. Most of the Norman-French loan words were derived from Latin. About ten thousand Norman-French words were added, and many Old English words were lost. Sometimes, the Old English and Norman-French words both stayed but took on differentiated meanings. One example is that the names for animals are based on Old English, but the words for the meat from the animals are Norman-French. This reflects the fact that English peasants cared for the animals, and the Norman-French rulers ate the meat in their castles. Figure 8–5 lists some of these pairs of words.

By about 1400, English was restored as the main language. During the Renaissance, many Greek and Latin scholarly terms were added to the English vocabulary, like *congratulate*, *democracy*, and *education*, along with many scientific terms, such as *atmosphere*, *pneumonia*, and *virus*. Brook (1998) points out that because of this infusion, especially of Latin terms, "One basic meaning could be expressed by three different English words that come from three sources—Anglo-Saxon, French, and Latin" (p. 26). Brook provides some examples listed here in Figure 8–6.

Anglo-Saxon	French	Latin
fear	terror	trepidation
win	succeed	triumph
kingly	royal	regal
holy	sacred	consecrated

Figure 8–6. Roots of English

English has many sets of words like these. Latin- and Greek-based words occur only seldom in everyday conversation, but they are typical of academic discourse. English learners must be able to use academic language to succeed in school settings. However, most of the English they hear or read comes from the conversational register.

Helping Students Develop Academic Language

Teachers can help students develop academic English by using techniques designed to make academic language comprehensible. We have written extensively about how teachers can make academic content comprehensible (Freeman and Freeman 1998a, 2001, 2002). Teachers can use a number of strategies to help students comprehend academic texts. They can activate or build background knowledge, preview texts, and teach ways to use graphic organizers to represent key ideas. Teachers can also involve students in extensive reading. The research reviewed earlier in this chapter shows that students acquire vocabulary most rapidly and effectively through extensive reading. If students are reading content area texts, they will acquire academic English.

Content-specific and general academic vocabulary Donley and Reppen (2001) point out that students encounter two types of academic language as they read: content-specific vocabulary and general academic vocabulary. Content-specific vocabulary includes technical words related to a specific academic discipline, such as *fault, ethnocentrism, protagonist,* and *googol*. General academic vocabulary consists of words that cut across disciplines and appear in many kinds of textbooks, such as *context, therefore, hypothesis,* and *longitudinal*.

Donley and Reppen conducted research that showed that students tend to acquire context-specific vocabulary more quickly than general academic vocabulary. Even though general terms appear more often in texts, they are less salient. That is, even though they are more frequent, these words are not as noticeable to readers. Donley and Reppen list several reasons for the difference in saliency between the two types of academic vocabulary.

Readers notice content-specific words because they are strongly connected with the topic. For example, someone learning about phonology would notice a word like *allophone* because of its close connection with the topic. In contrast, readers are less apt to notice general words like *therefore* because they are not related to a specific content. In addition, content-specific words are conceptually related to other words used to discuss a topic. For example, *allophone* is related to *phone* and *phoneme*. However, there are no conceptual relationships among general academic terms like *therefore* and *hypothesis*. This difference is partially the result of content-specific words being restricted in use to one discipline while general terms are used across different academic content areas.

Within a text, content-specific words are often typographically enhanced. They are boldfaced or italicized. This is not the case for general words. The content-specific words are also easier to explain, and they are often defined by glosses within the text or at the end of a chapter. General terms are much harder to define. How does one define an important causal connector like *thus*? Finally, students notice content-specific words because these are the words that often appear on tests. Again, this is usually not true for general academic vocabulary.

Donley and Reppen (2001) conclude their article by writing, "Although . . . students need to learn content-specific vocabulary, there is an even greater need for them to control academic vocabulary because it crosses disciplinary boundaries and is the foundation on which ideas are expressed in academic settings and texts" (p. 11). Academic vocabulary includes important concepts and connectors to help students understand content in all academic subject areas.

Cognate study   One way that teachers can help students develop both content-specific and general academic vocabulary is through the study of cognates. Cognates are words that come from the same root, that were literally "born together." If English learners speak a Latinate language, for example, they may understand many academic English words when they connect those words to related words they know in their first language. A Spanish speaker could understand the English word *hypothesis* by associating it with the Spanish cognate *hipótesis*. Knowledge of the Spanish word transfers to reading in English.

Support for the idea that what a person knows in one language can transfer to a second language comes from Cummins' (2000) theory of a common underlying proficiency. Cummins cites research that shows an interdependence among the concepts, skills, and linguistic knowledge in two languages. If a student understands the concept of the water cycle in one language, that concept transfers into science study in a second language. If a student knows how to summarize a chapter, that skill also transfers. Linguistic knowledge transfers as well. Students who understand the alphabetic principle, that there is a correspondence between sounds and letters, in their first language can apply that knowledge as they read in a second language.

Languages may be different on the surface, but a person who knows two or more languages develops an underlying proficiency of those elements common to the languages. Students can draw from this underlying proficiency when studying a second language. This helps account for the fact that students who arrive with adequate formal schooling in their first language succeed academically in English much more quickly than students who come with limited formal schooling

(Freeman and Freeman 2002). Students who have already developed literacy and content area knowledge in their first language can transfer that knowledge into academic studies in a second language. Students with limited previous schooling, on the other hand, have to learn both a new language and the academic concepts needed for school success.

Vocabulary knowledge can also transfer across languages. Since words may be thought of as labels for concepts, if a student knows a concept in the first language, the student can more easily acquire the vocabulary for that concept in a second language. In addition, if the two languages are related, the words used to express a concept may look and sound alike. Since many words that make up academic English have Latin roots, students who speak a Latinate language such as Spanish or French already know related words. By accessing these cognates, English learners can rapidly increase their academic English vocabulary. Figure 8–7, taken from *NTC's Dictionary of Spanish Cognates Thematically Organized* (Nash 1990), lists cognates from social studies and science.

Many everyday terms in Spanish are part of the academic language register in English. However, as they read or interact in classrooms, students often fail to draw on their knowledge base. Teachers can help students access cognates by engaging them in activities that increase their awareness of similar words across languages. Williams (2001) lists several strategies teachers can use. For example, a teacher might begin by putting book pages on an overhead transparency and having students find cognates. Then students could work in pairs to identify cognates. The teacher could also create a cognate wall. Pairs of students could add the cognates they find to the wall. This activity could extend throughout a unit of study, and students could list as many cognates as possible

Social Studies		Science	
English	*Spanish*	*English*	*Spanish*
civilization	civilización	geography	geografía
history	historia	biology	biología
past	pasado	analysis	análisis
pioneer	pionero	diagram	diagrama
colonial	colonial	experiment	experimento
diary	diario	formula	fórmula

Figure 8–7. English and Spanish cognates

related to the topic. They could also find general words that extend across units of study. The class could also develop a cognate dictionary, using the words from the cognate wall.

Rodríguez (2001) suggests that once students identify cognates, they can work together to categorize them. This is an excellent activity to raise word consciousness and increase the important academic skill of categorization. Rodríguez' students found several ways to classify cognates. For example, some, like *colonial*, have the same spelling. Others, like *civilization* and *civilización*, have a predictable variation in spelling. The derivational suffix *-ion* in English is spelled *-ción* in Spanish. Other cognates, like *sport* and *deporte*, have the same root. Some cognates share only one of the meanings of the word. An example is that *letter* in English can refer to a letter of the alphabet or a business letter, but in Spanish, the cognate *letra* means only a letter of the alphabet. Categorizing cognates is an activity that helps sharpen analytic skills and increases student's awareness of these words. Students can then apply their knowledge of cognates to academic English reading.

Linguistic Text Analysis

Older students can also benefit from linguistic study of content area textbooks. In the process of analyzing how writers use language, students become more aware of linguistic features of text, and they develop a greater understanding of academic content. Schleppergrell and Achugar (2003) report on a project that involved eighth-grade students analyzing a passage about the Missouri Compromise from a state-adoped textbook.

Students engaged in several activities over time designed to help them understand how the authors of the text used language to convey historical information. As Schleppergrell and Achugar write, "When historians write textbooks to explain how historical events came about and the reasons why they happened, they choose the information they want to present, decide how to organize the information, and select the appropriate words to construct the text. By doing an analysis of history texts, students can uncover those choices and develop an awareness of the ways language shapes what we learn and know" (p. 26).

Students examined the language of the text from three perspectives. They considered what the text tells about what is happening, the roles of the participants, and how the information is organized in the text. The activities teachers planned for students helped them investigate each of these areas.

First, students identified all the verbs in the passage. Teachers reviewed with students how to find verbs. In one activity, they gave students a Cloze passage with the verbs missing and then had them find verbs that would fit the passage. Then, they had students work together to list all the verbs in the Missouri Compromise passage. Next, students categorized the verbs as action verbs, thinking/feelings verbs like *resented*, saying verbs like *suggested*, and relating verbs like *was*. Most of the verbs in the passage were action verbs. Through class discussion, the teachers helped students recognize that historians use action verbs to recount events. At the same time, they include thinking/feeling verbs to provide their perspective on the events.

Students continued their analysis by looking closely at the sentences with action verbs. They identified the agent, the one doing the action, and the receiver of the action, the object of the verb. For example, in the sentence, "Missouri settlers had brought enslaved African Americans," the agent is "Missouri settlers" and the receiver of the action is "enslaved African Americans." In follow-up discussions, students considered more carefully how the authors of the text presented the information. This involved discussion of who the actors were in this account and who or what was being acted on, the receivers of the action. That is, students started to see the different roles groups played in the historical event.

Students also analyzed the point of view the authors took by analyzing the sentences with thinking/feeling verbs. In this process, students continually focused on both the historical content and the language used to present the ideas and events. Finally, students identified the connecting words in the text. Historical texts are usually organized by time or by cause and effect. By looking at the specific kinds of words the authors chose, students recognized that this passage was organized chronologically with little attention given to causes. They found phrases such as "By 1819" and "At the same time," rather than connectors like "therefore." This linguistic analysis drew students' attention to these important connectors and helped them understand the organizing principle for this passage.

Schleppergrell and Achugar point out that different kinds of analyses would be appropriate for different sorts of texts. They also note that students benefit from a careful linguistic analysis of one or two texts. These kinds of activities would not be carried out with most reading passages, only a few. However, this sort of careful analysis can raise students' consciousness of the academic language in their content area texts and help equip them to read these passages more effectively. The authors of this study conclude:

> Teachers find it difficult to scaffold language learners' reading of grade-level texts. We have suggested here that by analyzing the verbs that present the events in the text, the noun phrases that tell about the participants in those events, and the linguistic resources that indicate how the text is organized,

teachers can help students learn academic English at the same time they learn history. (p. 26)

The key here is that teachers and students study both language structures and academic content together. The two are closely interrelated. What we say is shaped by how we say it. Students gain both content area knowledge and greater linguistic awareness through this sort of close study of the language of their texts. In this process, they increase their ability to process the academic language needed for school success.

Conclusion

Morphology applies to both reading and second language teaching. Those who hold a word recognition view of reading suggest that students can use knowledge of word parts to recognize words. However, structural analysis is difficult because it is hard to recognize word parts, learn the meanings of the parts, and combine the parts to determine the meaning of words. However, the study of word parts can be interesting if carried out from a linguistic perspective. It can help students develop word consciousness. Students acquire many more words during reading than through direct study of vocabulary. Repeated exposure to a word is necessary for a person to develop a full understanding of the word, including phonological, morphological, syntactic, semantic, and pragmatic information.

Studies in the acquisition of morphemes form the basis for Krashen's Natural Order hypothesis. This research shows that grammatical morphemes are acquired in a fixed order. The order depends on the language being learned rather than the native language of the learner. The natural order of morpheme acquisition differs only slightly for first and second language acquisition.

English learners face the challenge of developing both conversational and academic English. Academic vocabulary can best be acquired through extensive reading. However, teachers can enhance students' learning by teaching general academic vocabulary and by engaging students in cognate studies. Knowledge of morphology can inform teachers as they make decisions about the best way to teach reading and to teach English language learners.

Applications

1. Many prefixes assimilate to the root of a word. Study a prefix like *in-* to find how it changes as it is attached to different roots. A comprehensive dictionary can provide information about prefixes.
2. Tompkins and Yaden (1986) list several animal names with interesting histories. Investigate these words to see which language they come from and

what the name means in the original language. For example, *aardvark* is an Afrikaans word meaning "earth pig." Try the following animal names:

alligator	crocodile	leopard	porpoise	penguin
beetle	duck	lobster	rhinoceros	porcupine
caterpillar	elephant	moose	spider	walrus
cobra	hippopotamus	octopus	squirrel	

3. We list several activities for investigating cognates. Try out some of these activities with your English language learners. Be prepared to share what you and your students did and how the students responded to each activity.

9

English Syntax

- *What are some basic aspects of English syntax?*
- *How do insights from syntax apply to teaching reading and teaching a second language?*

Four Views of Grammar

Linguists consider grammar to be the study of syntactic structures. However, the word *grammar* conjures up other meanings in the minds of most people. For many, the word brings back memories of worksheets and tests based on rules or on knowing the parts of speech. Most people admit they never really understood grammar very well or that they have forgotten it. Some people who studied rhetoric in college might say that grammar refers to the effective use of syntactic structures in writing or speaking. And still others might respond by saying that grammar is the built-in knowledge of a language that enables people to comprehend and produce language.

Weaver (1996) lists all four of these meanings of grammar:

- grammar as a description of syntactic structure
- grammar as prescriptions for how to use structures and words
- grammar as rhetorically effective use of syntactic structures
- grammar as the functional command of sentence structure that enables us to comprehend and produce language (p. 2)

Grammar as a Description of Syntactic Structure

These different definitions include the terms *grammar* and *syntax*. From a linguistic perspective, *grammar* and *syntax* are synonymous. Chomsky and other linguists argue that humans are born with a language acquisition device, a set of mental structures that enable them to use language input to form subconscious rules for how language works. Over time, humans develop an internal grammar, a set of rules they can use to understand and produce one or more languages. The internal grammar includes a syntactic component along with a knowledge of phonology, morphology, semantics, and pragmatics.

Although linguists study all the different aspects of language, the major area of study in recent years in American linguistics has been syntax. For many linguists, then, grammar is regarded as the study of syntactic structure.

Grammar as Prescriptions for Correct Use

For most people, *grammar* refers to a set of prescriptive rules they were taught in school. In Chapter 7 we explained that at one time schools were conducted in Latin. Teachers in these grammar schools taught Latin grammar. When the language of instruction shifted to English, these same teachers applied their knowledge of Latin grammar to English and began to teach English grammar. Since students could already understand and speak English, the focus was on written language. Teachers believed that if students learned about grammar, they could apply this knowledge to both writing and speaking. However, research consistently shows that students have trouble learning traditional grammar and applying grammar rules when they write or speak. Weaver (1996) has reviewed much of the research on teaching grammar and has come to the same conclusion.

In the first place, students find it difficult to learn and retain concepts from traditional grammar. In one series of studies, Macauley looked at students in Scotland. At the time of these studies, grammar was taught in both elementary and secondary schools for an average of thirty minutes a day. At the elementary level, the lessons emphasized knowing parts of speech and their functions. Thus, students were taught to pick out nouns in a sentence, and they learned that nouns served as subjects and objects in sentences. Macauley tested students at the end of elementary school. The test required students to read fifty sentences and decide whether the underlined word in each sentence was a noun, verb, pronoun, adjective, or adverb.

Even though the students had all had several years of daily study of parts of speech, the average score for the 131 students was only 27.9 percent right. Macauley had set 50 as a passing score. Students could get about 11 percent right just by guessing, but only one student scored 50 percent or better on all five parts of speech. When Macauley tested secondary students, they did somewhat better, but the mean for the top classes at the end of their third year of secondary school had risen to only 62 percent. Macauley's studies with students who received intensive training in traditional grammar showed that students have a great deal of difficulty even learning basic parts of speech.

Krashen (1998) has also reviewed research on the traditional prescriptive teaching of grammar. His conclusion is blunt: "Research on the relationship between formal grammar instruction and performance on measures of writing ability is very consistent: There is no relationship between grammar study and writing" (p. 8). For example, in a three-year study comparing the effects of traditional grammar, transformational grammar, and no grammar on high school students in New Zealand, Elley and his colleagues (1976) concluded that whether grammar study is traditional or transformational, it has almost no influence on the language growth of secondary students. This study found that students could not apply knowledge of grammar to their speech or writing.

One of the strongest statements on the teaching of grammar comes from a report issued by the National Council of Teachers of English, an organization with many members vitally interested in grammar and in the teaching of writing. The authors of the report (Braddock, Lloyd-Jones, et al. 1963) state:

> In view of the widespread agreement of research studies based upon many types of students and teachers, the conclusion can be stated in strong and unqualified terms: the teaching of formal grammar has a negligible or, because it usually displaces some instruction and practice in actual composition, even a harmful effect on the improvement of writing. (pp. 37–38)

Despite the research consensus, teachers continue to teach traditional prescriptive grammar. Weaver (1996) lists several reasons:

- teachers may not be aware of the research
- they may not believe the research
- they believe grammar is interesting and teach it simply for that reason
- they notice that some students who are good readers and writers are also good at grammar, so they assume that this correlation shows cause and effect
- they are required to teach grammar
- they feel pressure to teach grammar from parents or other community members
- they feel that although grammar may not help the average student, it still may help some students

Grammar as Rhetorically Effective Use of Syntactic Structures

Teaching grammar is firmly embedded in schools, especially secondary schools. Nevertheless, more teachers now teach grammar in the context of student writing, particularly during the editing stage. Weaver (1996) provides a number of useful minilessons that teachers can use to teach grammar in context. When instruction applies directly to student writing, it helps students produce more effective pieces. Students don't need to be able to label parts of speech, but they do need many opportunities for meaningful writing, and when they have produced a good piece of writing, they are ready to put it in conventional form and enhance the rhetorical effects through careful organization and choice of examples. At that point, a lesson on subject-verb agreement, using examples from student papers, or a lesson on transitional words can be useful. This approach is quite different from traditional grammar teaching.

Grammar as the Functional Command of Syntax

Chomsky has argued that humans are born with an innate capacity for language. Through exposure to language in meaningful contexts, humans are able to internalize rules of the language. These are not traditional prescriptive rules taught in school. Instead, they are a set of subconscious notions that allow humans to comprehend and produce meaningful utterances. These internal rules are refined to match the norms of the language community of which the speaker is a part. For a linguist, *grammar* is a term that refers to the set of rules each human internalizes that allows that person to produce and comprehend language. Over time, humans develop a full command of the syntactic structures of their community of speakers that allows them to function effectively.

Introduction to a Theory of Syntax

Modern linguistics builds on traditional approaches to teaching grammar, but the purpose is different. Rather than trying to develop a set of rules for students to learn, linguists attempt to make explicit the subconscious rules people use to produce and understand language. The current approach is descriptive, not prescriptive. In the following sections, we provide an introduction to a theory of syntax. This introduction covers some of the basic concepts and methods linguists use to describe the syntactic structure of English sentences. Then we consider how linguistic knowledge of syntax can apply to views of reading and views of teaching a second language.

In Chapter 1 we introduced Chomsky's theory of generative grammar. This theory is built on the idea that sentences have both a surface and a deep structure. Chomsky observed that some sentences in English are ambiguous, not because one of the words has two meanings, but because the sentence could be analyzed as having two different structures. For example, the sentence "He surprised the linguist with the question" could be taken to mean that "He" had the question or that the linguist had the question. The ambiguity is structural, not lexical. The words don't have double meanings, but the sentence does.

In addition to ambiguous sentences, English has some sentences that look different on the surface but are the same at a deep level. For example, the active-passive pair "The teacher read the book" and "The book was read by the teacher" express the same meaning even though the words appear in a different order on the surface. A theory of syntax is an attempt to describe the rules that govern the order of words at the deep-structure level and also to account for how deep-structure syntax is changed to create different surface-structure sentences.

In developing a theory of syntax, the first step is to decide what elements to include. For example, one could begin by simply saying that a sentence is an unstructured string of words, like "develop teachers creative lessons linguistics," but it is quickly apparent that the words must be put in some sequence. The first step in developing a theory, then, is to say that the linear order of the words needs to be considered. One possible sequence is "Teachers develop creative linguistics lessons."

The next step is to recognize that the words in a sentence are not all the same. A word like *creative* is different from one like *lessons*. This observation leads to the need to categorize words. In Chapter 7 we distinguished between content words (noun, verbs, adjectives, and adverbs) and function words, such as determiners and pronouns. Morphological evidence can be used to help identify content words. For example, only verbs add *-ing* to form progressive tense, as in "I am reading." The words in the example sentence in the previous paragraph could be categorized as shown in Figure 9–1.

A third step in developing a theory of syntax is to group the words. Some of the words seem to go together. This sentence could be divided into the following groups: Teachers – develop – creative linguistics lessons. The fourth step is to consider the function of each group of words. For example, *Teachers* functions as the subject, and *creative linguistics lessons* functions as the object of the verb. Building a theory of syntax involves determining the possible functions that groups of words, or constituents, perform in a sentence.

The final step is to find connections among the parts of the sentence. Some constituents depend on others. For example, the verb form *develop* is used because the subject, *teachers*, is plural. If the subject were singular, *the teacher*, then the verb would be *develops*. There is a dependency between the subject and the verb.

Noun	Verb	Adjective
teachers	develop	creative
lessons		linguistics

Figure 9–1. Categories of words

Building a theory of syntax, then, involves considering the order of the words in a sentence, the categories of the words, the way words are grouped, the functions different constituents have, and the dependencies among the constituents. Akmajian and colleagues (1979) write, "One of the most important ways of discovering why and how sentences must be structured is to try to state explicitly some grammatical rules for a given language" (p. 140). They offer the example of the rule for forming yes/no questions in English. For linguists, a rule is simply a description of some aspect of a language. The question rule describes the relationship between statements and questions that can be answered with yes or no. The assumption is that statements and questions have the same deep structure. Questions are formed by changing a statement in some way to produce a different surface structure. Investigating this rule involves examining the structure of English sentences. In examining such rules, linguists attempt to make explicit the subconscious rules speakers of a language normally use every day.

The Question Rule

There are different ways that a linguist might try to discover the rule for forming questions from statements. A first attempt might rely on the linear order of the words. For example, one could number the words in the following sentence, like so:

Teachers	can	develop	creative	linguistics	lessons.
1	2	3	4	5	6

Then, it would be possible, relying on linear order, to state a rule for changing the statement into a question. This first attempt at the rule might look like this:

1. To change a statement into a question, move word 2 to the front of the sentence.

This rule works fine for this sentence. If word 2 is moved to the front, the result is "Can teachers develop creative linguistics lessons?" However, for the rule to be adequate, it must apply to all statements. The scientific process involves forming a hypothesis and then looking for counterexamples. Are there statements that could not be turned into questions by following this rule? It is quickly apparent that a rule that relies only on the order of the words is not adequate. For example, let's try applying the rule to the following sentence:

Some	teachers	can	develop	creative	linguistics	lessons.
1	2	3	4	5	6	7

Applying rule 1, the question would be "Teachers some can develop creative linguistics lessons?" It is easy to find many other examples of sentences for which rule

1 would not work. This suggests that the hypothesis needs to be refined to take into account more than the linear order of words in a sentence.

It appears that the word that gets moved to the front of the sentence is a verb, not a noun, like *teachers*. To state the rule, then, one must rely on the morphological categories of words as well as the order of words. The second try for this rule could then be stated as

2. To change a statement into a question, move the first verb to the front of the sentence.

Applying this rule would produce the desired result and change "Some teachers can develop creative linguistics lessons" into "Can some teachers develop creative linguistics lessons?"

Rule 2 works for many English sentences. Nevertheless, it is still possible to find counterexamples, statements that can't be turned into questions by following this rule. Take, for example, the following sentence: "Teachers who read this book can develop creative linguistics lessons." Moving the first verb to the front produces "Read teachers who this book can develop creative linguistics lessons?" Obviously, this is the wrong result. The question that corresponds to "Teachers who read this book can develop creative linguistics lessons" is "Can teachers who read this book develop creative linguistics lessons?"

The rule needs to be stated in a way that ensures that the right verb gets moved. In a simple sentence, the right verb is the first one, but in a more complex sentence, the right verb might be the third or fourth verb in the sentence. English allows very long sentences, like this one: "Teachers who read this book and attend courses that enable them to learn a great deal about linguistics can develop creative linguistics lessons." Here, *can* is the fifth verb. There doesn't seem to be any limit, except for a listener's memory span, on how long sentences can be, and the verb that moves to the front can be any of the verbs in the sentence. Trying to specify that it is the first, second, or third verb doesn't result in the desired rule.

A better statement of the rule involves reference to *teachers* as the subject of the sentence and *can develop* as the predicate corresponding to this subject. Rather than referring only to morphological categories, it is necessary to refer to the functions of sentence constituents like subject and predicate to state the rule. The revised rule would then read as follows:

3. To change a statement into a question, move the first verb in the predicate to the front of the sentence.

To this point, the process of forming a rule for questions has involved the linear order of the words, word categories, and functional sentence constituents. The rule could be stated more precisely, however. In English it is possible to distinguish between auxiliary verbs and main verbs. In Chapter 7 we listed main verbs as content words and auxiliary verbs as function words. Main verbs take inflectional endings to show changes in tense. This is an open class, and new verbs are borrowed into English. Auxiliary verbs do not take endings, and new auxiliaries are not added to English. Main verbs seem to have semantic content that auxiliary verbs lack. It is hard to define an auxiliary verb like *can*. For these reasons, linguists differentiate between the two kinds of verbs.

The question rule applies to auxiliary verbs, not main verbs. It is auxiliaries like *can* that are moved to the left of the subject. Using the concept of auxiliary verbs, the rule can be stated as follows:

4. To change a statement into a question, move the first auxiliary in the predicate immediately to the left of the subject.

Linguists try to state rules that govern language processes as clearly as possible so that they can be tested against new sentences. The process is to state a rule, which becomes a hypothesis, and then test the rule against possible sentences in a language. Each time a counterexample is found, the rule is refined. The goal is to develop a small set of rules that accounts for all the possible sentences in a language. The rules for syntax would describe how sentences are structured at a deep level and the changes that take place to produce surface-level variations, such as questions.

Are there still apparent counterexamples to rule 4? Consider the following sentence: "Often, teachers can develop creative linguistics lessons." Application of rule 4 would produce "Can often teachers develop creative linguistics lessons?" This sentence seems to be a counterexample. However, rather than refining the rule at this point, a linguist might point out that the surface structure of a sentence starting with *often* does not match the deep structure. At the deep-structure level, *often* would be next to the main verb, and the sentence would read "Teachers can often develop creative linguistics lessons." Applying rule 4 to this sentence would produce the desired question, "Can teachers often develop creative linguistics lessons?" Rule 4 seems to work consistently when it is applied to the deep structure form of a statement.

In cases involving adverbs like *often* the difference between the deep structure and the surface structure involves the position of a word in the sentence. In fact, adverbs can move to a variety of positions, and linguists might debate where *often* should be represented in deep structure. However, moving a word like *often* to a different position in the sentence results in a match between the deep and surface structures. In other cases, some deep-structure words are deleted in the surface structure sentence. Speakers or writers can omit words that they think a listener or reader can infer. Re-creating the deep structure representation involves inserting deleted words. The fact that some words present in deep structure are deleted in surface structure helps account for other apparent counterexamples to rule 4.

Rule 4 refers to auxiliary verbs. However, some sentences lack auxiliary verbs at the surface structure level. For example, there is no auxiliary in the sentence "The teacher developed a creative linguistics lesson." Nevertheless, there is an auxiliary in the related question, "Did the teacher develop a creative linguistics lesson?" Evidence from related pairs of statements and questions such as this one lead linguists to hypothesize that at deep structure all sentences contain an auxiliary. In some cases, the auxiliary is deleted at surface structure. However, a theory of syntax would include a deep structure auxiliary since it shows up in questions. Native speakers of English automatically supply some form of *do* to form yes/no questions.

The assumption that AUX is present in deep structure is also supported by evidence from negative statements. Consider the following pair of sentences:

1. The teacher developed a creative linguistics lesson.
2. The teacher did not develop a creative linguistics lesson.

In the process of changing a positive statement like 1 to a negative statement like 2, speakers insert the AUX *did*. If the theory of syntax includes AUX in the deep structure, then that helps explain its presence in the surface structure of negative statements. In other words, the AUX is always there, but it doesn't show up in positive statements. However, it does form part of questions and negative statements.

A theory of syntax is based on the linear order of words, the morphological categories of words, and the functional constituents of sentences. Using these constructs, linguists attempt to describe the structure of English sentences at a deep level. Linguists hypothesize that sentences are structured because this allows them to explain why a series of unambiguous words like "The chicken is too hot to eat" can have an ambiguous meaning. The surface structure of this sentence can be associated with two different deep structures. In addition, if sentences are structured, then linguists can explain a rule like the question rule. Only by appealing to structure can such rules be stated.

Linguists have developed a set of rules to describe the structure of English sentences. The rules presented in this section provide an introduction to the kinds of rules linguists have written. Linguists have continued to refine their descriptions in their attempt to make the implicit rules that allow people to comprehend and produce sentences explicit. The rules presented here should be considered the beginning of a description of English syntax.

Phrase Structure Rules

The rules used in this description are referred to as *phrase structure rules* because they attempt to specify how the phrases in a sentence are structured. Phrase structure rules, like other scientific notations, are written following certain conventions. For example, the rule for the structure of a simple sentence is:

S → NP – AUX – VP

This notation means that a sentence (S) consists of a noun phrase (NP), an auxiliary verb (AUX), and a verb phrase (VP). The arrow can be translated as "can be expanded into." In other words, every sentence (S) can be expanded into, or rewritten as, a series of phrases that include a noun phrase (NP), an auxiliary (AUX), and a verb phrase (VP). These elements appear in this linear order. The claim is that every sentence in English at a deep-structure level follows this pattern. Questions follow a different pattern, but they are surface-structure variations on statements that do follow the pattern.

Noun phrases   Syntactic structure can further be described by defining each type of phrase. For example, an NP can contain several elements. Linguists might describe an NP as follows:

NP → (DET) – (Q) – (ADJP) – N – (PP)

This is a shorthand notation for the components of a noun phrase. It can be read as "A noun phrase can be expanded into a determiner, a quantifier, an adjective phrase, a noun, and a prepositional phrase." The parts of the NP go in the linear order specified by the formula. The abbreviations for determiner (DET), quantifier (Q), adjective phrase (ADJP), and prepositional phrase (PP) are placed in parentheses to show that they are optional. Only a few NPs have all of these elements. Every NP has a noun, however, so the N is not put in parentheses. Figure 9–2 illustrates some possible NPs that contain these different components.

As Figure 9–2 shows, an NP can have some or all of the elements. However, the elements must occur in the specified order. An NP like *two the hungry boys* or *hungry two boys* would not sound like English because it does not follow the specified order.

The rule for an NP contains two other phrases, ADJP and PP. Each of these also has an internal structure that can be defined. The rule for an ADJP could be written as follows:

ADJP → (INT) – ADJ

An adjective phrase can include an intensifier like *very* or *somewhat*. The INT is an optional element. Thus, two possible ADJPs are *very hungry* and *hungry*. In addition, an ADJP can have more than one adjective. A speaker can refer to

DET	Q	ADJP	N	PP
the	two	hungry	boys	in the kitchen
that		creative	teacher	
	several	lazy	linguists	at the conference
the		tall, green	tree	
			dogs	

Figure 9–2. Noun phrases

"an energetic, creative teacher," using two adjectives. In this case, the speaker could have also referred to the teacher as "a creative, energetic teacher." That is, the order of the adjectives could have been reversed. This is because *creative* and *energetic* are the same kind of adjective. However, consider the ADJP *the tall green tree*. In this case, reversing the order of the adjectives and saying, "the green tall tree" produces a phrase that does not sound like English. As children or English learners acquire a language, they acquire the syntactic structure of sentences, phrases, and the elements within phrases. For adjectives, it appears that adjectives of size, like *tall*, occur before adjectives of color, like *green*.

An NP also may contain a prepositional phrase (PP). The rule describing a PP is simply

$$PP \rightarrow P - NP$$

Both elements of the PP, the preposition (P) and the NP, are obligatory. Every PP has a preposition followed by a noun phrase. Figure 9–2 lists two PPs, *in the kitchen* and *at the conference*.

The rule for NP includes PP as optional. At the same time, the rule for a PP includes an obligatory NP. As a result, English syntax places no length limits on NPs. The upper limit is imposed only by the memory or attention span of the listener. For example, it is possible to describe someone as "the linguist at the conference near the door in the room with the table with the interesting carving." Including so many PPs would not be considered great writing, but English syntax allows such phrases. The rules for NP and PP are recursive because NPs can include PPs and PPs must include NPs. Recursive structural rules are those for which the output of one rule forms the input for the other. In mathematical terms, a recursive rule is like a circular reference in a formula. Computers can't handle such formulas because they are potentially infinite. English sentences can be infinitely long. Of course, a speaker would die before producing an infinite sentence.

What about the prescriptive rule "Don't end a sentence with a preposition"? The structural description of a PP as a preposition followed by a noun phrase seems to support this rule because the preposition precedes the noun phrase. However, the phrase structure rules we are considering here apply to deep structure, and it is possible to move elements around at the surface level. For that reason, it is possible to ask either, "Who are you looking at?" or "At whom are you looking?" The first question occurs more often in conversation and the second in formal writing. Both sentences are syntactically acceptable from a linguistic point of view because they are variations on the same deep structure. They differ in their level of formality and occur in different language registers. Students learning academic English encounter questions like the second one most often in lectures or textbooks. In most social situations, the first question is more common, and a danger of using the more formal variation is that the speaker might be regarded as a snob.

Many sentences that appear to end with prepositions actually end with verb particles. English has many two-word verbs, like *look up* or *write down*. If a sentence ends with one of these two-word verbs, the particle may be mistaken for a preposition. In questions such as "What word did you look up?" or "Which definition did you write down?" the last word is a particle. Trying to move the particle to a different position would produce questions like "Up what word did you look?" and "Down which definition did you write?" Clearly, these questions do not sound like English. The words *up* and *down* are particles that attach to the verbs, not prepositions that can be moved.

Auxiliaries English sentences begin with an NP. The second constituent is the AUX. English has a complex system for auxiliary verbs. This category includes modal auxiliaries, like *should* and *can*, along with forms of *have, be,* and *do*. Pinker (1994) points out that "there are about twenty-four billion billion logically possible combinations of auxiliaries . . . of which only a hundred are grammatical" (p. 272). For example, it is possible to say, "The linguist might have been napping," but other combinations of these three auxiliaries are not grammatical. Sentences like "The linguist have might been napping" and "The linguist been have might napping" do not sound like English. Part of what a child or an English learner acquires is this implicit knowledge of the order of auxiliary verbs. Linguists try to specify the order of the kinds of auxiliary verbs. For example, modals (*can, might*) go before auxiliaries showing tense, like *have*, and the form of *be* that indicates passive comes last.

V	NP	NP	PP	ADVP
sing				
sing	a beautiful song		in the morning	
study	linguistics			very diligently
give	the linguist	his homework	during class	

Figure 9–3. Verb phrases

Verb phrases   The third constituent in an English sentence is the verb phrase. The rule describing the verb phrase is

VP → V – (NP) – (PP) – (ADVP)

This rule specifies that a VP must have a verb and can have one or more NPs, one or more PPs, and one or more adverb phrases (ADVP). An adverb phrase, like an adjective phrase, can include an intensifier and must include an adverb. Thus, both *fast* and *very fast* can serve as ADVPs. Figure 9–3 shows some possible VPs.

In some sentences, like "Birds sing," the VP consists of just the verb. In other sentences, the verb is followed by one or more NPs. Thus, "The bird sang a song" has a VP with one NP, and "The student gave the linguist his homework" has two NPs, *the linguist* and *his homework*. Some verbs, called *intransitive verbs*, do not take a following NP. For example, no NP follows a verb like *go*. A speaker can say, "He went to class," in which there is a following PP, but not "He went class," with a following NP. Language development involves acquiring the knowledge of what other elements follow a verb. When students read extensively, they gain this kind of knowledge.

Prepositional phrases can be part of an NP or part of a VP. The following sentence illustrates the difference between these two roles of a PP: "The teacher assigned the problems in the book during class." This sentence has two PPs. The first one, *in the book*, is a PP that is part of the NP *the problems in the book*. This whole NP can be replaced by a pronoun like *them*. The sentence could read "The teacher assigned them during class." The second PP, *during class*, is not part of an NP. Instead it is an independent part of the VP.

228

Prepositional phrases that are part of NPs function like adjectives. They describe the noun. For example, *in the book* tells which problems the teacher assigned. The PP describes or modifies the noun, *problems*. On the other hand, a PP that is part of the VP acts like an adverb. It usually tells when or where. The PP *during class* tells when the teacher assigned the problems. It does not describe or define which problems the teacher assigned. PPs that serve as adverbs can be moved around in the surface structure. For example, the sentence could read "During class, the teacher assigned the problems in the book." In English, adverbs and PPs that function like adverbs can occur in different positions. It would also be possible to say "The teacher, during class, assigned the problems in the book." However, PPs that serve as adjectives, like *in the book*, cannot move out of the NP. A sentence like "In the book, the teacher assigned the problems at the end of the class period" does not sound like English. Another way of stating this is that PPs that are part of a VP can be moved around at surface level, but PPs that are part of an NP can not be moved out of the NP.

Grammatical Acceptability

In describing the syntactic structure of English, we have said that something "doesn't sound like English." This phrasing may not sound very scientific. However, linguists use intuitions of native speakers to determine grammatical acceptability. This is the approach of descriptive scientists, and it differs from prescriptive rules laid down by grammar teachers.

Linguists use people's judgments of what sounds right to describe syntactic structure. For example, most native speakers of English would say "a tall green tree," not "a green tall tree." The speakers might not be able to give a rule to explain why one sounds right and the other doesn't. However, native speakers acquire a set of subconscious rules that allow them to comprehend and produce English. They can use these same rules to judge whether or not a sentence sounds right. Because the rules are subconscious, a person may not be able to say why one sentence sounds better than the other.

Often, people studying a new language are frustrated when native speakers tell them they have used the wrong word but then can't explain the rule for determining which word to use. For example, Spanish has two words, *por* and *para*, that translate into English as *for*. Native Spanish speakers know that it is fine to say "Lo compro para ti" (I bought it for you), but it is not acceptable to say "Lo compro por ti," if you want to say that you are buying a gift to give someone. Even though both *por* and *para* mean *for*, they are used differently. The rule for their use is fairly complex. Native Spanish speakers will often say "Give me a sentence, and I'll tell you if it's right," but they find it difficult to state an explicit rule.

In the same way, English has three words, *at, in,* and *on* that can all be translated into Spanish as *en*. English speakers say "in the city," "at the airport," and "on the train." However, "at the city" sounds wrong, and "at the airport" and "in the airport" mean two different things. This is frustrating for Spanish speakers, who translate all three prepositions as *en*. Why do English speakers get "in a car" but "on a bus"? It would not sound right to say "I got on the car" or "I got in the bus." If someone gets on a car, she is on top of it. Most native English speakers can make these grammaticality judgments, but they would find it difficult to explain why one sentence is right and the other is not. Linguists rely on these grammatical intuitions to describe language structures.

Judgments of syntactic acceptability are not the same as traditional grammar rules. Telling someone not to end a sentence with a preposition or not to use two negatives in a sentence is different from saying something sounds like English. Teachers can tell students that periods go inside quotation marks. That is a rule to be learned. It is a convention of formal written language. Students can learn such rules and apply them in certain situations, such as when they edit their writing. However, in attempting to describe syntactic structure, linguists are attempting to describe how the language works. They are not attempting to prescribe correct usage.

Language Functions and Tree Diagrams

Linguists differentiate between syntactic structures and their functions. A phrase like *the creative teacher* is a noun phrase. That is its structure. However, the same structure can function in different ways in a sentence. For example, in the following sentences, this NP serves as a subject, as the object of the verb, and as the object of a preposition:

1. *The creative teacher* developed exciting linguistics lessons. (subject)
2. The principal admired *the creative teacher*. (object of the verb)
3. The student spilled her lunch on *the creative teacher*. (object of the preposition)

This NP serves as a different constituent of each of these three sentences. Its function is determined by its position in the overall sentence structure. Subjects come at the beginning of a sentence. Objects of verbs follow verbs. And objects of prepositions follow prepositions. Linguists use tree diagrams, sometimes called *phrase markers*, to visually represent the structure of sentences and the functions of phrases within a sentence. The three sentences above can be represented by the tree diagrams in Figures 9–4, 9–5, and 9–6.

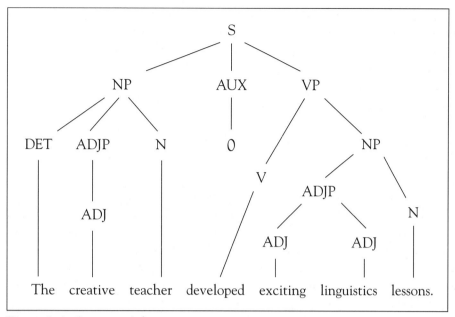

Figure 9–4. Sentence 1 diagram

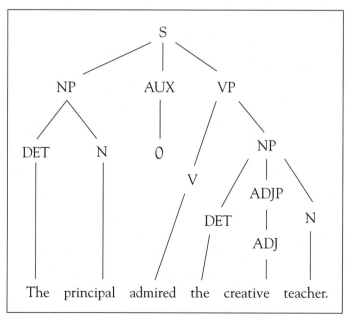

Figure 9–5. Sentence 2 diagram

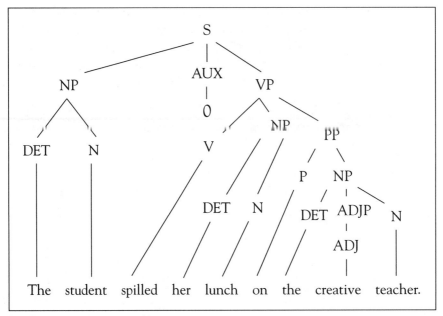

Figure 9–6. Sentence 3 diagram

These visual representations are called *tree diagrams* because they look somewhat like upside-down trees. They branch out as they move from the level of the sentence to the phrases and down to the words. At the top level, every diagram has the three components of the sentence, an NP, an AUX, and a VP. The first NP under the S is the subject of the sentence. Thus, the function of a constituent is defined structurally, not just semantically, as is often done in schools when students learn that the subject is "the doer of the action." In the same way, the object of the verb (the direct object) is the first NP under the VP.

Diagrams represent the different levels of sentence structure. At the top level, every sentence has an NP, an AUX, and a VP. In these diagrams the AUX is marked with a zero because no word occurs at the surface level representation. However, the AUX is shown because it is realized in questions or negatives. At the next level each of those parts of the sentence is expanded. For example, in Figure 9–4 the first NP is made up of a determiner (DET), an adjective phrase (ADJP), and a noun (N). In 9–5 and 9–6, the first NP consists of a DET and an N. All these expansions follow the phrase structure rules. The differences come because different sentences contain different optional elements. At the bottom level are the lexical items, or words, that make up a particular sentence.

Tree diagrams, like other graphic organizers, are useful because they help show relationships. For example, in Figure 9–4, it is possible to see that *exciting linguistics* is an adjective phrase. The two words are grouped together under one heading. In addition, the diagram shows that this ADJP is part of the NP that it is placed under. In Figure 9–6, the words *on the creative teacher* are all part of one PP, and that PP forms part of the VP. These relationships are more evident because of the visual display.

Sometimes students worry about having to learn how to diagram sentences. However, if sentence diagramming is considered just another kind of graphic organizer, students may be less apprehensive. In fact, some students who have difficulty reading about syntactic structure find that they can grasp many of the concepts more easily when they see them in a diagram. The diagram captures linear order, grouping of words into constituents, and labels for morphological categories of words. Such diagrams help students understand the structure of sentences and phrases. The best procedure is to write the sentence but then start the diagram at the top and, following the phrase structure rules, work down to the individual words. It is much more difficult to go from the words up to the top of the diagram. Working from the top down helps students understand the constituents of the sentence and the elements in the different phrases.

Using the morphological categories described in Chapter 7 and the rules listed in this chapter, students should be able to diagram any simple sentence. However, it is important to remember that diagrams represent the structure of sentences at the deep level, not the surface structure. Some sentences have to be rearranged into their deep structure before they can be diagrammed. For example, a sentence that begins with a prepositional phrase like "After class, the students will hold a meeting" must be a surface-structure variation, because at deep-structure level, sentences start with an NP, not a PP. In tree diagrams, lines don't cross. Figure 9–7 shows an incorrect representation of this sentence with lines that cross.

Moving the PP to the end would produce the deep-structure sentence "The students will hold a meeting after class." This sentence can be diagrammed following the rules listed previously. Figure 9–8 shows the correct diagram. The lines in this tree diagram don't cross over one another.

This section provides an introduction to the syntax of simple sentences. Many more details would need to be included to fully describe the structure of English sentences. However, linguists use the approach outlined here. The goal is to develop a small set of rules that can produce an infinite number of sentences. A description of syntax that contains this small set of rules would be psychologically real. Even though most linguists argue that humans have an innate capacity to acquire language, and even though language is complex, the underlying structure must not be so complex that it would be impossible to acquire. The rules outlined here suggest that all English sentences follow the same pattern at a deep level. Further, constituents like an NP and a PP each have a fixed structure that includes certain optional elements. The small set of rules listed previously can account for the structure of an infinite set of English sentences.

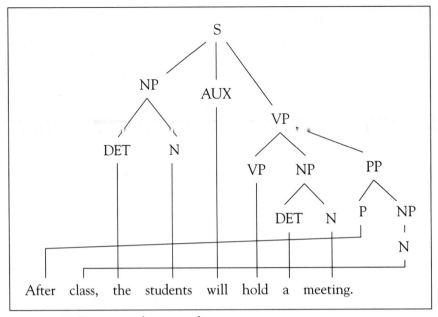

Figure 9–7. Diagram with crossing lines

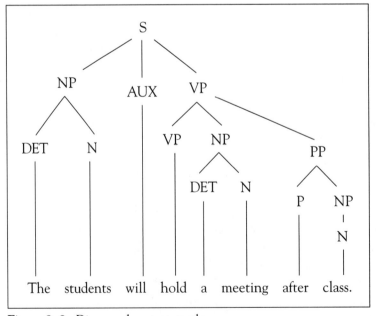

Figure 9–8. Diagram drawn correctly

Complex and Compound Sentences

The preceding sections described the structure of simple sentences in English. Simple sentences have one clause–one subject and predicate. Compound and complex sentences contain two or more clauses. The internal structure of each clause in a compound or complex sentence is the same as the structure in a simple sentence. The same phrase structure rules can be used to describe any English sentence. However, additional rules are needed to describe the organization of clauses in compound and complex sentences.

Compound sentences   Compound sentences consist of two or more simple sentences joined by a coordinate conjunction. The three most common coordinate conjunctions in English are *and, or,* and *but.* These three words capture the possible logical relationships between two ideas. The second idea can be an addition (*and*), an alternative (*or*), or an opposite (*but*).

A coordinate conjunction shows the relationship between two statements that are of equal importance. This is why these conjunctions are labeled "coordinate." A compound sentence can be represented in a tree diagram in which the two simple sentences are at the same level with the conjunction between them, as shown in Figure 9–9. The conjunction connects the two simple sentences but is not part of either one. Figure 9–9 uses the convention of representing some elements with a triangle. Linguists do this when they do not need to show complete detail to make a point. We follow this convention in discussing compound and complex sentences.

Beginning writers often string together their ideas with *and.* They present their ideas as being equally important. As writers develop, they learn to subordinate one

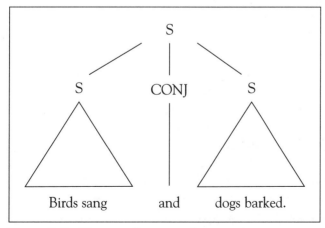

Figure 9–9. Diagram of compound sentence

idea to another. They structure their sentences to show that some ideas are subordinate to or dependent on other ideas. Rather than using a series of simple sentences or stringing together several ideas joined by *and*, they start writing complex sentences.

Complex sentences   Complex sentences consist of a main clause and one or more subordinate clauses. The main clause may also be referred to as an *independent clause* because it can stand alone as a complete sentence. The subordinate clauses may be referred to as *dependent clauses* because they depend on (literally "hang from") an independent clause. Just as complex words can consist of free and bound morphemes, complex sentences contain independent and dependent clauses.

Dependent clauses begin with a subordinate conjunction. Unlike coordinate conjunctions, subordinate conjunctions form part of the clause they attach to. Consider the following two sentences:

1.   Students represent syntactic structures when they draw tree diagrams.
2.   Students draw tree diagrams when they represent syntactic structures.

In the first sentence, the subordinate conjunction *when* attaches to *they draw tree diagrams*. In the second sentence, *when* attaches to *they represent syntactic structures*. The clause with *when* is the subordinate or dependent clause. It represents a less important idea than the idea in the main clause. Thus, sentence 1 emphasizes representing syntactic structures, and sentence 2 emphasizes drawing tree diagrams.

As people speak or write, they signal the important ideas by placing them in main clauses. They add extra information related to the idea in subordinate clauses. The subordinate conjunction shows the relationship between the ideas. In the previous sentences, the relationship is one of time. Using a different conjunction one could show a different relationship. For example, using *if* would show a condition: "Students represent syntactic structures if they draw tree diagrams." A conjunction like *because* could signal cause and effect: "Students draw tree diagrams because those diagrams represent syntactic structures." Effective writing involves deciding which ideas to emphasize and choosing the right conjunction to show the relationship between the ideas.

Dependent clauses can function in a sentence in the same way that an adverb, an adjective, or a noun functions. The clause is then represented in a tree diagram in the same position as the corresponding adverb, adjective, or noun. Adverb clauses tell when, where, why, how, or under what conditions. They answer the same questions that adverbs do. The conjunctions that begin adverb clauses are words like *after* or *because*. On the surface-structure level, adverb

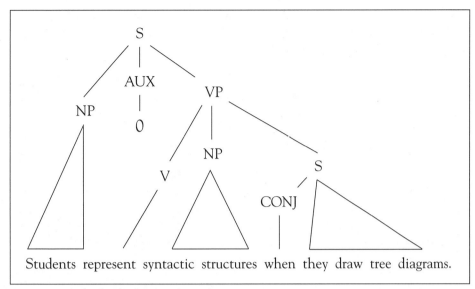

Figure 9–10. Adverb clause 1 diagram

clauses can appear at the beginning or end of a sentence, just like prepositional phrases that function as adverbs. However, at deep-structure level, sentences begin with the main clause, and the adverb clause forms part of the VP. Figures 9–10 and 9–11 show how sentences 1 and 2 above would be represented by a tree diagram. Again, the triangles indicate parts of the representation that are not important for this discussion. In addition, the zero under AUX shows that it is not pronounced in this sentence. We could also have included an AUX like *do* in these sentences, since that is the form that exists at the deep-structure level.

Adverb clauses, like adverbs, are placed in the VP. Adjective clauses, on the other hand, function as part of a noun phrase. Subordinate adjective clauses begin with one of the relative pronouns, *who, which,* or *that.* In formal registers, *whom* and *whose* also introduce adjective clauses. The following sentences contain adjective clauses:

1. Students *who draw tree diagrams* represent syntactic structures.
2. Diagrams *that represent syntactic structures* are often found in linguistics books.
3. I made an error in this tree diagram, *which I drew yesterday.*

Adjective clauses follow the noun in an NP in the same way that prepositional phrases can follow a noun. Adjective clauses are represented in tree diagrams as shown in Figure 9–12.

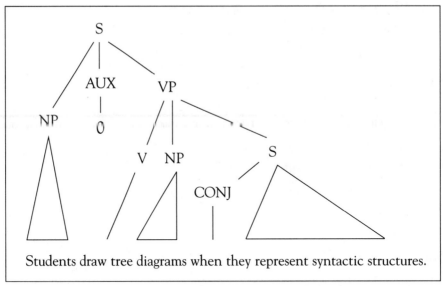

Students draw tree diagrams when they represent syntactic structures.

Figure 9–11. Adverb clause 2 diagram

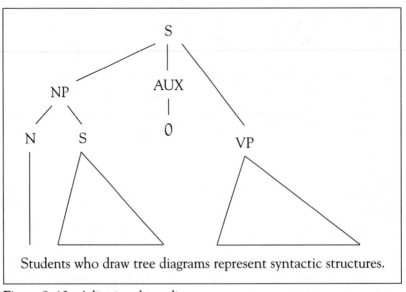

Students who draw tree diagrams represent syntactic structures.

Figure 9–12. Adjective clause diagram

In English, adjectives precede nouns at the deep level. However, adjective clauses, like prepositional phrases that function as adjectives, follow nouns. In fact, it could be argued that prepositional phrases following nouns are simply reduced forms of adjective clauses. Consider the following sentences:

1. The boy in that class drew the diagram.
2. The boy who is in that class drew the diagram.

In the first sentence, the PP *in that class* could be considered a reduced form of *who is in that class*, shown in sentence 2. A theory of syntax would need to specify the deep structure of these sentences.

Sentence 3 in the previous list shows one convention used with adjective clauses. When the clause contains extra information that is not needed, it is introduced with *which* and set off by commas. This is called a *nonrestrictive clause* because it isn't needed to restrict or identify the noun (*diagram*) that it refers to. The assumption is that the listener or reader knows which diagram the speaker or writer is referring to, and the fact that it was drawn yesterday is provided as extra information. The use of *which* and the commas rather than *that* is social convention used in formal writing. Teachers often give mini-lessons on conventions like these, and students can use this information when editing their writing.

The third kind of subordinate clause is a noun clause. Noun clauses replace noun phrases in some sentences. The following sentences contain noun clauses:

1. What you do is up to you.
2. Juan bought whatever appealed to him.
3. That Belinda studied hard was apparent.

Noun clauses often start with words like *what, whatever,* and *that*. In these sentences the subject or object is a whole noun clause rather than a noun phrase. Such sentences are diagrammed like corresponding sentences with NPs. For example, sentence 2 corresponds to a simple sentence, "Juan bought a linguistics book." However, instead of an NP (*a linguistics book*), there is a clause with a subject and predicate (*whatever appealed to him*). Sentence 2 would be diagrammed as shown in Figure 9–13.

Complex sentences are especially common in academic writing. Writers use complex sentences to signal the relationships between ideas. Sometimes, textbook writers attempt to simplify texts by shortening the sentences. Readability formulas often use sentence length as a measure of complexity. However, shortening sentences by changing a complex sentence into two simple sentences does not make reading easier. The word that is removed, the subordinate conjunction, signals the relationship between the ideas. Proficient readers attend to these key

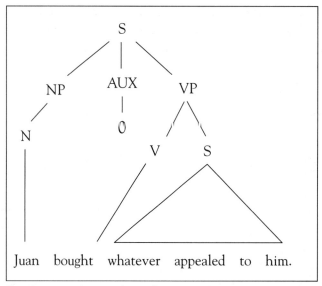

Figure 9–13. Noun clause diagram

words to determine which ideas are most important. Shortening the sentences actually makes reading harder, not easier.

This section provides a brief outline of the way linguists analyze and represent compound and complex sentences. Compound sentences contain equally important ideas, so the two or more clauses are drawn at the same level in a diagram. Complex sentences contain a main idea and one or more subordinate ideas. These less important ideas are placed lower on the tree. They are subordinated to and dependent on the main clause structure. Tree diagrams represent the relationships among the clauses in a compound or complex sentence. However, the structure of each clause in these longer sentences is the same as the structure of a simple sentence. People acquiring a language don't need to acquire new syntactic structures; they need to develop the knowledge of how the language combines basic structures.

Sentence Combining

Beginning writers often write simple sentences at first. Later they produce a series of simple sentences joined by *and*. As writers develop, they learn how to subordinate ideas to create complex sentences. One activity recommended by Weaver (1996) to help students write more complex sentences is sentence combining. Weaver cites research that shows that sentence combining exercises can improve student writing. Although students still need to do a great deal of reading, some activities that involve combining sentences can lead to more complex writing.

Strong (1993) has written extensively about sentence combining and has authored practice books for students. The exercises follow a consistent format. Students are given a series of simple sentences and asked to combine them into a more complex sentence. For example, students are asked to combine sentences like the following:

The linguist sits.
She sits in a chair.
The chair is red.
The chair is comfortable.
The linguist is content.

Students write one sentence that combines ideas from all five sentences. Students can compare their answers with those of classmates. They can discuss which sentences they think are most effective. Students can also work in small groups to produce their sentences. Most of the exercise books contain related series of sentences so that students can write paragraphs or longer pieces by combining them.

Sentence combining can help students see that there are different ways to combine sentences. Teachers can present minilessons on certain structures, such as adjective clauses and participial phrases, and then have students practice these structures as they combine sentences. Students can also generate a series of simple sentences for other students to combine. In addition, students can analyze good writing to see how published writers combine elements to form their sentences. Weaver suggests that sentence combining is one effective means of teaching grammar in context.

Syntax and the Two Views of Reading

Syntax is an important field of study for linguists. An understanding of syntax can inform teachers as they teach reading. Each of the two views of reading we have discussed assigns a different role to syntax. From a word recognition perspective, syntax plays a limited role. Since the focus is at the word level, little is written about the syntactic cueing system. Books such as *Put Reading First* (Armbruster and Osborn 2001) include a discussion of the use of context to identify words. The authors write, "Context clues are hints about the meaning of an unknown word that are provided in the words, phrases and sentences that surround the word. Context clues include definitions, restatements, examples, or descriptions" (p. 40). These authors refer to hints about the meanings of words that come from definitions, restatements, examples, or descriptions. All of these are semantic cues, not syntactic cues.

241

In their discussion of comprehension, the authors move from the word level to the text level. They discuss literal and inferential questions, metacognitive strategies, and use of graphic organizers, among other things. Nowhere in the discussion at the sentence or the text level do these proponents of a word recognition view discuss syntactic cues in any detail.

In contrast, those who take a sociopsycholinguistic view of reading regard syntax as an important component. Syntax is one of the three cueing systems Readers use acquired knowledge of syntactic patterns to predict the morphological categories of upcoming words. Proficient readers make substitutions that maintain the sentence syntax. For example, they substitute nouns for nouns or determiners for determiners.

In English, sentences follow the general pattern of NP – AUX – VP. Even though there are surface variations, this is the pattern readers predict. They also know that in an NP, there may be a determiner, an adjective, and a noun in that order. They use this knowledge to help them predict. If they see a preposition, they expect a noun phrase will follow.

Here is a sentence with nonsense words: "A phev was larzing two sleks." This sentence contains some function words and some inflectional endings. These provide morphological and syntactic cues for readers. This sentence appears to follow the usual NP – AUX – VP pattern. First, *a phev* looks like an NP because the determiner *a* precedes a word that must function as a noun. The auxiliary verb *was* comes next and signals that *larzing* must be the main verb. This is confirmed by the inflectional *-ing* on *larzing*. Finally, *two sleks* must be the object. This NP follows the verb, so it is in the right position. The quantifier *two* helps readers predict that a noun will follow. The inflectional *s* on *sleks* confirms that the word is a noun. Even though a reader could not construct meaning from this sentence because of a lack of semantic information, there are syntactic cues a reader could use to recognize the structure of the sentence. If only one or two words are unfamiliar, a reader may be able to figure out the meaning from context. As this example shows, there is a close link between morphology and syntax. The syntax provides a structural frame into which certain categories of words normally fit. Both the order of the words (the syntactic pattern) and the inflectional endings (the morphology) provide important cues.

Lexico-Syntax

Part of knowing a word is knowing how the word functions in a sentence. This knowledge goes beyond being able to categorize a word as a noun or a verb. It includes knowing what other kinds of words will follow. Linguists refer to the lexico-syntax to show the link between words and syntactic patterns. In English, verbs are especially important. Consider the following sentences:

The linguist *went* to the lecture.
The teacher *put* her keys on her desk.
The student *gave* the teacher her homework.

A reader who has acquired knowledge of each of these verbs can predict other constituents that will occur in the sentence. For example, a form of the verb *to go* such as *went* is usually followed by a prepositional phrase that indicates location, what linguists call a *locative*. A verb like *put* is followed by an object and a locative. People usually put something somewhere. *Give* requires two objects because people give something to someone. Verbs such as these are subcategorized to take different kinds of complements. Proficient readers have acquired knowledge of the kinds of words that will follow. This is not conscious knowledge. Good readers may not be able to explain that forms of *go* are often followed by locatives. However, readers can use this subconscious syntactic knowledge to make predictions as they read.

Teachers who take a sociopsycholinguistic view of reading provide strategies for students to use during silent reading to keep their focus on comprehension. One activity that helps students access syntactic cues is a Cloze procedure. Students are given a passage from which some words have been deleted and are asked to supply the missing words. Teachers can create passages with different types of deletions to help students focus on different aspects of syntax. For example, a teacher might delete adjectives that precede nouns. Or a teacher might take out the conjunctions.

Students can work together to figure out what words could go in the blanks. It is important for students to discuss why they chose the words they did. Consider the following short passage:

The linguist wished to _____ a new language. He wanted to _____ about the syntax of sentences in this language. He started to _____ a large corpus of language samples. Then he began to _____ the language to _____ to _____ patterns.

Normally, a longer passage would be used. Students could examine the passage and decide on words that fit the blanks. In the follow-up discussion, a teacher could point out that the missing words are verbs and then talk with students about the clues that a reader could use to predict a verb in this context. Through a series of lessons, a teacher could introduce different aspects of English. What is important is for students to think about the clues that tell them what kind of word might fit a particular blank. Getting the right word is not important. What is important is developing a strategy to be used later during silent reading.

One excellent source for Cloze exercises is *The Reading Detective Club* (Goodman 1999). This book contains a series of clever, contextualized Cloze activities. Students are invited to become detectives and solve the mystery of the missing words. Excellent suggestions for follow-up discussions are included. This book is a wonderful resource for lessons that would help students use both syntactic and semantic cues during reading.

Good readers use their knowledge of the lexico-syntax to make predictions as they read. Struggling readers often focus on individual words. In their attempts to sound out words, they lose the flow of the sentence or the passage. They develop what Smith (1985) calls *tunnel vision*. Their focus becomes so narrow that they miss important syntactic cues that could help them construct meaning from a text. Teachers can use Cloze activities and other strategies to help students move beyond a focus on individual words and use syntactic knowledge as they read.

Syntax and Second Language Teaching

Insights from linguistic studies in syntax have informed methods of teaching a second or foreign language. Many methods of teaching language have been based on contrastive analyses of the native language and the language students are attempting to learn. These methods identify grammatical aspects of the target language that should be taught.

ALM

One of the most widely used methods of teaching a second or foreign language has been the audiolingual method (ALM). Based on behaviorist psychology and structural linguistics, ALM includes dialogues and drills designed to help students learn English sentence patterns. ALM was introduced as a scientific method for language teaching because it relied on research in linguistics.

Linguists identified and described the basic sentence patterns of English. ALM texts incorporated these patterns in drills and exercises that provided students with many opportunities to practice the patterns. The simplest drills required students to put a target word into a sentence slot. The drills followed this format: The teacher holds up a pencil and says, "This is a pencil." The teacher then holds up a pen and points to a student. The expected response is "That is a pen." The teacher continues with other classroom objects. Students give complete-sentence answers.

Some exercises require students to transform patterns. For example, in one drill students change statements into questions. Given the prompt "Mr. Scott goes to work at eight o'clock in the morning," the students respond, "Who goes to work at eight o'clock in the morning?" The drill continues with more statements that students turn into questions that start with *who*. In other exercises students replace nouns with pronouns or change positive statements into negative statements.

In some exercises students practice using the correct verb tense. For example, given the sentence "Ann is studying her history lesson *now*" and the prompt "every day," the student is expected to respond, "Ann studies her history lesson every day." This exercise requires students to use the appropriate tense as the prompt changes. Some exercises focus very specifically on the order of words. In one exercise, students are given the sentence starter "Harry has" and then are presented with three phrases, "every Saturday afternoon," "lunch," and "with me and my family." The goal is to produce a complete sentence by putting the phrases in the right order.

In ALM, students were expected to learn the syntax without explicit instruction. This approach contrasted with the earlier grammar translation method, in which students were given the rule and then practiced it. In contrast, the grammar in ALM was presented inductively. The assumption was that students would develop good language habits by completing drills and exercises. Teachers provided immediate correction of errors. Every lesson focused on a specific grammar point.

Although ALM and other methods based on linguistic analyses may seem to be a good approach to second language teaching, students have had great trouble learning a language using these methods. In the first place, even though the grammar teaching was implicit, the assumption was that students could learn a language, not acquire it. For that reason, very little attention was given to the meaning of the sentences in the exercises and drills. It didn't really matter whether students could understand the words as long as they put them into the sentence following the pattern to be practiced. If a teacher who was conducting a drill gave the example "The teacher writes on the board with chalk" and then gave the prompt "whiteboard marker," a student could give the correct response, "The teacher writes on the board with a whiteboard marker," without understanding what the sentence meant. This focus on form over meaning blocks acquisition. People acquire language when they receive messages they understand.

A second problem with methods based on sentence patterns and transformations is that the exercises focus students on the surface-level features of language. Students are expected to learn the patterns through repetition. However, acquisition takes place only when a person can use the surface structure (what they hear or read) to construct a deep-structure meaning. Language is not developed by imitating what people say. Children use what they hear to develop rules for how a language works at a deep-structure level, and then they use these rules to generate sentences. That is why children produce sentences like "I goed to the store"—sentences they never could have heard, but sentences that reflect the rules children are constructing. Second language learners also need to construct rules so that they can comprehend and produce the new language. They use the surface structure to formulate rules for how the language works. They don't simply imitate what they hear.

Content-Based Language Teaching

Current methods of teaching English learners are based on an acquisition model of language development. Teachers use a variety of techniques to make the linguistic input comprehensible. They organize curriculum around themes and teach language through content.

Students acquire conversational language fairly rapidly, especially students living in an English-speaking environment. However, developing academic language takes more time. In Chapter 8 we discussed several aspects of academic vocabulary.

Academic language differs from conversational language in both vocabulary and syntax. Teachers who understand syntax can design lessons to help students acquire academic language. In general, academic writing and speech contain more complex syntax than conversational language. Some structures almost never heard in casual daily talk appear regularly in academic texts and lectures. Spurlin (1998) identifies five syntactic challenges for second language students reading academic texts: passive voice, comparatives and logical connectors, modal auxiliaries, verb phrases containing prepositional phrases, and relative clauses.

In English, sentences can be in either active or passive voice. The difference is that in active voice the subject is doing the action, and in passive voice the subject is being acted on. For example, "The linguist analyzed the phonology of the new language" is in active voice because the subject, the linguist, is doing something. In contrast, "The phonology of the new language was analyzed by the linguist" is in passive voice. The grammatical subject of the sentence, the phonology, is not doing the action. The grammatical subject and the logical subject (the linguist) are different. In active voice the grammatical and logical subjects are the same.

Passives appear frequently in academic writing because the person doing the action is not the focus of the sentence. For example, in describing an experiment, a textbook writer might say, "The rats were injected with insulin three times a day." Here, the person carrying out the experiment is not the focus of attention, so a passive construction allows the writer to emphasize the procedure. Since passives occur infrequently in conversation, they present a challenge for all readers, but especially for English learners.

Academic English presents other syntactic challenges. For example, there are more comparatives and logical connectors. In sentences like "English is a more analytic language than French" and "There are fewer phonemes in Spanish than in English," the reader has to use key words—*more* and *than* and *fewer* and *than*—that are separated but show the relationship between two ideas. The structure of these comparative sentences is complex. Yet, comparatives appear often in academic language. Similarly, readers have to understand how logical connectors like *if . . . then* and *not only . . . but also* work. These pairs of words show the relationship between two ideas in sentences like "If the mixture is heated too much, then the gas may explode" and "Not only did the colonists encounter harsh weather, but they also lacked food." The connecting words are separated from one another. Readers of sentences like these have to understand the two clauses and also keep the first part of the connector (*not only*) in mind and link it to the second part (*but also*). This is a cognitively demanding activity.

Academic writing also contains many complex verb constructions that contain modals like *should, would,* and *might.* These words indicate subtle shades of meaning such as permission, obligation, necessity, and possibility. The differences among "The researcher could have conducted a different experiment," "The researcher should have conducted a different experiment," and "The researcher might have conducted a different experiment" may not be clear to an English learner. In addition, modals often form part of a complex chain of auxiliaries in sentences like "The liquid *could have been* substituted for the gas."

Both prepositional phrases following verbs and relative clauses serve to create more complex syntactic structures. In a sentence like "Rainwater seeps into the ground after a storm," the first PP tells where and the second PP tells when, so the reader needs to process the action, the place, and the time. All this information is presented in one sentence. In the same way, in a sentence such as "The linguist identified a morphophonemic rule in Turkish that had not been found in other languages," the relative clause starting with *that* packs additional, important information into the sentence. Writing with prepositional phrases and relative clauses is more difficult to process because each sentence contains several related ideas.

Passives, comparatives, logical connectors, modals, prepositional phrases, and relative clauses are some of the features of academic language. Although these features may occur in conversational language, they are more common in academic talk and writing. Students need scaffolded instruction to help understand this complex language. Teachers who provide hands-on activities, collaborative projects, and graphic organizers can help make content instruction more comprehensible. In the process of learning academic content, students acquire academic language. This takes time and support. Teachers who are aware of the morphological and syntactic complexity of academic language carefully plan instruction to help students gain both academic content knowledge and the language forms needed to understand and express that knowledge. A specific focus on linguistic elements helps students become aware of the kinds of language in academic texts.

Conclusion

In this chapter, we have provided a brief introduction to syntax. Syntax is a complex subject. Linguists continually revise their theories of how language is structured. Their goal is to describe syntactic structure using a relatively small number of rules that can generate an infinite number of sentences. Such a description would be psychologically real. It would reflect the implicit rules that native speakers of a language acquire that enable them to comprehend and produce that language.

For linguists, *grammar* can refer to the internal rules native speakers construct. *Grammar* can also mean the descriptions of syntactic structure that linguists develop. However, for many people, *grammar* refers to a set of traditional rules to be learned in school. Traditional approaches to teaching grammar have not been effective in improving students' speech or writing. However, targeted minilessons based on students' writing are useful. Students can apply this knowledge as they edit their writing.

To describe the syntax of English, linguists use concepts such as linear order, morphological word categories, and sentence constituents. These concepts help linguists describe the structure of the phrases that make up sentences at the deep-structure level. In addition, linguists consider rules, such as the question rule, that describe how deep structures are changed to various surface structures. Further, linguists analyze the structure of compound and complex sentences to show the relationships among the clauses.

A knowledge of syntax can help teachers as they teach reading or teach a second language. The word recognition view of reading focuses at word level and pays little attention to syntax. In the sociopsycholinguistic view, on the other hand, syntactic cues are an important source of information that readers use to make predictions as they construct meaning. Some struggling readers read slowly, trying to pronounce each word. These readers fail to access syntactic cues. One procedure that can help struggling readers use syntax is Cloze.

Traditional methods for teaching English learners have often been based on linguistic analyses of the syntax of the target language. Exercises and drills have been designed to teach surface-structure patterns, often with little attention to meaning. Students learn to imitate the patterns but fail to construct the underlying rules that are needed to comprehend and produce the language. In contrast, teachers who use current methods teach language through content. Teachers with an understanding of syntax scaffold instruction to make academic language comprehensible.

Applications

1. Survey several colleagues. Ask them what they think *grammar* means. How do their definitions match up with Weaver's list? Discuss your results with classmates.

2. The position of a word in a sentence can change its function. Consider the following set of sentences:

   > Only he said that he loved linguistics.
   > He only said that he loved linguistics.
   > He said only that he loved linguistics.
   > He said that only he loved linguistics.
   > He said that he only loved linguistics.
   > He said that he loved only linguistics.
   > He said that he loved linguistics only.

   Discuss the meaning of each sentence. Do some sentences mean the same thing? How does changing the position of *only* change the meaning? What does this suggest about the relationship of syntax and semantics?

3. In this chapter, we describe how a linguist would formulate a rule for changing statements into questions. Using a similar procedure, develop a rule for changing an active sentence into a passive sentence. For example, your rule should be able to change

   > The linguist described the new language.
   >
   > to
   >
   > The new language was described by the linguist.

   Use linear order, word categories, and sentence constituents in forming your rule.

4. Some surface structures correspond to several deep structures. Pinker (1994, p. 209) offers the sentence "Time flies like an arrow" as an example. He lists five possible meanings of this sentence:

   > Time proceeds as quickly as an arrow proceeds.
   > Measure the speed of flies in the same way that you measure the speed of an arrow.
   > Measure the speed of flies in the same way that an arrow measures the speed of flies.
   > Measure the speed of flies that resemble an arrow.
   > Flies of a particular kind, time flies, are fond of an arrow.

Discuss the connection here between syntax and semantics. What morphological category does each word fit for each of the meanings? What words are not present in the surface structure that are understood to exist in the deep structure of these sentences?

5. In this chapter, we described sentence combining. In groups, generate series of sentences that could be combined into one sentence. Each group should write sentences on the same topic. Then trade sentence sets so that each group can write a combined sentence from the set it receives. Finally, share the results with the class. If possible, combine the resulting sentences to form a paragraph.

6. Examine a science or social studies textbook. Find examples of the different academic language structures Spurlin (1998) identifies. Can you find other structures that may cause English learners difficulty?

Afterword

Teachers can benefit from a knowledge of linguistics, the scientific study of language. Linguists generate and test hypotheses in their quest to make explicit the implicit knowledge that enables native speakers of a language to comprehend and produce that language. Linguistics includes a number of subfields. In this book we have looked in detail at those areas that are most important for teaching reading, ESL, spelling, phonics, and grammar. These areas of linguistics include phonology, morphology, and syntax.

Each area of linguistics provides useful insights into teaching reading and the related areas of spelling, phonics, and grammar. Reading theories can be divided into a word recognition view and a sociopsycholinguistic view. The goal of reading from either perspective is to construct meaning. The routes to meaning differ. Those who hold a word recognition view claim that readers first recognize words and then combine the meanings of words to get to the meaning of a text. Methods used to recognize words include phonics, sight words, and structural analysis. A careful study of phonology, orthography, and morphology suggests that these approaches to recognizing words are not consistent with linguistic realities. Teachers with a good understanding of linguistics realize the complexity of language and the problems underlying some current reading initiatives that emphasize word recognition.

Teachers with a sociopsycholinguistic view of reading hold that readers use background knowledge and cues from three linguistic systems to construct meaning. This view is supported by insights from linguistics. Since they recognize that language is too complex to be taught directly, these teachers provide strategies that enable students to comprehend texts. As they engage with meaningful texts, readers acquire the knowledge and skills needed for proficient reading.

Similarly, ESL has been taught from two perspectives. Traditional approaches attempted to teach, explicitly or implicitly, the surface patterns of a language. Students completed exercises and drills designed to help them learn the basic patterns and vocabulary of the language. However, people cannot learn a language by imitating surface structures. More current approaches are based on research that shows that students acquire a language when they receive comprehensible input. Teachers use techniques to make both oral and written language understandable for their students. They teach language through academic content so that their students can develop the academic language needed for school success. Second language teachers understand linguistics, but they do not attempt to teach phonology, morphology, or syntax directly or indirectly. They realize that language is complex, so they plan activities that lead to language acquisition.

Even though teachers who understand linguistics realize that language, oral or written, cannot be learned as a result of direct teaching, they also know that students benefit from language study for its own sake. Linguistics is an important and interesting academic content area. Students should learn about linguistics in the same way they learn about other areas of science and social science. They enjoy studying word histories, spelling patterns, and even syntactic patterns across languages if those studies are carried out using scientific concepts and techniques. In the process of doing linguistic study, English learners can become more proficient English users, and all students can become more proficient readers. The key is knowledgeable teachers who understand the essential linguistics for teaching reading, ESL, spelling, phonics, and grammar.

References

Adams, M. 1990. *Beginning to Read: Thinking and Learning About Print*. Cambridge, MA: MIT Press.

———. 1994. "Modeling the Connection Between Word Recognition and Reading." In *Theoretical Models and Processes of Reading*, ed. R. Ruddell, M. Ruddell, and H. Singer, 838–63. Newark, DE: International Reading Association.

Agee, J. 1999. *Sit on a Potato Pan, Otis! More Palindromes*. New York: Farrar, Straus & Giroux.

Akmajian, A., R. Demers, et al. 1979. *Linguistics: An Introduction to Language and Communication*. Cambridge, MA: MIT Press.

Anderson, R., and W. Nagy. 1992. "The Vocabulary Conundrum." *American Educator* (Winter): 14–18, 44–47.

Andrews, L. 2001. *Lingustics for L2 Teachers*. Mahwah, NJ: Lawrence Erlbaum Associates.

Armbruster, B., and J. Osborn. 2001. *Put Reading First: The Building Blocks for Teaching Children to Read*. Washington, DC: U.S. Department of Education.

Bach, K., and R. Harnish. 1979. *Linguistic Communication and Speech Acts*. Cambridge, MA: MIT Press.

Baugh, A., and T. Cable. 1976. *A History of the English Language*. Englewood Cliffs, NJ: Prentice Hall.

Berdiansky, B., B. Cronnell, et al. 1969. *Spelling-Sound Relations and Primary Form-Class Descriptions for Speech Comprehension Vocabularies of 6–9 Year Olds*. Inglewood, CA: Southwest Regional Laboratory for Educational Research and Development.

Braddock, R., R. Lloyd-Jones, et al. 1963. *Research in Written Composition*. Urbana, IL: National Council of Teachers of English.

Bradley, L., and P. Bryant. 1983. "Categorizing Sounds and Learning to Read—A Causal Connection." *Nature* 301: 419–21.

Brook, D. 1998. *The Journey of English*. New York: Clarion Books.

Brown, H., and B. Cambourne. 1987. *Read and Retell*. Portsmouth, NH: Heinemann.

Brown, H. D. 1994. *Principles of Language Learning and Teaching*. Englewood Cliffs, NJ: Prentice Hall.

Brown, R. 1973. *A First Language: The Early Stages*. Cambridge, MA: MIT Press.

Burgess, A. 1986. *A Clockwork Orange*. New York: Norton.

Carroll, L. 1981. *Alice's Adventures in Wonderland and Through the Looking Glass*. New York: Bantam Books.

Chomsky, N. 1959. "Review of Verbal Learning." *Language* 35: 26–58.

———. 1975. *Reflections on Language*. New York: Pantheon Books.

Clarke, A. 1957. *Space Pet*. New York: Harcourt, Brace, Jovanovich.

Clements, A. 1996. *Frindle*. New York: Simon and Schuster.

Clymer, T. 1963. "The Utility of Phonic Generalizations in the Primary Grades." *The Reading Teacher* 16 (January): 252–58.

Collier, V. P. 1995. "Acquiring a Second Language for School." *Directions in Language and Education* 1 (4): 1–6.

Cummings, D. W. 1988. *American English Spelling*. Baltimore: Johns Hopkins University Press.

Cummins, J. 2000. *Language, Power and Pedagogy: Bilingual Children in the Crossfire*. Tonawanda, NY: Multilingual Matters.

Dahl, K., P. Scharer, et al. 2001. *Rethinking Phonics: Making the Best Teaching Decisions*. Portsmouth, NH: Heinemann.

Donley, K., and R. Reppen. 2001. "Using Corpus Tools to Highlight Academic Vocabulary in SCLT." *TESOL Journal* (Autumn): 7–12.

Droop, M., and L. Verhoeven. 2003. "Language Proficiency and Reading Ability in First- and Second-Language Learners." *Reading Research Quarterly* 38 (1): 78–103.

Dulay, H., and M. Burt. 1974. "Natural Sequences in Child Second Language Acquisition." *Language Learning* 24: 37–53.

Elley, W. 1998. *Raising Literacy Levels in Third World Countries: A Method That Works*. Culver City, CA: Language Education Associates.

Elley, W., I. Barton, et al. 1976. "The Role of Grammar in a Secondary School Curriculum." *Research in the Teaching of English* 10: 5–21.

Farmer, A., and R. Demers. 1996. *A Linguistics Workbook*. Cambridge, MA: MIT Press.

Fraiser, D. 2000. *Miss Alaineus: A Vocabulary Disaster*. San Diego: Harcourt.

Freeman, D. E., and Y. S. Freeman. 2000. *Teaching Reading in Multilingual Classrooms*. Portsmouth, NH: Heinemann.

———. 2001. *Between Worlds: Access to Second Language Acquisition*, 2d ed. Portsmouth, NH: Heinemann.

Freeman, Y. S., and D. E. Freeman. 1996. *Teaching Reading and Writing in Spanish in the Bilingual Classroom*. Portsmouth, NH: Heinemann.

———. 1998a. *ESL/EFL Teaching: Principles for Success*. Portsmouth, NH: Heinemann.

———. 1998b. *La enseñanza de la lectura y la escritura en español en el aula bilingüe*. Portsmouth, NH: Heinemann.

———. 2002. *Closing the Achievement Gap: How to Reach Limited Formal Schooling and Long-Term English Learners*. Portsmouth, NH: Heinemann.

Freire, P., and D. Macedo. 1987. *Literacy: Reading the Word and the World.* South Hadley, MA: Bergin and Garvey.

Garan, E. 2002. *Resisting Reading Mandates.* Portsmouth, NH: Heinemann.

Goodman, D. 1999. *The Reading Detective Club.* Portsmouth, NH: Heinemann.

Goodman, K. S. 1965. "Cues and Miscues in Reading: A Linguistic Study." *Elementary English* 42 (6): 635–42.

———. 1984. *Unity in Reading. Becoming Readers in a Complex Society: Eighty-Third Yearbook of the National Society for the Study of Education,* ed. A. Purves and O. Niles, 79–114. Chicago: University of Chicago Press.

———. 1993. *Phonics Phacts.* Portsmouth, NH: Heinemann.

———. 1996. *On Reading.* Portsmouth, NH: Heinemann.

Goodman, Y. M., and A. Hepler. 2003. *Valuing Language Study: Inquiry into Language for Elementary and Middle Schools.* Urbana, IL: National Council of Teachers of English.

Goodman, Y. M., D. Watson, et al. 1987. *Reading Miscue Inventory: Alternative Procedures.* New York: Richard C. Owen.

Goodman, Y. M., and K. S. Goodman. 1990. "Vygotsky in a Whole Language Perspective." In *Vygotsky and Education: Instructional Implications and Applications of Sociohistorical Psychology,* ed. L. Moll, 223–50. Cambridge, England: Cambridge University Press.

Goswami, D. 1986. "Children's Use of Analogy in Learning to Read: A Developmental Study." *Journal of Experiemental Child Psychology* 42: 73–83.

Grabe, W. 1991. "Current Developments in Second Language Reading Research." *TESOL Quarterly* 25 (3): 375–406.

Gwynne, F. 1988a. *A Chocolate Moose for Dinner.* New York: Alladin.

———. 1988b. *The King Who Rained.* New York: Alladin.

Halliday, M. 1981. "Michael Halliday." *The English Magazine* (Summer): 9.

———. 1989. *Spoken and Written Language.* Oxford, England: Oxford University Press.

Halliday, M. A. K. 1975. *Learning How to Mean.* London: Edward Arnold.

———. 1984. "Three Aspects of Children's Language Development: Learning Language, Learning Through Language, and Learning About Language." In *Oral and Written Language Development Research: Impact on the Schools,* ed. Y. Goodman, M. Haussler, and D. Strickland. Urbana, IL: National Council of Teachers of English.

Heath, S. B. 1983. *Ways with Words: Language, Life, and Work in Communities and Classrooms.* Cambridge, England: Cambridge University Press.

Hoyt, L. 2002. *Make It Real: Strategies for Success with Informational Texts.* Portsmouth, NH: Heinemann.

Hughes, M., and D. Searle. 1997. *The Violent E and Other Tricky Sounds.* York, ME: Stenhouse.

Hymes, D. 1970. "On Communicative Competence." In *Directions in Sociolinguistics,* ed. J. Gumperz and D. Hymes, 35–71. New York: Holt, Rinehart, and Winston.

Krashen, S. 1982. *Principles and Practice in Second Language Acquisition.* New York: Pergamon Press.

———. 1993. *The Power of Reading.* Englewood, CO: Libraries Unlimited.

———. 1996. *Under Attack: The Case Against Bilingual Education.* Culver City, CA: Language Education Associates.

———. 1998. "Teaching Grammar: Why Bother?" *California English* 3 (3): 8.

———. 1999. *Three Arguments Against Whole Language and Why They Are Wrong.* Portsmouth, NH: Heinemann.

———. 2001. "Does 'Pure' Phonemic Awareness Training Affect Reading Comprehension?" *Perceptual and Motor Skills* 93: 356–58.

———. 2003. *Explorations in Language Acquisition and Use.* Portsmouth, NH: Heinemann.

———. In press. "Phonemic Awareness Training: Both Boring and Ineffective?"

Kucer, S. 1985. "Predictability and Readability: The Same Rose with Different Names?" *Claremont Reading Conference Forty-Ninth Yearbook,* ed. M. Douglass, 229–46. Claremont, CA: Claremont Graduate School.

Kucer, S., and J. Tuten. 2003. "Revisiting and Rethinking the Reading Process." *Language Arts* 80 (4): 284–90.

Lado, R. 1957. *Linguistics Across Cultures.* Ann Arbor, MI: University of Michigan Press.

Lederer, R. 1991. *The Miracle of Language.* New York: Pocket Books.

Lindfors, J. 1987. *Children's Language and Learning.* Englewood Cliffs, NJ: Prentice Hall.

Lorge, I., and J. Chall. 1963. "Estimating the Size of Vocabularies of Children and Adults." *Journal of Experimental Education* 32: 147–57.

McWhorter, J. 2000. *Spreading the Word: Language and Dialect in America.* Portsmouth, NH: Heinemann.

Medina, J. 1999. *My Name Is Jorge on Both Sides of the River.* Honesdale, PA: Boyds Mills Press.

Miller, G., and P. Gildea. 1987. "How Children Learn Words." *Scientific American* 257 (3): 94–99.

Mills, H., T. O'Keefe, et al. 1992. *Looking Closely: The Role of Phonics in One Whole Language Classroom.* Urbana, IL: National Council of Teachers of English.

Moustafa, M. 1997. *Beyond Traditional Phonics: Research Discoveries and Reading Instruction.* Portsmouth, NH: Heinemann.

Nagy, W., R. Anderson, et al. 1985. "Learning Words from Context." *Reading Research Quarterly* 20: 233–53.

Nash, R. 1990. *NTC's Dictionary of Spanish Cognates Thematically Organized.* Chicago: NTC Publishing Group.

Neumann, S. 1999. "Books Make a Difference: A Study of Access to Literacy." *Reading Research Quarterly* 34 (3): 286–311.

Opitz, M. 2000. *Rhymes and Reasons: Literature and Language Play for Phonological Awareness.* Portsmouth, NH: Heinemann.

Pallotta, J. 1986a. *The Icky Bug Alphabet Book.* New York: Scholastic.

———. 1986b. *The Ocean Alphabet Book.* New York: Trumpet.

———. 1993. *The Extinct Alphabet Book.* New York: Scholastic.

Pally, M., ed. 2000. *Sustained Content Teaching in Academic ESL/EFL: A Practical Approach.* Boston: Houghton Mifflin.

Parish, P. 1976. *Good Work, Amelia Bedelia.* New York: Avon Books.

Partridge, E. 1983. *Origins: A Short Etymological Dictionary of Modern English.* New York: Outlet Books.

Paulson, E., and A. Freeman. 2003. *Insight from the Eyes: The Science of Effective Reading Instruction.* Portsmouth, NH: Heinemann.

Petitto, L. 2003. *How Children Acquire Language: A New Answer:* www.dartmouth.edu /~lpetitto/langAc.html.

Piaget, J. 1955. *The Language and Thought of the Child.* New York: Meridian.

Pinker, S. 1994. *The Language Instinct: How the Mind Creates Language.* New York: William Morrow.

Prelutsky, J. 1986. *Read-Aloud Rhymes for the Very Young.* New York: Alfred A. Knopf.

Read, C. 1971. "Pre-school Children's Knowledge of English Phonology." *Harvard Education Review* 41 (1): 1–34.

Rice, M. 2002. "Children's Language Acquisition." In *Language Development: A Reader for Teachers,* ed. B. Power and R. Hubbard, 19–27. Upper Saddle River, NJ: Merrill/Prentice Hall.

Rodríguez, T. A. 2001. "From the Known to the Unknown: Using Cognates to Teach English to Spanish-Speaking Literates." *The Reading Teacher* 54 (8): 744–46.

Samoyault, T. 1998. *Alphabetical Order: How the Alphabet Began.* New York: Viking.

Saragi, T., P. Nation, et al. 1978. "Vocabulary Learning and Reading." *System* 6: 70–78.

Schleppegrell, M., and M. Achugar. 2003. "Learning Language and Learning History: A Functional Linguistics Approach." *TESOL Journal* 12 (2): 21–27.

Schumann, J. 1978. *The Pidginization Process: A Model for Second Language Acquisition.* Rowley, MA: Newbury House.

Schwartz, A. 1972. *A Twister of Twists, a Tangler of Tongues.* Philadelphia: J. B. Lippincott.

Seashore, R., and L. Eckerson. 1940. "The Measurement of Individual Differences in General English Vocabularies." *Journal of Educational Psychology* 31: 14–31.

Skinner, B. F. 1957. *Verbal Behavior.* New York: Appleton.

Smith, F. 1971. *Understanding Reading.* New York: Holt, Rinehart, and Winston.

———. 1973. *Psycholinguistics and Reading.* New York: Holt, Rinehart, and Winston.

———. 1985. *Reading Without Nonsense.* New York: Teachers College Press.

———. 2003. "The Just So Story—Obvious but False." *Language Arts* 80 (4): 256–58.

Spurlin, Q. 1998. "Purposeful Science Instruction for Bilingual Learners." *The Journal of the Texas Association of Bilingual Education* 4 (2): 22–35.

Stanovich, K. 1986. "Matthew Effects in Reading: Some Consequences of Individual Differences in the Acquisition of Literacy." *Reading Research Quarterly* 21: 360–407.

———. 1996. "Word Recognition: Changing Perspectives." In *Handbook of Reading Research: Volume II,* ed. R. Barr, M. Kamil, P. Moosenthal, and P. D. Pearson, 418–52. Mahwah, NJ: Erlbaum.

Strong, W. 1993. *Sentence Combining: A Composing Book*. New York: McGraw-Hill.

Swain, M. 1985. "Communicative Competence: Some Roles of Comprehensible Output in Its Development." In *Input in Second Language Acquisition*, eds. S. Gass and C. Madden, 235–53. Rowley, MA: Newbury House.

Terban, M. 1982. *Eight Ate: A Feast of Homonym Riddles*. New York: Clarion Books.

Thomas, W. P., and V. P. Collier. 2001. *A National Student of School Effectiveness for Language Minority Students' Long-Term Academic Achievement: Final Report*. Santa Cruz, CA: Center for Research on Education, Diversity, and Excellence.

Tompkins, G., and D. Yaden. 1986. *Answering Students' Questions About Words*. Urbana, IL: National Council of Teachers of English.

Treiman, R. 1985. "Onsets and Rimes as Units of Spoken Syllables: Evidence from Children." *Journal of Experimental Child Psychology* 39: 161–81.

Trelease, J. 2001. *The Read-Aloud Handbook*. New York: Penguin Books.

Valdés, G. 2001. *Learning and Not Learning English: Latino Student in American Schools*. New York: Teachers College Press.

Van Lier, L. 1988. *The Classroom and the Language Learner*. New York: Longman.

Villaume, S., and E. Brabham. 2003. "Phonics Instruction: Beyond the Debate." *The Reading Teacher* 56 (5): 478–82.

Watson, D. 1996. *Making a Difference: Selected Writings of Dorothy Watson*. Portsmouth, NH: Heinemann.

Weaver, C. 1996. *Teaching Grammar in Context*. Portsmouth, NH: Boynton/Cook.

Wells, G. 1986. *The Meaning Makers: Children Learning Language and Using Language to Learn*. Portsmouth, NH: Heinemann.

Wilde, S. 1992. *You Kan Red This! Spelling and Punctuation for Whole Language Classrooms, K–6*. Portsmouth, NH: Heinemann.

Williams, J. 2001. "Classroom Conversations: Opportunities to Learn for ESL Students in Mainstream Classrooms." *The Reading Teacher* 54 (8): 750–57.

Wolfram, W. 1991. *Dialects and American English*. Englewood Cliffs, NJ: Prentice Hall Regents.

Wolfram, W., and D. Christian. 1989. *Dialects and Education: Issues and Answers*. Englewood Cliffs, NJ: Prentice Hall Regents.

Wylie, R., and D. Durrell. 1970. "Teaching Vowels Through Phonograms." *Elemenary English* 47: 787–91.

Yopp, H. K. 1992. "Developing Phonemic Awareness in Young Children." *The Reading Teacher* 45 (9): 12–19.

Index